D1326076

MY LIFE AND TIMES
OCTAVE ONE:
1883-1891

A

BY COMPTON MACKENZIE

Novels and Romances

SINISTER STREET
SYLVIA SCARLET
GUY AND PAULINE
CARNIVAL
FIGURE OF EIGHT
CORAL
THE VANITY GIRL
ROGUES AND VAGABONDS
THE ALTAR STEPS
THE PARSON'S PROGRESS
THE HEAVENLY LADDER
HUNTING THE FAIRIES
WHISKY GALORE
KEEP THE HOME GUARD
    TURNING
THE MONARCH OF THE GLEN
THE RIVAL MONSTER
THE RED TAPEWORM
ROCKETS GALORE
THE LUNATIC REPUBLIC
POOR RELATIONS
APRIL FOOLS
RICH RELATIVES
BUTTERCUPS AND DAISIES
WATER ON THE BRAIN
VESTAL FIRE
EXTRAORDINARY WOMEN
THIN ICE
EXTREMES MEET
THE THREE COURIERS
OUR STREET
THE DARKENING GREEN
THE PASSIONATE ELOPEMENT
FAIRY GOLD
THE SEVEN AGES OF WOMAN
THE OLD MEN OF THE SEA
THE FOUR WINDS OF LOVE:
    THE EAST WIND
    THE SOUTH WIND
    THE WEST WIND
    THE NORTH WIND
MEZZOTINT

Play

THE LOST CAUSE

Verse

POEMS 1907
KENSINGTON RHYMES

History and Biography

EASTERN EPIC. VOL. I
ALL OVER THE PLACE
GALLIPOLI MEMORIES
ATHENIAN MEMORIES
GREEK MEMORIES
AEGEAN MEMORIES
WIND OF FREEDOM
MR ROOSEVELT
DR BENES
PRINCE CHARLIE
PRINCE CHARLIE AND HIS
    LADIES
CATHOLICISM AND SCOTLAND
MARATHON AND SALAMIS
PERICLES
THE WINDSOR TAPESTRY
THE VITAL FLAME
I TOOK A JOURNEY
COALPORT
REALMS OF SILVER
THE QUEEN'S HOUSE
MY RECORD OF MUSIC
SUBLIME TOBACCO
GREECE IN MY LIFE
CATS' COMPANY
CATMINT

Essays and Criticism

ECHOES
A MUSICAL CHAIR
UNCONSIDERED TRIFLES
REAPED AND BOUND
LITERATURE IN MY TIME
ON MORAL COURAGE

Children's Stories

SANTA CLAUS IN SUMMER
TOLD
MABEL IN QUEER STREET
THE UNPLEASANT VISITORS
THE CONCEITED DOLL
THE ENCHANTED BLANKET
THE DINING-ROOM BATTLE
THE ADVENTURES OF TWO CHAIRS
THE ENCHANTED ISLAND
THE NAUGHTYMOBILE
THE FAIRY IN THE WINDOW BOX
THE STAIRS THAT KEPT ON
    GOING DOWN

1. The Author aged 4

MY LIFE AND TIMES

OCTAVE ONE
1883-1891

Compton Mackenzie

1963
CHATTO & WINDUS
LONDON

Published by
Chatto & Windus Ltd
42 William IV Street
London, W.C. 2

★

Clarke, Irwin & Co. Ltd
Toronto

Printed in Great Britain by
T. & A. Constable Ltd
Hopetoun Street, Edinburgh

To my brother
FRANK

CONTENTS

*

PLATES

*

Note

There will be an index in Octave Two, to be published next year, which will have all entries in Octaves One and Two.

PROLOGUE AND APOLOGIA

IT is four o'clock on the afternoon of October 16th, 1961, with the moon coming to her first quarter as I set out to write the first octave of My Life and Times beginning with my birth at West Hartlepool in County Durham on January 17th, 1883, and ending in September 1891 with my going to Colet Court, the Preparatory School of St Paul's, called in these days the Junior School. This octave will be published (D.V.) on my eightieth birthday in January 1963, after which I hope to write an octave a year, each one to be published on as many birthdays as I am left to keep in this world.

For many years now friends have urged me to set out upon an autobiography, but I have resisted their exhortations because I did not feel I could bring myself to indulge in what amounts to undressing in public until old age had removed me far enough from the past to be able to regard that youth as somebody for whose behaviour I was no longer responsible. Thus I hoped I should have the courage to write with frankness about that self of once upon a time without feeling embarrassed by breaches of what I consider good manners or by sins against what I regard as good taste.

My old friend Eric Linklater has always argued in favour of an autobiography in the style of Benvenuto Cellini, who compressed his life into a single volume. However, I have always felt that one justification for writing my life was the exceptional memory I have of my childhood. So far I have not met anybody who could claim a practically continuous memory of his life from before he was two years old, and not merely of incidents in that life but of what he thought about those incidents at the time. I have used that memory of childhood in my novel *Sinister Street*, but every incident in that novel was reshaped to suit the narrative and I hope it may be of service to those who contemplate becoming novelists to learn how the autobiographical material of the author himself can be applied to the chief personage in a novel who yet is not exhibited as a portrait of the author. Some of the experiences of Compton

Mackenzie were given to Michael Fane as his own, but most of the experiences of Compton Mackenzie were impossible for Michael Fane if he was to be presented as Everyboy with a similar social and educational background to that of Michael Fane. That *Sinister Street* is still in print both in hard covers and as a paper-back all but fifty years after it was first published suggests that I was more or less successful in doing what I had attempted.

If I had tried to portray myself I should have had to strain the reader's credulity. Few children teach themselves to read at the age of twenty-two months; I should have been accused of portraying a freak instead of Everyboy.

Neither Dickens nor Thackeray lived long enough to write a full autobiography, although both used autobiographical material in their novels. Whether either could have written a frank autobiography in the climate of opinion at the time when they were writing may be doubted, and therefore the loss is less severe. I think that Somerset Maugham has chosen the best way by writing his autobiography when an octogenarian but leaving it to be published after his death. That is what I should have liked to do, but I have not been able to save enough money to spend half the year on writing a series of books which would earn money only after I was dead.

I have not kept diaries and therefore inevitably there will be occasional errors in chronology, but I prefer to make a mistake in months rather than to exhume from a diary a forgotten impression or experience and try to restore it to life by what can only be a faded effect of the original many years later. This is not a slight upon the great diarists like my Pauline predecessor Samuel Pepys. His diary was the perfect expression of himself; it was not an *aide mémoire* to an autobiographer.

My theory is that memory will preserve what was worth preserving if responsibility be laid upon it, but that the use of a diary relieves it of responsibility and renders sterile the creative force of memory. I have sometimes read a half-condescending half-contemptuous allusion by modern critics to the part played by memory in a work of imagination with the suggestion that the use of memory deprives it of the right to be saluted as a work of imagination. Such critics forgot (if most of them ever knew) that Mnemosyne was by Zeus the mother of the Nine Muses. The mythopoea of Hellas had no doubt of the importance of memory to art.

When the second volume of *Sinister Street* was published in 1914, fourteen months after the first volume, I wrote in the course of an epilogical letter to my friend John Mavrogordato: "Many critics have persisted in regarding *Sinister Street* merely as an achievement of memory . . . you know from many hours of talk that, if I were to set down all I could remember of my childhood, the book would not by this time have reached much beyond my fifth year."

Now, within nine months of fifty years ago when I began to write *Sinister Street* at 6 North Street, Westminster, I start to set down all I can remember of childhood that seems worth recording. Naturally I hope for the sake of my publishers that what I record will be readable today, but the inspiration of the ambitious task I have set myself is self-indulgence, or in other words to relive as much as I can of what has been a full and fortunate life.

I originally intended to call my autobiography *The Keyboard*, and it was this title that gave me the idea of dividing my life into octaves. Then I thought of calling it *The Eternal Present*; finally I have decided to call it *My Life and Times*. I have retained, however, the original scheme of octaves which, sometimes a little over and sometimes a little under, will provide each volume with a suitable serial ending.

This first octave from January 1883 to September 1891 will cover my childhood until I went to Colet Court. The second octave from September 1891 to February 1900 will cover my life until by a stratagem I escaped from the boredom of school. The third octave from February 1900 to October 1907 will wind up with my starting to write my first novel. The fourth octave from October 1907 to April 1915 will see me on the way to Gallipoli. I have already written in four volumes my war memories, but in writing them I avoided saying much about my personal life. That gap will be filled in the fifth octave from April 1915 to June 1923 when I retired to the seclusion of the small island of Jethou. The sixth octave from June 1923 to October 1931 will conclude with my election as Rector of Glasgow University and going at last to live in Scotland. The seventh octave to September 1939 will end with the beginning of the Second World War. The eighth octave will carry on until Britain's abdication from the Empire of India in August 1947. I aim at writing two more octaves from memory, slim volumes those to show how much faster time flies after sixty, but on my eightieth birthday I shall start a diary which will stop when my end comes. If by God's grace I should succeed in keeping what many will think is a presumptuous time-table, I shall be eighty-nine when the tenth octave is published in January 1972 and I shall leave the diary of an octogenarian for posthumous publication.

Many years ago now a reviewer in the *New Statesman* said that the trouble with me as a writer was that I was suffering from arrested development. Perhaps I am. I enjoy looking at Westerns on television and I never miss Sports Report in the Light Programme at five o'clock on Saturday afternoon. I feel when I am talking to Charles Snow that I am talking to an elderly uncle, although I am old enough to be his father. I find myself at ease in the company of children. I am aware of much more common sense in the young people who protest against the absurdity of our country's trying to compete with the U.S.A. and the U.S.S.R. by sitting down on the pavement of Whitehall than I can discern in those who sit there on more comfortable seats. I should like to have spent my prime in Periclean Athens or Medicean Florence; having been born when I was, I have tried to make the best of it. Anyway, if I have failed to grow up it was certainly *not* under the influence of Peter Pan.

FIRST YEAR: 1883

IN the late evening of Sunday, January 14th, 1883, Edward
Compton, the young founder and actor manager of the
Compton Comedy Company, set out on his twenty-ninth birthday to find a doctor in the unfamiliar town of West Hartlepool.
His wife, Virginia Bateman, who was his leading lady, had
been expecting her baby to be born two months hence and a
small house at Keswick had been taken for the event. Now
suddenly without warning the first labour pains had begun,
and it was imperative to find a doctor.

The journey that Sunday from somewhere in the Midlands
had been tiring—a long wait at York before the carriage
reserved for the Company had been hitched on to the train for
Darlington, where there was another long wait before it was
hitched on to the North-Eastern train to West Hartlepool.
Here rooms had been booked at 23 Adelaide Street. They were
far from being up to the standard of the best theatrical digs of
those days; the bedroom was over an archway leading to a
stable-yard into and from which waggons were continually
lumbering. However, on that Sunday evening the archway
had been undisturbed by traffic, and the landlady tried to
console the young actress with a vivid account of what torments
she had gone through when her own eldest was born thirty
years ago while her husband was at sea.

"At any rate Mr Compton's not at sea," she pointed out.

But Mr Compton was almost as much at sea as the landlady's
husband when he stood looking at two red lamps separated
from one another by two houses. Which of the two doctors'
bells should he ring? In the end, fortunately for myself, he
chose the right-hand lamp. If he had chosen the left-hand
lamp, as I in his position should have done, being left-handed,
I should never have been born at all, for that particular doctor
was a drunkard whereas Dr Swanwick on the right hand was
as good a doctor as could have been found in all County
Durham.

Many years later my mother would tell me one day about

B

those agonising three nights and two days before I was born. When I was writing the first chapter of *Carnival* and was describing the birth of Jenny Pearl, a fragment of what she had told me came back. "She stared at herself in the glass, and thought how pretty she looked and, flushed by the fever, how young." My mother had indeed a most exquisite complexion and never used so much as a powder-puff except on the stage.

The labour continued during the next two days, and on the Tuesday evening before my father went down to the theatre Dr Swanwick told him that if by next morning the baby had not been born it would be necessary to kill it to save the mother's life. However, he had telegraphed to London for some new instrument, and if this arrived next morning it might be possible to save the baby. Fortunately for me the postal service was more efficient in the eighties of the last century than it is today. The instrument did arrive by the first post, and on Wednesday, January 17th, I was born at 10 a.m., the sign Pisces being in my ascendant. I was a very feeble and small baby with a disproportionately large head, and I had to be flicked with a towel to extract a cry. My mother was in such a critical condition that I was put into another room and left there. Here I was visited by my father, who thought I was being neglected, and in order to put this right decided it would be a good idea to give me some spoonfuls of milk. He was scolded by the monthly nurse for doing this, but apparently the excess of zeal for his first-born's inside had no ill effects. Anyway, he was soon out of reach of rash displays of paternal solicitude because the tour had to go on and he had to leave for Newcastle on Sunday.

Four weeks after I was born I was christened in Christ Church, West Hartlepool, Edward Montague Compton, my surname being set down as Mackenzie in the parish register. This seems the moment to explain about the use of 'Compton' by those in my family who go on to the stage.

In the *Dictionary of National Biography* my grandfather appears as Henry Compton, whose real name was Charles Mackenzie. On his tombstone in Brompton Cemetery is inscribed Henry Compton (Charles Mackenzie). He was born in 1805, the son of John Mackenzie who married Elizabeth Symonds; she was an aunt of John Addington Symonds, Senior. This was truly Puritan stock. There were several generations of doctors from father to son, ending up with Horatio Symonds, who was Physician to the University when I went up to Oxford in 1901.

This is how John Addington Symonds, Junior, described that Symonds stock in a fragment of autobiography: "A Nonconformist ancestry of several generations, complicated by ineradicable family pride. How this pride had formed itself I am incapable of saying. They knew little about what is really interesting in their genealogy. A tradition survived of ancient gentry sacrificed to a religious and political creed. They were proud of being members of a family which had relinquished the world and dedicated all its energies during two centuries to the maintenance of an ideal."

My grandfather was taken into the business of an uncle, Samuel Symonds, who was a London merchant of West Country cloth. However, instead of sticking to a business career with a prosperous future before him, as soon as he became of age he reversed Dick Whittington's behaviour and turned his back on the City of London in order to go on the stage. He realised what a disgrace this would be to his mother's relatives, not least to her uncle and former guardian. Dr John Addington, of whom in old age his great-great-nephew John Addington Symonds would write: "His carriage, conversation, and deportment combined aristocratic hauteur with the sarcastic wit and frankness of expression which characterised professed free-thinkers at the beginning of the nineteenth century. This was remarkable in the case of a man whose father was a non-juror and Nonconformist minister and who had acquired a moderate fortune by the practice of medicine in London. The gradual emergence from narrow intellectual conditions in a Puritan pedigree is always interesting. We see the process going forward in the case of Quakers, and of Dissenters who have acquired importance at the present time. . . . In 1881 I deliberately burned the correspondence of five generations—that is to say the letters of my grandfather [who was the brother of my own great-grandmother] and of his immediate ancestors through four generations . . . the perusal of them left a deeply painful impression on my mind. The intense pre-occupation with so-called spiritual interests; the suffocating atmosphere of a narrow sect resembling that of a close parlour; the grim stern dealing

with young souls not properly convinced of sin . . . caught me
by the throat and throttled me. I could not bear to think that
my own kith and kin, the men and women who had made me,
lived in this haunted chamber. . . . No doubt these documents
. . . epitomised the spiritual archives of a race who scorned
their ancient and decaying gentry, and who boasted—I
remember the phrase in one of those letters—that they had
been renowned for their piety through two centuries. This was
written by the head of the family to one of the younger members
who innocently asked for information about such insignificant
trifles as Sir Richard FitzSimon, K.G., temp. Edward III. He
was told that seats and crowns in the heavenly Jerusalem had
far more value and were far more difficult to win, than coronets
or garters bestowed by kings."

I have in me an eighth of that Puritan stock and I ask myself
what I have inherited from it. I think it may be punctuality
and a sense of responsibility towards publishers and editors. I
certainly cannot trace any other relic of it in my character unless perhaps my inclination to be a minority man may be a Nonconformist heritage. Perhaps, too, I owe my great-grandmother,
besides the blood of generations of Worcestershire surgeons,
some of my brain. In 1925 W. T. J. Gun published a
paper in *The Eugenics Review* called 'Further Studies in Heredi-
tary Ability' in which among the descendants of John Symonds,
the last Worcestershire surgeon, are set down: John Addington
Symonds; Sir Morell Mackenzie; Sir Stephen Mackenzie;
Henry Compton; Sir Rowland Hill; Professor Louis Miall,
F.R.S.; Rosamund Hill; George Birbeck Hill; Lord Strachie;
St Loe Strachey; Sir Maurice Hill, the judge; Sir Leslie Scott;
Dame Katherine Furse; and my sister Fay, to which might
have been added the names of Canon G. A. Cook, the Regius
Professor of Hebrew at Oxford; Sir Francis Aglen, the Inspector-
General of Chinese Customs; Miss Compton (Mrs R. C.
Carton); the Rt Hon. John Strachey; and Dame Janet Vaughan
the Principal of Somerville College, Oxford—a good mixed
bag for a Worcestershire surgeon.

My grandfather withdrew for some years from any com-
munication with his family after that twenty-first birthday,
when he decided to become an actor, and he took the name
of his paternal grandmother, Susannah Compton of North-

amptonshire. That was in 1826. He not only changed his surname; he changed his Christian name as well, from Charles to Henry. Why this offspring of a father who kept a private school and wrote a life of Calvin and a mother with that two centuries' weight of puritanism heavy upon her should have suddenly broken away was for a long time a complete mystery to me. Two of his brothers had become distinguished doctors, one of them the father of Sir Morell and Sir Stephen Mackenzie. Another brother had become an Independent minister in Glasgow and lost his life in the wreck of the *Pegasus* on the Goldstone Rock off Holy Island in 1843. In the *Annual Register* of that year one of the six survivors out of fifty spoke of his admiration for the conduct of the Reverend John Morell Mackenzie in calming the panic of the passengers by prayer as the ship sank. "All present knelt around him and he in the calmest manner commended their souls to God." A favourite actor called Elton from the Edinburgh Adelphi Theatre was among those drowned, and by a coincidence which much appealed to my grandfather the actor's haresfoot was found inside his brother's bible when it was washed ashore.

Henry Compton toured the provinces, in some of the circuits of the time, for eleven years before he obtained an engagement in London. I have a beautiful silver snuff-box "Presented by the Frequenters of the Theatre Royal, Leeds, to Henry Compton in testimony of their admiration of his professional excellence as a Comedian". The date is November 1st, 1836, and there were seventy-eight subscribers.

From the supper at which the presentation was made I find recorded in the *Memoir of Henry Compton* by two of his sons that one of the guests, who had been rebuked by the Chairman for interrupting the speeches, rose unsteadily to his feet and addressed my grandfather: "Mr Compton, I'm drunk—in fact I'm *very* drunk; and on an occasion like this I would be ashamed of myself if I were not!"

My grandfather may have been as much puzzled as his Noncomfornist relatives to know whence originated this sudden break from Puritan respectability to follow the stage. I discovered in tracing the history of his Mackenzie predecessors a fact of which he was probably ignorant. The first cousin of his great-great-grandmother Janet Ross was David Ross, a contemporary of Garrick. David Ross was the son of an Edinburgh writer to the signet who in his will charged his daughter Elizabeth to pay her brother a shilling a year "to put him in mind of his misfortune he had to be born". David Ross successfully contested this will as being against Scots law. The Edinburgh W.S. who had migrated to London in 1722 and practised as a solicitor of appeals had forgotten his Scots law, with the result that David was the richer by £6000. David, who had been educated at Westminster, came back to Scotland and obtained a patent for the old Edinburgh theatre in the Canongate. Edinburgh was so much shocked by this profanation that there were riots before the theatre was opened in 1767 with the first play legally performed in Scotland. The play was the *Earl of Essex*, for which James Boswell wrote a prologue. Ten years earlier Dr Alexander Carlyle, D.D., had been hauled up before the General Assembly for attending a performance of John Home's *Douglas*, the fact that the play was written by a Presbyterian minister adding to the offence. What would the General Assembly have thought of their clerical representatives two centuries later, who as landlords of the Gateway Theatre would encourage stage-plays to be presented to the citizens of Edinburgh; stage-plays, moreover, in which the conduct of the juvenile lead sometimes sets nothing like as good an example as the Reverend John Home's Young Norval? However, the devout will be glad to know that drink is still taboo as a subject for drama and that whatever tolerance might be extended to other human frailties a proposed stage version of *Whisky Galore* was discouraged.

In spite of being an actor, my grandfather in his private life seems to have maintained a Puritan standard of behaviour throughout his life, and the only form of indulgence I can trace recorded of him are a pipe and a glass of toddy after he had walked back at night from the Haymarket Theatre to the house he had built for himself in Stamford Road, Kensington. His diversions were boxing, sculling, riding, walking and skating. No doubt if golf had been introduced into England by the middle of the nineteenth century he would have been a devotee of that game.

My father used to tell a story about one of these long walks. On one occasion Henry Compton found himself near Epsom at midday, and feeling hungry went to the nearest inn, where he was told he could not be given lunch because a rural decanal meeting was being held and there would be no room at table for anybody except the parsons. Henry Compton, who always wore black clothes on these walks of his, asked the inn keeper to let the rural dean know that a brother of the cloth was asking for hospitality from his brethren. The rural dean at once spotted who my grandfather was and sent a cordial invitation to join them at the ordinary. When his guests was seated he announced that it was always their custom when entertaining a visitor from another rural deanery to ask him to say grace. The Haymarket comedian was taken aback for a moment, but only for a moment. He rose and said, "O Lord, open Thou our lips, and our mouths shall show forth Thy praise."

Henry Compton's first London engagement was in 1837 at what was then called the Theatre Royal Lyceum and English Opera House. An extract from the acting-manager's letter to him reflects the attitude of the stage twelve days after Queen Victoria had succeeded to the throne:

"Theatricals must turn for the better, as they are now at their worst. The young queen must be fêted. She will encourage the stage; all young persons love it."

In 1839 Henry Compton was playing the Apothecary in a production of *Romeo and Juliet* at Drury Lane. This was the first meeting between him and Miss Emmeline Montague, whom one day he would marry. Emmeline Montague, the Juliet, was then hardly nineteen. She was a daughter of Henry Montague, a Somerset man who for many years was the leading light comedian at the Bath theatre. Her mother was the daughter of a Somerset doctor. Daniel Maclise painted her as Ophelia in his picture of the Play Scene from *Hamlet* which used to hang in the Tate Gallery. Probably it is considered too old-fashioned to hang there today and like several of the favourite pictures of my youth may have been relegated to the cellars.

Henry Compton did not meet Emmeline Montague again until they found themselves playing together at the Theatre Royal, Liverpool, nearly ten years later; in 1848 they were married in London, the wedding breakfast being held in the house of Mark Lemon, the editor of *Punch*.

My grandfather, who was now forty-three, decided that his wife, fifteen years younger than himself, must quit the stage. However, he did allow her to tour with Charles Dickens' amateur company, who were raising money for the Guild of Literature and Art, one of the chief promoters of which was Bulwer Lytton. Dickens, himself a first-rate actor, Douglas Jerrold, Mark Lemon, Cruikshank and Tenniel all played parts. The tour was a great pecuniary success, but for some reason or other the Guild never materialised.

Lytton wrote a comedy for them called *Not so Bad As We Seem* which was first performed at Devonshire House in the presence of Queen Victoria and Prince Albert in the year of the Great Exhibition. Seventy years later, in November 1921, the play was revived for a performance in which some of the descendants of those who played in the original production took part. My sister Fay Compton played her grandmother's part; Neville Lytton played; so did I; so did various Dickens descendants. And when the play was over in those George I costumes we danced a côtillon for which Margot Asquith and Adeline Gênée were added to the cast. Then after the final bows and curtseys the sound of hammering was heard. The housebreakers had begun to demolish Devonshire House. How utterly unimaginable such a final curtain would have seemed in 1851.

My grandparents lived first at 16 Charing Cross, but when one of those Victorian families began to grow too large my grandfather built Seaforth House in Stamford Road, Kensington. Seaforth House was a double-fronted residence with four large bay windows set in nearly half an acre of garden which my grandfather, under the advice of his friend James Veitch of Chelsea, planted with the latest rhododendrons. It is now buried under some flats called Cottenham Court.

From this house twice a day Henry Compton walked to and from the Haymarket Theatre for nearly eighteen years, and brought up a family of seven sons and two daughters on a salary that never exceeded £20 a week. His sense of responsibility as a paterfamilias was so strong that he resigned from the Garrick Club when he moved to Kensington in case he should be tempted to dally there, after the theatre, in the congenial company of friends. Not surprisingly, in spite of the rigorous economy with which his household was conducted, he was unable to save money. His last London engagement after he left the Haymarket was at the Lyceum in 1875, when at the age of seventy he played the First Gravedigger in my American grandfather's production of *Hamlet* with Henry Irving. His last performance was at the Prince of Wales's Theatre, Liverpool, when on Saturday, July 19th, 1877, he wound up a fortnight's engagement by playing Mawworm in *The Hyprocite* and Dr Pangloss in the last two acts of *The Heir At Law*. He was in pain all the time, but showed no trace of it in his performance. The next day he returned to London; exactly two months later he died of cancer. When it was known that his widow would be left in straitened circumstances by his death, a monster benefit was given at Drury Lane for which the Queen took two boxes; of course she was not present in person, not having attended any theatrical performance since the death of the Prince Consort. Lytton's *Money* was performed by all the leading actors and actresses of the day, and the £4000 taken remained a record sum from any theatrical benefit for nearly a quarter of a century, until it was exceeded by the £7000 raised for Nellie Farren at Drury Lane. At the same time as the London benefit there was a great benefit at the Theatre Royal, Manchester, which raised another £2000.

The feeling at the time was expressed in a letter to *Punch* from 'A Clergyman of the Church of England' in which he wrote of Henry Compton as "an actor who, more than any living comedian, has helped me and thousands of others to understand certain sides of Shakespearian comedy, and who is, furthermore, one of the truest, most self-respected, most artistic actors the stage in our time has seen".

Henry Compton's attitude to his art seems as serious as any of his Symonds forefathers to their profession. When at the age of twenty my father was playing in stock at Kilmarnock my grandfather was writing:

"So you're a-going it you are, as Romeo, Iago, Claude Melnotte, *cum multis aliis*. What on earth could the performance of the above three parts have been like? . . . I would rather you had climbed the ladder more slowly and steadily. 'They stumble' etc.; but it has been good hard practice, and you will get into some steady work at Newcastle, better than 'doing the lead' within a twelvemonth of entering. Don't let this 'flash-in-the pan' sort of work unsteady you for quiet, even, thoughtful practice, which is more important."

And again:

"I don't know what you and your professional friends are thinking about when they advise you to take not only an injudicious but an impossible step . . . your friends may tell you and with a kind feeling believe you equal to an engagement of the sort proposed in London, but I should think it a very dangerous experiment to cheek a London public in such a style of theatre . . . This sort of thing is not to be done at a leap. Light Comedy is not learnt by playing two or three parts in a second-rate theatre. I have a strong impression you are getting on right well, and have got the stuff in you; all the more important that you should perfect yourself by thoughtful study and painstaking practice, so that, when you open, wait your opportunity to appear in a first-class London theatre, and let us see an accomplished actor with the real 'finish' about him, which is not to be picked up in a twelvemonth."

In spite of his father's doubts about the advantage of getting on so fast in his profession, Edward Compton continued to do so. He was exceptionally good-looking and had inherited talent on both sides. Some of his ability as an actor was devoted to killing any possible comparison with his father by avoiding the least suggestion of imitation. The son of a distinguished father, whether he be a politician, a writer, a barrister or an actor, is always handicapped.

By the time he was twenty-four he was the leading man to Miss Wallis, playing with her in various Shakespearian parts and of course Claude Melnotte in the perennial *Lady of Lyons*. Later he accompanied Adelaide Neilson to the United States, playing Romeo, Benedick, Claudio in *Measure for Measure*, Orlando, Malvolio, and again of course Claude Melnotte to her Pauline. Of Lilian Adelaide Neilson the *Dictionary of National Biography* says: "As a tragedian she had had no English rival during the last half of this century. Her Juliet was perfect, and her Isabella had marvellous earnestness and beauty. . . . She was thoroughly loyal and quite devoid of the jealousy that seeks to belittle a rival artist or deprive her of a chance.

In the popularity she obtained her antecedents were forgotten. Her social triumphs were remarkable."

Adelaide Neilson was born at Leeds in 1848, the only child of an obscure actress called Brown by a father whose name she never knew. She lived as a child at Skipton and was taken away from school at twelve to work as a mill hand. Then she became a nursemaid, and on learning the circumstances of her mother ran away secretly to London before she was sixteen. Here among other experiences she served behind a bar at a public-house near the Haymarket, where she attracted customers by reciting Shakespeare. Finally, in July 1865, she appeared at the Royal Theatre as Juliet before she was seventeen and a half years old. The theatre was nearly empty but fortunately for her one or two critics of repute were present and within less than a year she was a star of the London stage.

"She possessed remarkable beauty of a somewhat southern type," says the *D.N.B.*, "girlish movement, and a voice unusual and caressing."

About this time she married the son of an Anglican parson. It was a completely unhappy marriage, but she did not succeed in divorcing him for more than ten years. That was in 1877, after she had made three triumphant tours in the United States.

I have a tattered copy of the *Memoir of Henry Compton* bought at the sale of a library in 1897 and presented by the purchaser to my father. This is inscribed 'Miss Neilson with best regards from Edward Compton, June 7th /79'. My father was then twenty-five; Miss Neilson was thirty-one. He was playing with her at the Adelphi at this date and in the autumn he toured with her all over America, not returning to England until July 1880, by which time they were engaged to be married in September. A small party was made up to go to Paris, probably for Miss Neilson to deal with her trousseau. Just before they left for France Miss Neilson, who had already left my father £2000, felt a presentiment of death and wanted to change her will to leave him all she had, some £40,000. My father (typically of him) dismissed the presentiment as fanciful, and the party set out. Almost at once after arriving in Paris, Adelaide Neilson drank a glass of iced milk in the Bois de Boulogne and collapsed in my father's arms. She died that night and they brought her body back to be buried in Brompton Cemetery. Presumably it was the emotional shock to my father that cost him the loss of almost all his hair. So there was the best-looking young actor of the day completely bald before he was twenty-seven. Fortunately he had enough courage and common sense to realise that there was no career before him except in costume plays, and he did not make the mistake of trying to seek London engagements in modern plays with the aid of a toupée. Instead he decided to start a company of his own to tour the provinces in old English comedy, to which in earlier days were added *As You Like It, The Comedy of Errors* and *Twelfth Night*.

Thus it came about that on February 7th, 1881, the Compton Comedy Company was born at Southport to enjoy a life of thirty-five years. From the £2000 left to him by Lilian Adelaide Neilson, Edward Compton was able to equip his company with costumes. In those days touring repertory companies did not carry scenery. Every theatre in the provinces was expected to have a stock of its own. There would be what was called a drawing-room set, a library set, a parlour set, an inn set, two open-air backcloths with wood wings, and about four front cloths of interiors and exteriors. The women had to find their own dresses; the men had to find their own wigs and buckles. The tour lasted forty-six weeks with five weeks' 'rest' in June and July, and in Holy Week, with a week of rehearsals before the new tour began in the first week of August. A stage-struck young woman in those days certainly knew by the end of a tour with a provincial repertory company whether she was meant to be an actress or not.

It must have been a strain on my mother's courage to be left alone with a week-old baby at 23 Adelaide Street, West Hartlepool, but the play must go on and the Compton Comedy Company had to appear in Newcastle five days after I was born and from there go on to Scotland. My mother was just thirty at this date, having been born on January 1st, 1853, in Walker Street, New York. I will deal presently with her family. I find it tiresome to write family history because I am always under the impression that too much of it at a time is tiresome for the reader. Many years after 1883 I was searching the playbills in the Mitchell Library in Glasgow to find out what was the opera that Madeleine Smith attended on the night that L'Angelier had his first attack after that coffee (it was not chocolate the first time) handed to him from her bedroom window, and enjoyed the agreeable thrill of discovering that the opera played that night was *Lucrezia Borgia*. While searching through those playbills I came across one of the Compton Comedy Company three weeks after I was born, and learned that *The Comedy of Errors* was played three times together with *The School for Scandal*, *The Rivals* and *She Stoops To Conquer* at the Royal Princess' Theatre, Glasgow.

Fortunately my mother was able to obtain a very good nurse whom I dearly loved. Her name was Bush, and although she had to leave us before the end of the year I still have a clear picture of her in my mind's eye. She was a tall young woman, wearing a blue cloak and a bonnet.

Eight weeks after I was born my mother and Bush brought me to rejoin the Company at Belfast. A scribbled note by my mother says:

"'You were a very good baby and always ready to be interested. You were always taken to visit every one we knew. On one occasion Frankfort Moore was very proud of putting you to sleep when neither mother, father nor nurse could do so."

Frankfort Moore was a lovable Irish novelist and playwright who a quarter of a century later would write to Hutchinsons (his publishers) and ask them to pay special attention to my first novel; it had already been turned down by Murray and Heinemann, whose example Hutchinsons quickly followed. My mother's note goes on:

"In Dublin you were taken to every party, though of course you were still in long clothes. Several Irish priests took a lot of notice of you. You were brought to the theatre to be fed at the breast during performances."

When I was three months old I was covered all over with a vicious eczema, and for over a month I was swathed in bandages from top to toe. A doctor in Southport cured it by prescribing cod-liver-oil, but recurring attacks of eczema were the curse of my early childhood, and the only advantage was having to use Vinolia instead of Pears' Soap because the latter had too astringent an effect on the skin. I was certainly not that baby in the Pears' Soap advertisement who was depicted

everywhere reaching out of his bath for the cake of soap on
the floor beside it with the motto 'He won't be happy till he
gets it'. Later, when I was about ten, I used to hum a one-line
catch I made up about Vinolia which went, "Vee, Vi, Vin,
Vinó, Vinól, Vinolli, Vinolia."

When I was six months old the holiday from acting was
spent at Keswick, where my parents had taken a little house
in which it had been intended I should be born. It was now
mid-June, and for six weeks not a drop of rain fell in the Lake
District, which must have surprised the people of Cumberland
and Westmorland. By now my interest could always be held
with picture books and I was saying a few words, but being
still without a tooth I could not pronounce 's' with a consonant.
Indeed, 's' with a consonant was a problem for me until I was
nearly three, though 's' with a vowel was manageable and I
never lisped.

My first vivid memory of the past must date back to not
more than seven months, because in the last week of July we
went to Scarborough, where the company would open in
August at the Spa Theatre. I was being wheeled in my perambulator along a country road just outside Keswick when
suddenly Bush picked me out of the perambulator and held
me up in her arms to look at black rabbits and white rabbits
running about in a field sloping up from the road. People have
questioned the possibility of remembering an incident from
the age of seven months, but as I write these words I can see
those rabbits and am aware of being in the arms of my nurse.
After we left Keswick towards the end of July I was not in any
town or city where within reach of a perambulator I could
have seen rabbits of any colour. Bush would have to leave us
in December to attend on her mother. The little Welsh nursemaid who succeeded her is as clear in my mind's eye as Bush
herself, but it was not my equally loved Minnie who held me up
to look at those rabbits. I asked my mother whether she remembered anything about those rabbits and she did not recall the
incident. Therefore I can rebut the inevitable suggestion that
I must have imagined the incident because I had been told
about it later. Throughout these memories of early days I
shall always make it clear when I am narrating an incident of
which I was told later.

In Scarborough I was presented for the first time to one of my two godfathers. This was John Bolton, an elderly Yorkshireman of considerable means. I shall say no more about him yet because he and his house are a vivid memory later on and I do not recall this first meeting at which he gave me a christening mug. This was a silver Queen Anne mug on which he had had embossed the scene where Robinson Crusoe and Man Friday sighted the savages in the distance. This mug fed my fancy in early childhood, but it was to vanish as part of the spoils of a burglary sixteen years later. My mother did not want me to have John Bolton as a godfather because she did not think him sufficiently religious. On one occasion she said something about the Crucifixion and he shocked (but also amused) her by saying, "Oh well, Jenny, it's all very sad to be sure, but it happened a long time ago. Let's hope it never happened at all."

During that autumn of 1883 the C.C.C. as it was always called visited a different place every week and sometimes two places in a week. I look back as far as I can remember to the bills posted in the towns that were visited. It was a big black C round ompton, omedy and ompany, in red letters within it. David Allan of Belfast, who was a great friend of my father, devised these bills. The ladies of the company were very kind to me. I was particularly fond of Miss Elenor Aickin who played Mrs Malaprop, and all the other matronly parts in old comedy, and of Miss Nellie Harper, then in her very early twenties, who played the parts like Maria in *The School for Scandal* and Julia Melville in *The Rivals*. The first I called 'Aiky' and the second 'Newwiarp'. Fifty-five years later Mrs Molyneux, who as Eleanor Molyneux had acted in many West End productions and whom I had not met since the first two years of my life, told me that once when I was sitting on her knee in the train she had nearly dropped me off it when the train stopped and I said 'tation' in what was apparently an absurdly deep voice for a child only nine months old. Not having a tooth yet, I could not manage the 's'. I was told my first tooth arrived a month later in Leeds. On another occasion —Mrs Molyneux thought it was in Llandudno but could not be sure—she was carrying me up the steps of an hotel where a caryatid with bare breasts stood on either side of the entrance.

I stretched out a hand to touch one breast, saying 'Aiky' and then leaned across to touch the other and say 'Newwiarp'. I had then just been weaned and no doubt I was finding the tin of Benger's Food less physically appealing than the female breast.

In December of my first year the Compton Comedy Company played a short London season of six weeks at the Strand Theatre. The plays performed were *Twelfth Night*, in which my father played Malvolio and my mother Viola, with O'Keefe's *Wild Oats* and Holcroft's *Road to Ruin*. The last named remained in the repertory of the C.C.C. for over twenty years. It was now that Bush left us, her place to be taken by that pretty and lovable little Welsh girl called Minnie.

My only memory of that time in London is of being photographed by Faulkner, the popular child-photographer of the time, whose studio was in Baker Street. He used to keep various toys with which to amuse his young clients; one of them was a toy elephant which captivated my fancy so much that for several weeks after I had been photographed standing up with my hand on its back I was often begging to revisit this elephant. At last one day I was taken to the Zoo to be shown a real elephant. I have been told that in a voice of profound disillusionment I declared that the great animal was not an 'effytant' but an 'olibus'. To the eyes of a twelve-month-old an elephant with a cargo of children on its back must have seemed like one of those knife-board omnibuses of long ago.

My mother told me that during those weeks in London Harry Mackenzie used to come round from Harley Street after breakfast and carry me off to play with his sisters. He was Morell Mackenzie's eldest son and soon after this went on the stage, calling himself H. H. Morell. After a few years he went into partnership with a French Jew called Mouillot and they rebuilt the Theatre Royal, Dublin, among other theatrical enterprises. In later life Harry Morell looked like a heavy dragoon who had been wounded in the Crimea. He had broken a leg in a smash with a dog-cart, and strangely enough his brother Kenneth had done the same thing; moreover, their grandfather had died after a smash with his gig. Harry Morell took to drinking heavily and his partner, believing he would not last long, suggested buying him out and allowing him

2. Great-grandfather John Mackenzie

Photo: T. G. Keown

3. My great-great-grandmother's house

£6000 a year for life. So Harry Morell retired to his father's old house at Wargrave-on-Thames, gave up drink completely and outlived Mouillot by several years.

One of those sisters of his in Harley Street was Ethel McKenna, whose granddaughter is Virginia McKenna. In the *D.N.B.* Morell Mackenzie is stated to be descended from the Mackenzies of Seatwell. This is inaccurate. John Mackenzie who married Elizabeth Symonds was the only son of John Alexander Mackenzie, a prosperous wharfinger on the Thames. He gave up the business which had been started by his grandfather and took to running schools and preaching in Independent chapels. Perhaps this was his way of going on the stage. His half-sister Mary Jane Mackenzie wrote a novel which was published in 1820 by Cadell, the first publishers of Jane Austen. I have a first and second edition of *Geraldine* By A Lady. It is much better than the average novel of that period, which, of course, is not saying much. Later she took to writing works of tedious piety.

John Mackenzie's great-grandfather, another John Mackenzie, was a ship-master, the third son of the Reverend Bernard Mackenzie, Episcopalian priest of Cromarty until he was deprived in 1690. He was descended from Murdoch Mackenzie, the fourth of Kintail, and his great-grandfather, Colonel Daniel Mackenzie, who was in the Dutch service, married a kinswoman of the House of Nassau. It was he who presented Seaforth with the golden bed of Brahan. Through Janet Ross, the wife of John Mackenzie the ship-master, the family is descended on the spindle side through Mackenzies of Redcastle, Kincraig, Tolly, Fairburn and Achilty, from Kenneth Mackenzie the seventh and Kenneth Mackenzie the tenth of Kintail. The ship-master, who died shortly before the '45, would often take his schooner to Venice from Cromarty, and tradition in Cromarty said that he was a Jacobite agent. I hope that tradition is based on fact.

C

ONE YEAR OLD 1884

EVERY week, except for five weeks in the summer at Lowestoft, a different place and sometimes two different places in the same week. Sunday after Sunday in the train. From that faraway year of 1884 comes back the metallic sound of the footwarmers being pushed into the compartment, and after that my being put to sleep, and as I lie looking up at the roof I see the oil swinging to and fro in the lamp that sheds a rather feeble light. I have one picture that is still vivid in the mind's eye. I am looking out of the window and suddenly below a steep embankment I see the wreck of a train. It must have been somewhere on the Midland Railway because the carriages lying on their side are a rich brown. As I recall the scene the wrecked train seems to be lying far below, but to the eyes of a child distance always seems much greater than it actually was. However, it must have been a bad enough accident to be recorded in the *Annual Register*, such a much more valuable publication once upon a time than the expensive *Annual Register* of today with its interminable statistics. Why does the *Annual Register* now ignore the needs of the social historian of the future?

I found in the *Annual Register* of 1879 what may have been the railway accident whose remains I saw when I was about fifteen months old.

"August 29.

"The Midland Railway's express train from the North was completely wrecked in its approach to London—engine, tender, and some carriages turning over on the up side of the line, the Post-Office van and a carriage being thrown down the embankment on the other side . . . and the permanent way being altogether effaced for a space of about 50 yards. Beyond a few bruises to the engine-driver and scalds to the stoker, no persons were injured."

Of course, the embankment could not have been the height it seems in memory, but it can hardly have been less than forty feet, and how the passengers escaped bruises when those carriages crashed down and turned over is extraordinary. It may seem odd that the Midland Railway should have left the remains of that train wreck lying about for at least five years. However, if British Railways had existed in 1879 those carriages would probably still be lying there today.

My next memory of the early part of 1884 is of an agreeable visitor who used to play with me and make me laugh. This must have been Charles Flower, who came up several times to persuade my father to bring the Compton Comedy Company to Stratford-on-Avon for the Memorial week as he had done in 1882 and 1883. Charles Flower came up to towns in the north of England and as far as Scotland, but my father refused in spite of my mother's adding her persuasion to Charles Flower's arguments. By now he was set on the revival of old English comedies, and although he still kept *The Comedy of Errors* and *Twelfth Night* in his repertory he obstinately refused to include any others. The result was that in 1886 Frank Benson took on the Shakespearian festival at the Memorial Theatre for the next thirty-three years.

I was told that Charles Flower was amused by my unusual powers of conversation for an infant who was still cutting his teeth, and used to give me a lot of attention.

So instead of playing at Stratford the C.C.C. played at the Gaiety Theatre, Dublin, that April, and afterwards went to Cork, where I was much frightened by a Punch and Judy show performing somewhere in the spacious Cork Opera House. This I do not remember.

From Ireland the C.C.C. went to Scotland. A year or two later it would always be the other way round, but in those days my father was not yet in a position to dictate his tours. This was my first visit to Glasgow, and I am told I made my first appearance in a crimson pelisse and a ruby bonnet, a forerunner of the LL.D.'s gown I should be given forty-seven years later.

By chance a torn programme from the Royal Princess' Theatre of that visit of the 'celebrated Compton Comedy Company from the Strand Theatre, London' has survived among some odds and ends of papers. It was for the week beginning May 26th, and in spite of that adjective 'celebrated' it is a sign of the comparative newness of my father as an actor-manager that a brief testimony from the *Referee* of December 23rd, 1883, is quoted: "As a genuine comedian, Mr Edward Compton has few equals and no superiors on the English stage." By this time *Twelfth Night* had vanished from his repertory, and of Shakespeare only *The Comedy of Errors* remained.

About this time I had invented a game which gave me considerable pleasure. It was called 'Walkie, Walkie' and consisted of my sitting on the floor and making a bottle of Guinness or Bass walk. My father, who had a sympathy with childish games, improved on this by sitting on the floor opposite to me, when the pair of us with a bottle in each hand would walk them towards one another until they met with an exhilarating clink. On this occasion in the Glasgow lodgings two of the bottles broke when they met just as the landlady came in and scolded my father for making such a mess of her carpet. After this my mother forbade 'Walkie, Walkie'.

The holiday of six weeks in June and July of that year was spent in Lowestoft where I do remember being frightened by a Punch and Judy show. I can see it now with the sea beyond, and no sooner have I recovered from Punch and Judy than I am being alarmed by niggers with tambourines and bones and huge mouths and straw hats, wriggling and singing against the glitter of the sea.

My father's mother, who was now sixty-five, came to stay with us in Lowestoft and I remember the joy of driving about every afternoon with Grandmama in a pony chaise, seated on my mother's lap. I was cutting the double teeth at the back and as a sedative for whatever pain there was I started to suck my thumb. The general belief is that thumb-sucking is the result of premature weaning, but I was assured by my mother that in my case it did not start until eight months later and that when the time came for the morning rest or the night's sleep I used to say 'take lill' rest with lill' thumb'. Incidentally I never used 'I' but was always Monty in the third person. Indeed, I was nearly four years old before I spoke of myself in the first person or used a possessive 'my'.

My grandmother joined us again that September in Bournemouth, where she was staying with her younger daughter Emmie, who was married to Duncan Hume, the organist of

St Peter's Church. Sir Henry Taylor, who was then living in Bournemouth, was interested to meet her because she had acted in one of his plays over forty years earlier. Taylor was by now in his mid-eighties. According to my mother I made friends with him and Lady Taylor. I wish I could record that I made friends with Robert Louis Stevenson, who had arrived in Bournemouth that July and himself made friends with the Taylors just about the time we were there.

Towards the end of that week in Bournemouth a cata-strophe occurred the indirect consequences of which had a profound effect upon my childhood. My much-loved Minnie, the pretty little Welsh nursemaid with whom I slept, developed a very bad sore throat. A doctor was called in that afternoon, and he diagnosed it as diphtheria. My mother was urged to take Minnie to a cottage hospital some way out of Bournemouth and to be sure that it was in an open fly. Minnie fell into hysterics as soon as she heard she had to be taken to a hospital and remained in hysterics throughout the drive. My father became nurse until Grandmama could be fetched from the Humes to take over. My mother managed to get back from the hospital just in time to dress for the part of Lady Gay Spanker in Boucicault's play *London Assurance* and of course my father also had to go off to the theatre. So to Grandmama fell the task of putting me to bed. It was my habit to sleep with a rubber ball, a woolly lamb and a deeply cherished india-rubber cat which I called 'Ay'. Did my unwillingness to refer to myself as 'I' originate in a desire to make clear it was not the cat speaking? No, I suppose it was the budding extravert, to use the current jargon. I still think that the old distinction between the objective and subjective approach to life was a clearer definition.

My three night companions were all gathered safely to-gether, but there was a fourth missing. This was a hank of cotton known as 'Cottony'. It had been my habit to go to sleep with the fringe of the coverlet twisted round my fingers and when it became too warm for this coverlet I was given this hank of cotton instead. To this day I find myself twisting my handkerchief round and between my fingers when I am preoccupied with some problem of the next sentence. On that night in Bournemouth just on seventy-seven years ago as I

write these words, Cottony was not to be found, and my
unfortunate grandmother did not know who or what Cottony
was. I can see her now, dear amiable woman from whom I
think I inherit my own amiable temperament today, offering
me reels of cotton which one after another I flung away in
indignation until at last, exhausted by the emotion of Cottony's
absence I fell asleep.

The next morning my father took me up to London to
stay with my mother's younger sister, Isabel Bateman, my
godmother, who was playing with Charles Warner in *In the
Ranks*, a melodrama by G. R. Sims and Henry Pettitt which
had been running since October 1883 and was to run on until
well into 1885 at the Adelphi Theatre. Isabel Bateman was
living in St John's Wood with Lizzie Dillon, who had been the
loved nurse several years earlier of my cousin Sidney Crowe.

I enjoyed being with the Dillons in St John's Wood. I
cannot remember the name of the road, but from the far end
of the big garden I could gaze at the occasional barge going
along the Regent's Canal and, although the Dillons did not
have any children, they had a lot of rabbits. My godmother
whom I called Little Auntie, a manner of address which was
carried on by my brother and sisters, had a blue Skye terrier
called Laddie to whom I was devoted. His pedigree name was
Auld Reekie and he had once belonged to my mother. My father
did not care for dogs, and so when she married my mother
gave him to her sister, for which Laddie never forgave her.
If she came to see Isabel, Laddie would retire under a sofa and
refuse to greet her. I was photographed with him that autumn
by Faulkner of Baker Street. The very next day Laddie was
stolen and never found again.

I spoke just now of the profound effect upon my childhood
caused by the catastrophe of Minnie's diphtheria. This was the
engagement that autumn of Annie Curry to be my nurse and
the nurse of the child that my mother was expecting in the
spring. Looking back on it now, I think that having to deal
with unreasonableness in an elderly woman was a valuable
preparation for life because it taught me very early to expect
people to be stupid and to be agreeably surprised when they
were not.

When Nanny brought me up to rejoin my father and mother,

who were playing in Hull that week, I was sharply aware of
this old woman's intrusion between me and my adored mother.
I suppose in fact that Nanny was not much more than fifty-
five at this date, but to me she seemed the oldest and ugliest
woman in the world. My mother was always convinced that
anything she herself very much wanted to do was the wrong
thing to do, and so from the first she allowed Nanny's early
Victorian notions about what children should and should not
do far too much latitude. I remember soon after we arrived
in Hull being depressed at tea because it would so soon be
time for Pappa and Mamma, as they were still being called,
to go to the theatre, and Nanny's saying that if they did not
go to the theatre there would be no money to buy biscuits for
my tea. Preferring my parents' company to 'bickies', I refused
to eat them. Nanny tried to force a biscuit into my mouth.
I picked up the plate and flung it on the floor. Thereupon she
put me to bed and managed to persuade my mother for the
sake of discipline not to come and say good-night before she
left for the theatre. In fact, of course, my mother was gratified
by my contempt for biscuits if biscuits for me meant being
deprived of her company. However, she was always fearful
of being accused of spoiling me and therefore surrendered.

Shortly after this my mother was laid up and had to be
left behind in some town. When she rejoined the Company
at Huddersfield she was horrified to see all my curls had been
cut off. It was my father's idea. He thought that by doing
this he would preserve my head from the baldness which had
spoiled his own prime. He must have had his doubts about
the way my mother would receive this haircut, because I have
to this day an envelope of golden-brown curls, on which is
written in my mother's hand 'Baby's hair'. Therefore obviously
he must have asked the barber for the curls as a peace-offering.
I need hardly add that Nanny thoroughly approved of that
haircut, because the golden-brown faded and she was able to
sniff and call my hair 'mousy'. For her, mousiness was a kind
of disgraceful tint.

By that November I was able to read nursery rhymes and
fairy stories. This must have been by a kind of mental photography because I was never taught to read. I knew the rhymes
by heart and if I failed to remember a line I could recover it

from the printed page. My father used to tease me by saying the nursery rhymes wrong, which used to distress me a good deal, but if I showed him on the page where he was wrong and he refused to accept my correction I used to become speechless with rage and despair at his stupidity. My mother was not particularly impressed by my being able to read before I was two. She and her sister Isabel had read Rollins' long Roman history before they were two and a half. Their mother had taught herself to read at two and by the time she was four was reading Sterne's *Sentimental Journey* as a favourite book.

That Christmas the C.C.C. played at Coventry, and my father learned Tennyson's *Lady Godiva* in order to recite it at his benefit night. I can recall listening to him with absorption as he went over and over the lines to memorise them. It amused my father to give me one or two cues from Shakespeare to which one of my favourite responses was 'Lay on, Macduff, and damn'd be he that first cries hold enough', after my father had cried 'Turn, hellhound, turn.' Even more appealing to my fancy was when my father announced, 'My lord, the Duke of Buckingham is taken', at which I thrust out a menacing hand and proclaimed in that strangely deep voice for one not yet two years old, 'Off with his head', to be followed by crossing my arms and shaking my head as I reflected sternly 'So much for Buckenum.'

This is certainly dramatic precocity, but it seems insignificant when I remember that my mother's two elder sisters, in the year of the Great Exhibition filled the St James's Theatre for a hundred nights when they were eight and six years old.

And this seems to be a suitable cue for an account of my mother's family.

INTERLUDE

IT begins with my great-grandfather Joseph Cowell, who wrote an entertaining set of reminiscences called *Thirty Years Passed among the Players in England and America*. This was published by Harper and Brothers, 82 Cliff Street, New York, in 1844.

The *Dictionary of National Biography* calls this work 'clever and amusing', and when at last I got hold of a copy, thanks to the kindness of an American reader, I was able to agree with that description myself. Mr Munsen Havens of Cleveland, Ohio, having noticed in some article of mine that I had not been able to read these reminiscences of my great-grandfather, bought a copy at the sale of the library of William Winter, the most famous of all American dramatic critics. It was originally published as a paper-back, and I doubt if many copies still exist. Among the publishers' announcements at the back is 'A Christmas Carol in Prose; being a Ghost Story of Christmas. By Charles Dickens. Price 6¼ cents.' Threepence! The Americans were doing better then out of ignoring copyright than the Russians are doing today.

Joe Cowell's real name was Joseph Leathley Whitshed; he makes a mystery of it by quoting from *Childe Harold*:

> But whence his name
> And lineage long, it suits me not to say.

The *D.N.B.*, with signs of careless proof-reading, says that his real name was Witchett, but in the next line that Admiral Whitshed was his uncle. Neither is true. The Admiral's name was Hawkins, the son of a Bishop of Raphoe. In 1791 Captain Hawkins, R.N., added Whitshed to Hawkins with a hyphen, under the terms of a cousin's will, Whitshed being the name of his maternal grandmother. This cousin was Colonel Whitshed, which means that my great-grandfather was a posthumous child and Captain Hawkins-Whitshed who became Admiral Sir James Hawkins-Whitshed, Bt., Admiral of the Blue, was a kind of guardian to him. His mother was a

devout Roman Catholic, and I surmise that the marriage with
Colonel Whitshed was one of those pre-emancipation marriages
lawful in the eyes of the Church but illegal in English law
which at that date only recognized marriages performed in an
Anglican church by an Anglican clergyman. I surmise further
that if Colonel Whitshed had married a Catholic legally he
would have been cut out of his grandmother's will and not
enjoyed her money while he was alive.

The reminiscences begin:

"The only spot on earth to which my memory turns with
that peculiar feeling which they alone can appreciate who
can remember the cot where they were born, is the little
village of Tor-Quay in Devonshire. But it was not where I
was born: all I can recollect of the place of my nativity is a
very large dark-looking room, and a very large, black-looking
chimneypiece. . . . I remember no little window 'where the
sun came peeping in at morn', as Hood says so prettily; nothing
but the large dark room, and large black chimney-piece;
perhaps a sad prognostic of my future fortunes."

In recalling Torquay he becomes more cheerful:

"The local inhabitants of this insignificant little village were
fishermen, pilots and boat builders; a simple, industrious kind-
hearted people. How often have the little shoeless urchins
shyly thrust me a slice of their dark-brown bread through the
trellis-work of the flower-garden in front of the house; and
many a weather-beaten handful of forbidden fruit has been
dropped imto the ready pin-a-fore of 'Master Joe' and
devoured with ecstasy in the most private place on the
premises."

He recalls a masked ball given on Lord St Vincent's birthday
at Carey Sands, of which the children were allowed to see the
commencement and after walking through the rooms sent
home. This would be in January 1801 when the Channel fleet
was in winter quarters off Torbay and Joseph Whitshed was
just nine years old.

"Here I first saw Lord Nelson, a mean-looking little man,
but very kind and agreeable to children; he prophesied a very
different fate for me from what it has been, and some trifling
anecdotes of himself made so strong an impression on my mind
as greatly to influence my conduct while in the navy."

A company of actors from Totnes had been engaged for this festive week to play in a hall fitted up as a theatre.

"The fireworks, ox-roastings, balls and concerts were all described and explained to us and all perfectly understood excepting the play, and that was incomprehensible. To satisfy our tortured curiosity, this angel-woman[1] (her name is too sacred to be put on record with the adventures of a poor player) actually engaged a portion of the company to give an entertainment at our house to please the children. . . . The dining-parlour was speedily unfurnished. . . . Chairs, sofas, and ottomans were placed in rows, and elevated in the back apartment, where the servants and the humble neighbours were to be accommodated to peep through the open door over our heads. . . .

"We children were placed in front, the governess at our backs, ready to explain any doubtful point and direct our deportment, our general instructions were to clap our hands when she did and not to laugh; this latter command I made up my mind to disobey; and I did. To her supposed superior judgment in juvenile matters had been left the control of the entertainment; and she had selected scenes from *Hamlet*. . . . She was a romantic little body. She hated me with all her heart, but was too prudent to say so. She had a very pretty ill-natured looking face, and small neat figure, in despite of one very crooked leg; this fact I discovered in consequence of her tumbling head-foremost over a stile one slippery day, and for laughing most heartily I was locked up in a cupboard, at the door of which I kicked so lustily for half an hour they were obliged to let me out. . . .

"Presently the ghost flitted in from behind a French flag— there was one on each side of the room with the English ensign over it—enveloped in a white sheet, his face whitewashed, and a white truncheon in his hand. . . . Before he had time to reply to Hamlet's earnest enquiries I shouted out with all my might 'That's the man who nailed up the flags!' . . . The Governess gave me one of her withering looks, but all the rest of the audience laughed most heartily, so did Hamlet, so did the ghost, till his white sheet shook.

"Hamlet was a slim, round-faced, good-looking young man,

---

[1] His mother.

and rather effeminate in his manner; we all agreed that he was like our pretty housemaid, Sally.

"Horatio was a greater success with the children and the servants than Hamlet. Partly this was due to his costume. His waistcoat was nearly covered with gold, and his cloak was spangled all over; he wore light blue pantaloons and red shoes. Besides, in the course of the evening he sang a fine loud song about ships and the navy, and danced a sailor's hornpipe. . . . He appeared to have twice as much to say as Hamlet and what he did say he said three times as loud. . . . The coachman said he heard one speech while he was feeding the horses, and the stable was at least one hundred yards from the house; no doubt the same speech which frightened two of the youngest children. They cried, and at their own request were sent to bed.

"Hamlet made several long soliloquies, and as he looked me straight in the face, I thought he addressed me in particular; so when he enquired

'Whether 'tis nobler in the mind to suffer
The slings and arrows of outrageous fortune
Or to take arms against a sea of troubles'

I replied 'If I were you I'd go to sea.' This called forth a joyous shout from the next room, for even then I was the low comedian of the household; but my governess said I was a very bad boy and if I spoke again I should be sent to bed. So when I thought Hamlet was going to make me another long speech I shut my eyes and made up my mind to go to sleep till it was over. But my friend Horatio soon roused me. . . .

"At last exhausted with wonder and delight I went to bed. I prayed every night that I might be *made a good boy and go to heaven.* I fell asleep, and dreamt that I had got there, and was surrounded by dozens of Hamlets, and Horatios, and ghosts in red wings and striped stockings, dancing and singing, and the angels applauding them in the most boisterous fashion; but when I wakened to my astonishment I heard Horatio singing away with all his might in the housekeeper's room, amid clapping of hands and shouts of laughter.

"Before I closed my eyes again that night, I made up my

mind that I would rather be that Horatio than be Horatio Nelson, though he had lost an eye and banged the French."

Beyond the fact that he entered the Navy as a midshipman when he was thirteen either in 1805 or 1806, Cowell says nothing more about his early life. His mother must have left Torquay soon after that performance of *Hamlet* to live in South Audley Street, in that little house which still stands by itself next to the Grosvenor Chapel. Some ten years ago the owner, an old lady, died and I made enquiries about that rarity, a Mayfair freehold. The price asked was £21,000 and beyond my means. Shelley once lived in it for a few months with poor Harriet.

My great-grandfather resumes his story in August 1809:

"I was just turned seventeen, but in manner and appearance much older. Three years in the navy, the usual hardships of a sailor's life, a complexion stained with salt water and the sun of many climes, are materials to make boys into men at very short notice. I had three weeks' leave of absence prior to a twelve months' cruise on the West Indies station. My mother lived next door to the Grosvenor Chapel; and on Sunday morning, determining to see all that could be seen (as my days were numbered) I 'dropped in' to witness the service . . . having been educated a rigid Roman Catholic, my entering an Episcopal house of God was induced by pure curiosity. In the adjoining pew was an elderly tradesmanlike-looking man with a pug nose and a round, unmeaning face, resembling altogether a good-natured bulldog; with him a plump old lady, and an elegantly dressed young creature— their daughter of course; but where could she get such an abominable plebeian-looking father and mother? I felt angry that nature had made herself so ridiculous. . . . Her fine eye, I thought, sometimes wandered towards me; a naval uniform in those days was quite as attractive as a soldier's is in these; she sat close to me, nothing but the abominable bulkhead of the pew between us. . . . I had been in love two or three times before, and have been in love ever since, and perfectly understood the symptoms in this case. In my own mind, I had got the consent of my mother, and had retired on a British midshipman's pay to a cottage near a wood with a cow, cabbage-garden, chickens and children. The only impediment that appeared to cross my path to pre-eminent felicity was her pudding-faced, pug-nosed parents; my mother would decidedly object to them, whatever she might think of their daughter. In my confusion of thought I stood up in the pew, and popped on my hat with the cockade behind; the old gentleman pointed out my error; I thought I saw a child-like giggle play over the beautiful face of my adored; I would have given two years. pay to be mast-headed out of sight of land or petticoats for the rest of my life. The service ended, I gained the door as they did, and tendered an awkward acknowledgement of thanks to the old man for correcting my ridiculous position.

" 'Sir,' said he, with a kind of plethoric chuckle, 'you gentlemen of the navy, sir, don't often get to church, I suppose; but, sir, I love a sailor, sir; I'm a loyal subject, sir; God bless the king, sir, and God Almighty bless the queen, sir. And I'm blessed if she oughtened to be blessed, sir, for blessing the country with such a blessed lot of royal highnesses, sir. Sir, I'm a true-born Englishman, and have the honour to be leather-breechesmaker, sir, to His Royal Highness the Duke of Sussex,' pointing at the same time to a sign over a bow-window, by the side of which he stopped and rung a bell at the private entrance. The door was opened by a boy in undress livery; we bowed and parted. I looked up at *William Creek, Tailor and Breeches-maker in Ordinary to H.R.H. the Duke of Sussex* in green and gold letters, and the King's Arms in a semi-circle over it, exactly four doors away from my mother's house. I had followed my charmer at a regular distance of about three feet, sometimes on the curbstone, sometimes in the gutter, or, as a sailor might say two points to leeward. Now this was not *mauvaise honte* on my part but prudence; for upon coming alongside in the first instance I found, to my astonishment, she was at least three inches taller than myself. In everyday language, she was what is called a magnificent creature. Over her sculptured form she had thrown a splendid scarlet mantle, trimmed with white ermine; a white hat with a drooping red feather adorned her classic head. . . . I was in love, but she was (oh horrible thought!) the daughter of a leather-breeches builder. But then he made breeches for His Royal Highness the Duke of Sussex! How might that soften down the bowels of my mother's aristocratic authority? There was hope in that thought, and I determined to be measured for a pair the next day; though I had but little time to wear them, for on the station to which I was ordered, even if the service would permit the costume, the climate would not.

"On the following morning I called on Mr Creek.

"'Sir, he's at breakfast,' said the knock-kneed boy in the grey livery, 'but, if 'tis anything partic'lar, I'll call him, sir.'

"The bow-window apartment I had entered was covered with a handsome carpet; in the centre a billiard-like table on which were writing materials and the papers of the day; and the walls decorated with numerous mirrors. My prospect of consent began to brighten. If he was a breeches-maker, he didn't breakfast till ten o'clock and kept a sort of livery servant. I had barely time to peep through a glass case the width of the shop, covered with a demi-transparent green curtain, behind which at least thirty men were employed on a platform, stitching away at his royal highness's small-clothes, I suppose, when Mr Creek appeared. His fat face was buttered from ear to ear, which he proceeded to wipe with his folded hand-kerchief, while in his peculiar style he paid me the compliments of the day. When he came to a pause, I begged him, in my most urbane manner, to measure me for a suit of clothes.

"'Sir, with pleasure, sir. A uniform suit of course? I pride myself on my uniform fits, sir. This coat is a little too much—'

"I interrupted by quickly saying,

"'I wish a plain coat, Mr Creek.'

"'A plain coat, sir? Bless me, sir, have you left your ship for any length of time?'

"'I may shortly leave the navy altogether,' said I, with a sigh. I thought of the cottage and the cow; and as my mother cheerfully paid my bills at the time, and might not after I had retired from the service and married the tailor's daughter, prudence prompted me to order a green coat, red waistcoat, and leather breeches—a very fitting dress for rural felicity. The red vest I intended in compliment to the colour of my wife's cloak—that was to be; and I hinted that if it could be made of the same piece of cloth that his daughter's mantle was composed of, I should praise it more highly.

"'Oh sir,' said the old man, his little blue eyes twinkling on either side of his putty-like nose, 'she's not my daughter. I—'

"'God be praised!' exclaimed I.

"'Sir!' said he, his face suddenly assuming an expression of gravity which its fat-encumbered muscles seemed impossible for it to achieve; 'sir—I beg pardon, sir,—but I should like to know why you appear so thankful, sir, that Anna is not my daughter!'

"Anna! I heard her name for the first time, a pastoral, poetical and pretty name—a real sailor's name.

"I blundered out that I had thanked God that, in addition to her natural protector, she had a friend of his age and respectability to guide her moral deportment, of which I judged from the sacred place to which he had conducted her when we first met. A shade of doubt passed over his countenance, but he recollected I was his customer, and his natural good-humour and common sense prevailed. He went on to explain that Anna had no father; he had died when she was an infant, and had left her mother 'well to do in the world' with three children, all girls, two much older than Anna, and one long since married to a cousin of his wife. She was a native of —— in Berkshire; at her father's death, her mother had taken a milliner's shop, where Anna had learned the rudiments of the business, but had been sent to London under his care, and was now articled for three years (two and a half of which were yet to stretch their slow length away) to the Misses Twicross, the celebrated dressmakers in Bond-street, with a premium of fifty guineas, to be 'finished'.

"Upon giving my name and address, the old man exclaimed, 'Why, bless me, sir, I have the honour, sir, to be in great favour with your mamma, sir, my neighbour, sir; and you know, sir, it's very few people as is, sir'—with a kind of confidential chuckle. 'You see, sir, her kitchen-chimney was on fire, and the maid-servant set up a terrible screeching; and there was so much smoke, sir, that you couldn't see where the fire was; and the parish engine, sir, being in the basement story of the chapel, next house to hers as one may say; I and my boy and the poor apple-woman that she kindly gives leave to sit at the corner of the court pulled it out, sir, and I dragged the hose into the passage; but the fire went out before we could get any water, but your good mamma, sir, coming down stairs and seeing me with the brass nozzle in my hand,

4. C. M.'s maternal grandparents, Mr and Mrs Bateman

5. My grandfather, Henry Compton

5. My grandmother, Mrs Henry Compton

sir, thought I had extinguished it; and so, sir, whenever she speaks of me, sir, she always says "The good man that saved my property by putting out the fire, Mr—What's his name? Something that puts my teeth on edge?" " 'Mr Creek, ma'am," says Mary. "Yes, Mr Squeak, that's it."'

"The jolly old man chatted himself into a most familiar good-humour. I recounted some of my ship-shape adventures and, well pleased with each other, we parted, with my promising (oh, how gladly!) to take a cup of tea with himself, and wife and Anna 'just in the family way' that evening. I am not going to tantalise my readers with a rodomontade of love-making; suffice it to say that my Anna had received an education far above her station; affable, nay, even free in her manner, but with a mind as simply pure and unpolluted as the stream that wanders through and adorns her native village. I readily obtained permission to save Mr Creek the trouble of conducting her to Bond-street in the morning. The jovial old tailor had made us stand back to back to decide our height; and he declared, 'Anna, sir, is only an inch taller than you are—good measure, sir.'

"When at an early hour the next day we met, I had heels to my boots that placed me on a level with her at any rate; and before we had crossed Grosvenor Square, I had good reason to believe that our hopes and wishes were more on an equality than our persons. Doubt not I was most punctual in my attendance to and from South Audley-street to Bond-street. Three times that week and four times the next, accompanied by the old people, we attended the theatre. The first legitimate play I ever beheld Anna sat beside me—'twas Romeo and Juliet. 'They must have played it on purpose,' said the innocent Anna in a whisper, and her cheek wet with tears, and I in my heart damned the author for not letting them live and be happy.

"I passed two whole, dear, delicious Sundays in her society. Oh how sweet

> To walk together to the kirk,
> And all together pray.

"I spoke not of any difference of creed; for her sake I would have turned Turk.

D

"The old man was our confidant and counsellor. 'Sir, you must join your ship, sir, at the proper time; and Anna, sir, must finish her time with the Misses Twicross, and get the worth of her fifty guineas, sir; and you must fight the enemies of Old England! Oh, I'm a loyal subject, sir; and when you're a lieutenant, sir, and the old lady won't consent, sir, if you both think as you do now, and there should come a peace, sir, you'll get your half-pay, sir; you can teach transportation, navigation I mean, sir, and drawing and painting. (I had been well instructed and had taken his and his wife's portraits, and Anna's picture in little:); and she will be mistress of her art, sir; I am well to do in the world, sir; have neither chick nor child; Anna's father was a good friend of mine, sir—lent me money when I first went into business; but never fret, sir; take things cool as I do, sir,' wiping the perspiration from his fat forehead; 'all will be right, sir; take my advice, sir.'

"*I wish to God I had.*

"The fatal second Sunday at length arrived—I thought, in the middle of the week I had to set forth at 5 p.m., to ensure my being on board by gunfire on Monday morning, but it was past seven before I could finish all my oaths of constancy, and exchange those tokens sailors think so sacred.

"With hope decking the future on the rainbow-colours of love at seventeen, I rushed into the chaise on a bright autumnal evening and, faster than the sun, I seemed to travel on the road to Portsmouth, to overtake him in a few weeks in the West Indies. The tedium of many a weary middle-watch in that sunburned sea has been relieved of its monotony in (castle-) building the cottage, and the cow, the chickens and the children; and then

> Look'd on the moon,
> And thought of Nancy.

Midshipman Joseph Leathley Whitshed made a mess of his naval career by striking a bully of a lieutenant on the voyage home from the West Indies. He was put in irons with the prospect of a court-martial when the ship reached England and the likelihood of being sentenced to be shot at the end of it. Luckily his own ship was engaged by a Frenchman and he was allowed to fight his gun. He did this well enough to justify

Admiral Sir Robert Calder in pre-dating his discharge from the service by sick list. So when his ship reached Plymouth Dock—the modern Devonport—Midshipman Joseph Leathley Whitshed became Mr Joseph Leathley Cowell. He had fifty pounds of pay in his pocket and when he had gone through that he kept himself for over a year by painting. To quote his quotation from Shelley:

'Tis easy then for a new name,
And a new life, fashioned on old desires.

In other words there returned the desire to be an actor which had been at the back of his mind since the performance of *Hamlet* at Torquay over ten years earlier and had been revived by those visits to the theatre with the Creeks. So he wrote the manager of the Dock Theatre.

> *Plymouth Dock,*
> *January 11, 1812*
>
> *George Sanford Esquire,*
> *Sir, I wish to become an actor. I will be content to receive a small amount of pay until I get acquainted with the duties I have to perform. I have learned 'Iago' in Shakespeare's play of Othello, and could easily get perfect in 'Belcour', in Cumberland's comedy of The West Indian; I have seen Elliston in that character in London, and have vanity enough to believe I could play either of them. Your early reply through the post office will oblige.*
>
> *Yours respectfully,*
>
> *Leathley Irving*

An odd coincidence that for his next pseudonym he should have chosen the pseudonym of an actor not yet born who would be given his great chance by his own future son-in-law.

Mr Sanford gave 'Mr Irving' an appointment and 'Mr Irving' sent in his card with Cowell on it and received a lecture on changing his name for the stage.

"You assume another name because you are ashamed of a pursuit either your taste or your necessities induce you to adopt. Now, sir, with such a feeling you can never be an actor. No man can never be eminent in a profession he considers it a disgrace to follow. Keep the name you say you have a claim to, and now are known by."

However, Sanford evidently found his young visitor an attractive personality and agreed to give him a trial. My great-grandfather wrote of him over thirty years later:

"Poor George Sanford. He died a few years since, regretted and respected by all whose good opinion he would have condescended to care for while living. He was a native of the city of New York, and 'tis somewhat strange that my first theatrical friend and manager first saw the light in the same city where my last born opened her eyes [this was my grandmother] and in a country I by choice have been a citizen of for more than half of my thinking life."

In the end Sanford gave the novice a chance to face an audience.

"The night arrived—January the twenty-third, 1815. *The part of Belcour by a gentleman, his first appearance on any stage*, attracted a full and very fashionable house. Admiral Calder, the commander of the port, and a large party occupied the stage-box. I had many shipmates in harbour at the time, and some relatives; all, of course, attended, induced by pity; how I hate the word—scorn or curiosity.

"I had been used to danger in many shapes, and fear is not an attribute of my nature, but I was most damnably frightened on that occasion. I spoke the words mechanically, but I could neither see nor hear; my mouth was parched; what to do with my hands I knew not; if both arms had been amputated I feel assured I should have been relieved of an abominable encumbrance."

However, after his first scare the young actor's confidence returned.

"At the conclusion of the performance 'Three cheers for the blue jacket' was announced and performed in full chorus. This little compliment I was in the habit of receiving upon the slightest occasion, during the season; for, though I had been dismissed the navy with a flea in my ear, my offence was a feather in my cap in the estimation of many comrades of my own grade, or those beneath me."

For the next four or five years Cowell acted with various provincial circuits and established himself as a favourite low comedian. He married, first, a sister of W. H. Murray, the Edinburgh theatrical manager and friend of Scott, in spite of his being a grandson of Sir John Murray of Broughton, Prince Charles Edward's secretary about whom Sir Walter Scott was always so bitter. By her he had a son, Sam Cowell, an immensely popular singer of popular songs who made his first appearance upon the stage at Boston, Mass., in 1829 at the age of nine, and like his father earned a place in the *Dictionary of National Biography*.

About the time of Queen Caroline's trial Cowell was acting at Drury Lane under Elliston's management.

"To keep his own name and that of his theatre constantly before the public, he knew, from every quack's experience, was most important, and every means to achieve this object was resorted to by Elliston. . . . The poor persecuted Queen Caroline had arrived in England to demand redress from the unmanly accusations brought against her by her husband, and Elliston . . . showed his one sided loyalty and ignorance at the same time, by omitting 'et regina' at the bottom of the playbills, and leaving 'vivant rex'. And so the *singular plural* remained for weeks. . . . But this paltry attempt to wound the feelings of a suffering female, for the dirty desire of pandering to the malignity of her depraved husband, was held in contempt and derision by every thinking mind, and I hope by even his King among the number."

That singular plural is certainly a sad reflection on the Latin taught to Elliston at St Paul's School.

Cowell evidently did not hit it off with Elliston and he left Drury Lane for the Adelphi, his 'pet theatre'.

"The trial of Queen Caroline," he writes, "created the most intense and universal excitement among all classes of persons ever witnessed in London during my recollection. There were two parties, equally violent in their opinions— the King's cruel and vindictive in their accusations; and the Queen's, boisterous and vehement in their declarations of her innocence. It absorbed every then topic of conversation; and the rancour with which either position was maintained severed the bonds of old friendships and ruffled the social comfort round the domestic hearth. . . . I was one of her most enthusiastic supporters; for, admitting all they brought against her were true, *she was a woman*, and I always make it a rule, in taste, to be on their side, whether they are right or wrong. . . .

On the night of her acquittal the excitement was terrific; the
military were ordered out, to intimidate the multitude by their
presence, and instantly suppress any treasonable outbreak by
the joy-intoxicated myriads who were parading the streets
and rending the air with shouts of triumph. Our theatre was
crowded and it so happened that in the first piece some fifty
supernumeraries were employed. Highly elated by the success
of my party, I met these fellows ready dressed for the stage,
awaiting the commencement of the performance; and without
thought in the fulness of my feeling, I proposed '*Three cheers
for the Queen!*' which was instantly given in a voice of thunder!
. . . At the conclusion of the first act there was a universal cry
for 'God save the Queen'. The number and temper of the
audience were too dangerous to trifle with, and old Lee, the
stage-manager, who was foolish enough to adore the king and,
in consequence, hate the queen, had to address them in his
'official capacity'. After stating that he was instructed to
inquire their pleasure and being answered by a thousand
voices that they wanted 'God save the Queen!' he went on to
say that 'we recognize no anthem called "God save the Queen,"
but if it be the wish of the audience, at the end of the first
piece, the company will sing "God save the King".'

"As he had stated, the whole of the ladies and gentlemen
(as is usual on such occasions) appeared at the appointed time,
and Mrs Tennant commenced the first verse, amid some
interruption by the audience,

> 'God save great George, our king;
> Long live our noble king;
> God save the—'

'Queen!' I shouted with all my might. The effect on the
actors and audience was electrical, and peal on peal of applause
drowned the hearing of the termination of the verse."

The result of this ebullience of chivalry was that the management decided to punish Cowell by retaining his week's salary.
To the treasurer, as he was then called (the Friday night of
salary payments is still called 'treasury') the Queen's champion
replied:

"Understanding that this stretch of power was to be assumed,
I prepared for *The Times* newspaper this little paragraph,

which, to prove how anxious I am to exonerate you from any participation or approval of my conduct I'll read to you.

"And I produced the following:

UNPRECEDENTED CRUELTY AND OPPRESSION

On the night our beloved queen was acquitted of the vile and infamous charges that were fabricated to achieve her ruin, a poor actor, in the fulness of his heart, substituted 'queen' for 'king' in a fulsome song the over strained loyalty of the managers of the Adelphi Theatre endeavoured to thrust upon the patience of the audience, and for this heinous offence, in their opinion, these lawmakers have taken from him his week's wages, and his only means of support for a wife and large family of children."

The large family of children consisted of two small sons but the threat of publication was enough. The salary was not retained by the management.

Soon after this Cowell received an offer from an American theatrical manager to go to the United States.

In these days when the representatives of Hollywood and American theatrical managers and publishers are familiar figures it may be amusing to have an impression of what was a rare bird nearly 150 years ago.

"I got a note from Stephen Price, suggesting that I would breakfast with him at ten o'clock the next morning. He lodged in Norfolk-street in the Strand. The door was opened by a servant-girl; in answer to my inquiry, she said 'I'll see' and in a minute a negro man appeared, and showed his own teeth and me into the parlour where a cloth was laid for breakfast. In a short time he returned to say Mr Price would be glad to see me upstairs. I was conducted to a chamber and on the bed, with his feet wrapped in flannel, and his body in a wadded silk morning-gown, lay Stephen Price. In a peculiarly distinct, drawling manner, which till you got accustomed to it, had a very singular effect . . . small, bright, mischievous eyes, an abominable nose—looking like a large thumb very much swollen and nearly coming to a head, but decision and firmness strongly marked around his mouth; his appearance and manner were greatly at variance for he looked like fifty, and talked like twenty.

"'I must apologise to you, Mr Cowell,' said he, 'for asking you to take your breakfast in my bedroom; but after calling in at Astley's to see you, James Wallack and myself finished the evening at Vauxhall, and I didn't get home till four this morning; and the consequence is I caught cold and have a fit of the b——y gout. I'm very subject to the d—— thing. But Wallack's the d——dest b—— I ever met with. Nothing ever hurts him. Mr Oxberry informs me, sir, that you have a desire to visit New Yo-ork.'

"I have, sir," I replied.

"'Well, sir,' said he, 'I'll tell you candidly that I'm d——d if you'll do for New Yo-ork, if you are not a better actor than you appeared last night. I'll tell you what 'tis, there's a little b—— in the Park Theatre of the name of Nexon, who can play that character quite as well as you can, and he merely d'livers messages *there*.'

"You have, I conclude, then, an excellent company," said I, a little nettled, "on your side the water?"

"'A d—— deal better company than they have in any theatre in London,' said he, faster than anything he had said yet.

"Well, sir, surrounded as you are by such a galaxy of talent, it will be advisable for me to remain in London."

"'Why, sir,' he replied quickly, 'I'll tell you what 'tis; James Wallack and sev-eral of my friends say that you're a b——y good actor, but that you won't act at Astley's. What will you take to go to New Yo-ork?'

"Fifteen pounds a week," I replied.

"'I'll give you ten pounds a week for the first season,' said he, 'but twelve for the second.'

"Agreed," said I.

"'When can you go?' said he.

"Tomorrow," said I.

"'Well, sir,' said he, smiling, 'I'm d——d but you are certainly the easiest man to make a bargain I ever dealt with.'

"If he had known, however, as much as I did he would have offered me a guinea a week, and I would have taken it, but, Heaven be praised he didn't, and he continued;

"'There's an eternal fine ship, called the *T'ames* sailing from London on the first of September and another called the

Albion, on the same day from Liverpool, in which I shall sail. The only difference in the thing is, you get to sea a d—— deal quicker by going to Liverpool.'

"I gave the London ship the preference, as more convenient on account of baggage, and that I might once more visit my old cruising ground the British Channel, and perhaps for ever bid farewell to the scenes of my boyhood.

"The Captain was Charles H. Marshall, a very good-looking and very fine fellow, with 'no drowning marks upon him.' The mate was a weather-beaten, humorous, 'sea monster'; upon asking his name, he replied,

"'If you're an Englishman, and I once tell you my name, you'll never forget it.'

"I don't know that," I replied; "I'm very unfortunate in remembering names."

"'Oh, never mind,' said he, with a peculiarly sly, comical look; 'if you're an Englishman you'll never forget mine.'

"Then I certainly am, "I replied.

"'Well, then,' said he, dryly, 'my name's Bunker! and I'm d——d if any Englishman will ever forget that name!' "

The *Thames* left the Downs on September 8th 1821, and was off Staten Island by October 23rd 'after a tedious and most boisterous passage'. My great-grandfather and one or two of the other passengers were allowed to row ashore and take the ferry boat to New York. He was surprised to find that "the feeling created by the war with England, then long since over, was still rankling in the minds of the lower order of Americans, and their hatred of an Englishman they took a pride in showing whenever in their power".

"New York was then a very different place of accommodation for travellers from what it is at the present day; oyster-cellars that you could tumble into at every corner; 'restaurant' staring you in the face in every street. . . . The only two places of the kind in existence then was Morse's, a very humbly fitted up cellar, where a table-cloth was never seen and a clean knife only by waiting till the operation was performed, under a store in Park Row where now, I suppose, there are thirty . . . and one of a little better class, kept by a Frenchman, under Washington Hall, then the second-best hotel in the city. . . .

"Feeling hungry and fatigued I entered what in London would be called a chandler's shop, put some money on the counter, and enquired if they would sell me for that sum some bread and butter and a tempting red herring or two I saw in a barrel at the door.

"'Why, what coin is it?' said a fellow in a red flannel shirt and a straw hat.

"English shillings," I replied.

"'No,' said the fellow. 'I know nothing about English shillings, nor English anything, nor I don't want to.'

The newcomer managed to change a few shillings for dollar bills at a Jewish Exchange Office and then went back to eat his red herrings.

In his own words, "Relieved in mind and body, I sallied forth again up Wall-street and through Broadway. The pavement was horrible, and the sidewalks, partly brick and partly flagstones of all shapes, put together as nearly as their untrimmed forms would permit. The Park I found to be about the same size as Portman Square, but of a shape to defy any geometrical term to convey the form of it. It had been surrounded by a wooden, unpainted, rough fence, but a storm on the first of September had prostrated the larger portion, together with some fine old cottonwood-trees, and the little grass the cows and pigs allowed to remain was checkered o'er by short cuts to the different streets in the neighbourhood.

"I continued my walk up Broadway, and as I went the houses diminished both in size and number, and in less than a mile I was in the country."

That evening Cowell went to a performance of *Lionel and Clarisse* at the Park Theatre at which he was presently to make his first appearance on the American stage.

"The house was exceptionally dark; oil, of course, then was used, in common brass Liverpool lamps, ten or twelve of which were placed in a larger sheet-iron hoop, painted green, hanging from the ceiling in the centre, and one, half the size, on each side of the stage. The posts of the boxes were decorated with one continuous American ensign; the seats were covered with green baize, and the back of the boxes with whitewash, and the iron columns which were supporting them with burnished gold! . . . The audience came evidently to see the

play and be pleased with everything; the men generally wore
their hats, and the ladies all came in bonnets, but usually
dispossessed themselves of them and tied them in large bunches,
high up to the gold columns, the varied colours of the ribands
and materials of which they were made, being a vast improvement to the unfurnished appearance of the house."

Cowell was encouraged for his own prospect of success by
the intelligent appreciation of the Park Theatre audience, and
having made an appointment with an Irish boatman to row
him out to rejoin the ship, which was expected on the morning
tide, he set off again for Wall Street.

"The night was very dark, not a lamp was to be seen, save
a twinkle from a little light through the closed glass door of
a solitary chemist's shop, in the whole distance; 'Twas about
eight o'clock, and every store was shut; nor did I meet more
than thirty persons during my walk. Look at Broadway and
Wall-street now!"

The Irish boatman met him at the grocery at the foot of
Wall Street with the news that the ship would not be in for
another two hours at least.

"I enquired of mine host if I should be an intruder by
remaining in his shop, and I ordered some more bread and
butter and a herring. . . . To make myself as amiable as possible
in the estimation of four or five gentlemen, short of shirt and
long in beard, I treated them to two or three rounds of grog
and cigars. I was then no connoisseur in the latter article,
having never smoked tobacco in any shape in my life, but I
undertook a 'long nine' and a couple of glasses of 'excellent
brandy' as old red shirt said. On the passage I had never even
tasted wine or spirits, though these luxuries were included in
the thirty-five guineas apiece cabin fare. So ill prepared, the
long nine soon knocked me over as flat as a *nine pounder*. . . .
I was perfectly in my senses, but was incapable of voice or
action. In these days the march of progress in such matters
would have doomed me to the certainty of having my throat
cut, then stripped and thrown into the dock; and the next
thing a coroner's inquest would have quickly brought in a
verdict of *found drowned*, and no more said about the matter.
But at the untutored period I speak of they were content to
take only my movables, *id est* my hat, cravat, watch, snuff-box,

handkerchief and the balance of the dirty dollars. My in-
capacity to make resistance, saved my coat, for I was so limber
they couldn't get it off whole and after splitting it down the
back they concluded it would be more honourable to let
me keep it—carried me down to a boat and rowed me off to
the ship where I was delivered on board as a 'gentleman very
unwell'."

His first night at the Park Theatre was more successful than
his first night in that Wall Street grocery.

"Two tunes, which I couldn't discover to be at all like
any air I had ever heard before were *Yankee Doodle* and *Hail
Columbia*. Unexpectedly introducing these then unhackneyed
tunes in a song I manufactured for the occasion produced a
great effect, and my success altogether was immense. . . . I
became at once a decided favourite with the audience; and
that enviable position, I am proud to say, I have maintained
in all the principal cities of the Union, up to the present hour."

After he had found rooms for himself Cowell notes:

"There is still a remnant of the custom, but then it was
universal for all classes of citizens, tradesmen or otherwise,
no matter how advantageously they were situated for either
business or comfort, to change their abode on the first of May.
From that date all houses and stores were rented for one year;
and the hurry, bustle, turmoil and confusion into which that
day threw the whole population of New York cannot be
conceived; it could be compared with nothing but itself. A
town besieged would fail to convey an idea of the ridiculous
effect of an immense mass of men, women and children loaded
with articles of household utility or ornament, taking shelter,
with much seeming anxiety, in some abode, from which
another party, loaded in the same manner, were making their
escape. The streets crowded with carts, waggons, and carriages
of every denomination, teeming over with chairs and tables,
in the hurry apparently packed on purpose to tumble off, to
the great delight of the cabinet-makers and others, who took
no interest in the matter beyond the mischief. No better proof
of the national forbearance and government of temper natural
to Americans, than such a trial of patience as this could
possibly be invented; and yet even the demolition of a favourite
basket of china, or a dray carrying a load of furniture nobody

could find out where; or the porter's placing a ponderous piece of furniture in the fourth storey of No. 80, when it was expected in the first parlour of No. 1, were causes of merriment, especially to those who had the right to be annoyed; and with the exception of some disputed points of etiquette among the Irish carmen the whole day's 'toil and trouble' appeared to be considered an excellent frolic.''

Cowell played on until the season ended on the fourth of July 1822 to begin again on the first of September.

"About the middle of August great alarm was created by some cases of yellow fever occurring in the northern part of the city. In a day or two the contagion crossed Broadway, and a death being reported at the Custom House in Wall-street, the panic became universal and frightfully ridiculous. The whole population in that section of the city who were well or able, beat a retreat with bag and baggage—the sick and poor at the expense of the authorities—the movement of the first of May would have been no comparison. Well-dressed women were seen hatless, dragging a squalling child through the blazing sun, and the fond father following with a bed on his head, and perhaps a gridiron or a pair of tongs in his hand. All the ferry-boats to Hoboken, Powless Hook, Staten Island, and Brooklyn were constantly plying loaded down with passengers, who seemed to think drowning a secondary consideration; and in *one hour* the thickly-inhabited and largest portion of New York was deserted by every human being, the district supposed to be infected was boarded up, the streets covered ankle deep with lime, and all intercourse prohibited....

"John Kent and I kept bachelor's hall, for not a soul would venture to pay us a visit. He was a faithful old negro from Jamaica, who for years had been employed in the theatre as a sort of deputy property-maker. . . . Twice a week we made it a rule late at night to trespass in the uninhabited region, John loaded with a huge basket of coarse provisions for the starving cats, and after a donation or two of the sort, the numbers that would surround us, the moment they heard our approach, would be past belief: I found it a most whimsical mode of cheating a long, dull night of part of its death-like solitude; not another thing that breathes or stirs would we meet in our walk except a single horse, perhaps, trotting along

with an unattended hearse, and the driver smoking a cigar,
or whistling 'Yankee Doodle'. . . . . Some of the retail dealers
from Broadway and Pearl-street, after the first alarm had
subsided, had erected temporary sheds for the sale of their
various merchandise at Greenwich Village, which could then
only boast of a state-prison and some dozen scattered houses
and, in consequence, the place suddenly assumed the appearance of a fair."

From now on most of the autobiography is taken up with
reminiscences of actors and actresses in this or that part, and
the performances of forgotten players make tedious reading.
However, interlarded with these are some good tales.

Here is a memory of a gambling scene on one of the Missis-
sippi river boats in 1829. The game is by now non-existent.

"Two men played at it, and three cards were dealt singly
to each, and a trump turned up; and the opponent to the
dealer might order it to be turned down, and then make it
another suit more agreeable to his hand, or play it as it was.
The great point in favour of the opponent to the dealer was
to know if he held *any* trumps and *how many* he had. . . . Sitting
by me was an apparently uninterested looker-on like myself,
peering over my Virginian friend's hand, and marking by
his fingers stretched upon the table, the number of trumps he
held. The eagle eye of the Virginian soon detected the villainy,
and taking out his hunting-knife—it was before Bowie christened them—began paring his nails with well-acted indifference,
as if entirely absorbed in the game, and laid it quietly on the
table without its sheath. The next hand dealt him one trump,
and the spy placed his fore-finger on the table, which my
friend instantly chopped off!

"'Hallo! stranger, what are you about?' shouted the dis-
membered gentleman. 'You have cut off one of my fingers.'

"'I know it,' said old Virginia, coolly, 'and if I had had
more trumps, you would have had less fingers.'

"This was considered an excellent practical joke, and we
all took a drink together, and I lent the wounded a hand-
herchief to bind up his hand."

And here is an interesting sidelight on poker as it was being
played in 1829. The Oxford Dictionary's earliest allusion to
poker is from 1846.

"One night, while I was getting instructed in the mysteries of *uker* (this was the original spelling of *euchre*) close by was a party playing *poker*. This was then exclusively a high-gambling Western game, founded on *brag*, invented as it is said by Henry Clay when a youth.

"The aces are the highest denomination; then the kings, queens, jacks and tens; the smaller cards are not used; those I have named are all dealt out, and carefully concealed from one another: old players pack them in their hands, and peep at them as if they were afraid to trust even themselves to look. The four aces, with any other card, *cannot be beat*. Three aces or three kings with another pair is called a *full* and is considered a very good bragging hand. The dealer makes the game or value of the beginning bet, called the *ante*—in this instance it was a dollar—and then everybody stakes the same amount, and says '*I'm up*'."

Presumably the flush and the straight did not yet exist, and the fact that Cowell thought it worth while as late as 1844 to explain a card-game suggests that poker had not by then made much headway in the Eastern States.

"During the time Lafayette was travelling through the Union, receiving the enthusiastic homage of all classes or persons, and, by the only mode in his power, showing his gratitude by kissing all the young women, shaking hands with the old, and blessing the little children, it so happened that my company was up in some city where he was not; but on his return to New York, I fortunately encountered him, and he honoured the theatre with a visit, which, of course, produced an overflowing house. The box appropriated for the use of himself and suite I had decorated with as many flags as I could borrow from volunteers and fire companies, mechanic and masonic societies, with the French and American ensigns enfolding each other in divers affectionate attitudes interspersed with a profusion of every description of vegetable matter with the exception of oak and laurel which Billy Rider, a delicious specimen of the Emerald Isle, had been desired exclusively to obtain.

"'There, sir, that's what you sent me for,' said Billy, throwing down a huge bundle of shrubs.

"No, sir, it's not; I said oak and laurel.'"

"'Divil a sprig of laurel is there, I believe, in the whole State of Jersey. By my word, sir, it was down to Werhawk I was, and back again twiced. As to oak, by the powers, there's plenty of that at the tops o' the trees where no mortal man could touch a leaf of it, av he had the legs of Goliath. By my troth, now they are mighty green and pretty—see the red berries on that darling there—depend on it, sorr, d—— the difference will the ould Gineral know; he's had something better to do than to be bothering his brains about bothany; and all those flags and finery that's the thing itself, sorr, to tickle a Frenchman.'

"And I believe Rider was partially right, for upon conducting the marquis to his box, for the sake of saying something, I apologised for the lack of preparation in consequence of the shortness of the notice I had received of the honour he intended; and with earnest sincerity of manner, he exclaimed:

"'Sir, it is most superb!'

"It was notorious that he never remained more than half an hour at any theatre he attended; but (in my opinion) he showed his taste by witnessing the whole of our performance. . . . I had, of course, sent refreshments to the party, which the committee, like all committees, appeared to enjoy most heartily; but observing the General did not partake, I inquired if there was anything he particularly wished, and he requested a glass of sugar and water. Old Hays, the celebrated police-officer, whom I had stationed at the door to prevent the General's being killed with kindness I despatched for the desired beverage; and, wishing to take a drink with the good old man, I ordered two glasses, slyly whispering Hays to put some gin in mine: when in returning he gave me a cunning sort of thief-catching wink to direct me to my 'sling'; but the General, having the first choice, got the gin, and I the sugar and water. He drank without a remark; I don't know if the marquis ever repeated his dose, but I pledge my honour I have never repeated mine."

In the month of February 1826 my great-grandfather resolved to give the people of South Carolina an opportunity to see Edmund Kean at the Charleston theatre. Kean had been having a bad time in places like Boston and Philadelphia where he had appeared on the stage drunk.

"Every means in my power I artfully used to smooth the path of Kean's reception . . . but still the Eastern papers were torturing his offence into a *national insult*, and calling on the chivalry of the South to avenge the wrongs this immoral play-actor had heaped upon the country. I had determined that there should be no time allowed to organise a plan of hostility by having the bills already printed, announcing '*Kean's first appearance this evening*', and intending no matter when he arrived that he should perform the same night, but in this point of policy I was in part defeated, by the ship *Othello*, in which he was a passenger, being reported early on Sunday morning. I boarded the vessel before she crossed the bar, and found this wreck of better days feeble in body, and that brilliant, poetic face a Raphael might have envied for a study, 'sicklied o'er with the pale cast of thought'. His first inquiry was if the public were hostile to his appearing, and like a child he appealed of me: 'Cowell, for God's sake, by the ties of old fellowship and countrymen I entreat you not to let me play if you think the audience will not receive me. I have not strength of mind and body—look how I'm changed since you saw me last—to endure a continuance of the persecutions I have already endured, and I believe a repetition of them would kill me on the spot.'

"I, of course, encouraged him to hope all would go well; but on coming from the boat, some twenty idlers collected, and as we turned from the wharf hissed and groaned; the well-known, hateful sound, seemed to enter his very soul, and looking up in my face, with 'God help me!' quivering on his parted lips, he clung to my arm as if for succour, not support. I assured him the disapprobation was meant for an officer of the customs, in whose boat he had landed, who was objectionable to the people; and doubting, yet hoping it was true, I conducted him to my house next the theatre which I had hired for the season.

"He passed the day with me and some new-found friends, and made himself, as he always could when he thought proper, most agreeable.

"Early in the evening I conducted him to his quarters which I had prepared for him at St James's. He was delighted with his black landlord, and astonished to find that a negro

E

could amass a fortune, and possess all the material advantages of a well-behaved white man in the same situation in life, in a slave state. His notions of slavery had more than likely been altogether formed by acting in the opera Paul and Virginia.

"Though most comfortably lodged, he assured me the next day he had never closed his eyes; his anxiety had brought alone such rest

> As wretches have o'er night
> Who wait for execution in the morn.

"What would be the night's event, who could tell? The public is a hard riddle to find out, but when you do happen to hit upon it, how simple it is. Fifty friends gave fifty different opinions each with an 'if'. For my part, I most earnestly desired his success, and therefore honestly believed his genius would triumph.

"Not a place was taken, but the house was full soon after the doors were opened. Before it was uncomfortably crowded, I stopped the sale of tickets, for nothing puts an auditor so soon out of humour as a disagreeable seat.

"Kean had set his 'soul and body in the action both' and I never saw him play better. At his entrance all was 'hushed as midnight'—a quiet so profound 'that the blind mole might not hear a footfall' and this *awful attention* continued during the whole performance, whenever he was on the stage; and when the curtain fell, some few amazed spectators hummed applause. *There was but one lady in the whole house!* the wife of the district attorney, and a warm friend of the drama. *Woman, in thy purity, how powerful thou art!* The presence of this *one* acted like a charm. She sat alone, the beauteous representative of the moral courage of her sex, and awed to respectful silence the predetermined turbulence of twelve hundred men!

"Poor Kean was in ecstasies at his escape. The next morning nearly all the places were secured for Wednesday, and a splendid houseful of ladies, as well as gentlemen, assembled to witness his master-piece Othello. At his entrance some ill-advised applause was instantly drowned in a shower of hisses; and in the early portion of the play, several sudden expressions of disapprobation occurred; and in the third act, at nearly the end of his fine scene with Iago, the storm so long pent up burst forth; some oranges, thrown on the stage, appeared to be the signal for a general tumult in the midst of which I had the curtain lowered, opened the stage door, and presented myself to the audience. It was my intention to have made an appeal to their indulgence on my own account, but remembering

> The silence, often, of pure innocence
> Persuades when speaking fails

I assumed as innocent an expression as I knew how, proceeded quietly and slowly to pick up the atoms of oranges and apples, looked unutterable things and once

> I lifted up my head and did address,
> *Myself* to motion like as *I* would speak
> But even then—

I bowed my self across the stage and departed, amid thunders of applause! and, before it had subsided, thrust Kean on with Desdemona, and the same people who, a minute before, were pelting him with rubbish rose on their seats and with 'caps, hands and tongues applauded to the clouds' and the play proceeded with undisputed approbation!! At the end, Kean was loudly called for; but, from experience, knowing that for him to open his mouth filled with language of his own would probably ruin all, I pleaded his exhaustion as an excuse for his making me the means to express the grateful sense he had of their kindness, and tendered his respectful acknowledgements.

"The next day some of the first men in the city left him their cards, dinner-parties were made expressly for him, carriages were proferred for his use; the rarities of the season and climate poured in upon him, and the numerous attentions shown him by the kind, yet aristocratic inhabitants of Charleston, equalled and were more gratifying to his feelings than the hollow-hearted homage paid to him by a crowd of flatterers in the sunshine of his career. He received fifty pounds sterling per night; that is, two hundred and twenty-two dollars and twenty-two cents. . . . Kean was so delighted with the place and the people that he determined to remain until the season was concluded. A friend gave him the use of a country house in Sullivan's Island—a most romantic sandbank in the centre of the harbour. With two Newfoundland dogs of mine, a pet deer and the mare *Fanny* he was 'alone in his glory'; for it was literally uninhabited in the winter with the exception of a few soldiers in the fort. He played Bertram for my benefit, on the last night, to the largest amount ever received at the Charleston theatre. He took his passage with me in the ship *Saluda* and with

Calm seas, auspicious gales, and sail so expeditious

that in three days, recreated in mind and body he arrived in New York in the merry month of May 1826.

"Poor Kean! I never more saw him act; and though, for years after his brightness flickered at intervals on the gloomy path of the declining drama, it soon blazed again with his uniform, unequalled brilliancy. His neglected early life had grafted habits on his nature totally at variance with his pure poetic taste, and giant-like strength of admiration of all that was great and noble in art, and made him the contradictory and, at times, objectionable creature which, in general, he is so exclusively described. The truth of the adage in his case was painfully proved: *he knew not who was his father*. When all the thinking world were awe-struck contemplating his genius, several were named as having a title to that honour, and among them the late Duke of Norfolk; and Kean was weak enough to appear proud of this parental appropriation. A Mrs Curry, who was an inferior actress at one of the minor theatres, claimed him as her son and whether he believed her to be his mother or not, he supported her and her daughter for years.

"The startling effect of his style of acting boldly and suddenly setting at defiance the law and decorum of the long-accustomed school of which a Siddons and a Kemble were the models, cannot be conceived at this day, when every aspirant to dramatic fame totters in the path his genius boldly trod; for though he left behind no parallel to his excellence, he created a host of imitators.

"The novelty of his manner may be understood by the following anecdote which he told me himself. At his first rehearsal at Drury Lane, 'steeped in poverty to the very lips', wrapped in an old, rough greatcoat—though it was warm weather—and his appearance altogether bespeaking his estate, several of the well-clothed and well-fed minions of the drama did not condescend to rehearse with him at all; and those who did refused to deviate from the accustomed business of the stage, which, right or wrong, they had followed for years, and turned into unconcealed ridicule his temerity in presuming to suggest any alteration of the acknowledged laws. Among others, he particularly named Dr Camp—he, poor fellow, long since died of a dysentery, mixed up with old age and abject poverty, in Texas! He eloquently, yet playfully, described the laceration of his feelings at having his peculiarities of voice imitated behind the scenes by

The loud laugh, that speaks the vacant mind.

"Amid these outward and visible signs of contempt for his talent, old Miss Tidswell, who had played small characters in the theatre since Garrick's time, and who afterwards called herself his aunt, poked him in the back with her umbrella, beckoned him to the wing, and petitioned him not to persevere in playing; explaining that all the actors and good judges were laughing at him; and pointing out to him the horrible disgrace of his inevitably being pelted from the stage *would be to her*, as she had acknowledged him as a distant relation, and introduced him as such to some performers of her own class in the second green-room!

"Wounded in spirit, he left the theatre, half inclined to follow her advice, not in consequence of any doubt in his own mind of his capacity—for true talent is always self-informed—but to shrink from the dirty annoyances attending his assertion. But, fortunately, he met at the door an old comrade, from some country theatre, to whom he unburdened his 'o'er-wrought heart' and the poor disciple of Thespis being in possession of the extraordinary sum of five shillings, Kean accompanied him to a tavern. After a good dinner, a pot of porter, and the warm encouragement of his ragged but sincere friend, he went to the theatre, desperate in his determination to succeed; played Shylock to a very indifferent house, but sealed his fame forever."

After this portrait of Edmund Kean it seems worth while to give my great-grandfather's impression of Junius Brutus Booth, who crossed the Atlantic to the United States about three months before Joe Cowell himself.

"Booth, though not a servile imitator of Kean, founded his manner exclusively on his style. He played precisely the same round of characters, dressed them exactly in the same costumes and being naturally like him in appearance the similitude was extraordinary. Kean's transcendent genius had so dazzled the public taste that his defects of voice and figure were actually considered necessary attributes and Booth possessed the same advantages. Old Dowton morosely said, when Kean first appeared 'God renounce me! 'tis only necessary nowadays to be under four foot high, have bandy legs, and a hoarseness, and mince my liver! but you'll be thought a great tragedian.'

"Soon after Booth's arrival in this country he declared his intention of becoming a citizen, and purchased a small farm near the village of Belle-Air in Maryland—the only sterile section of land I know of in the whole state; deposited his wife and family in a log cabin, and shone himself periodically as a star of the first magnitude through the theatrical hemisphere. Scrupulously avoiding all ostentatious display, he adopted the reverse extreme; attired in a conspicuously plebeian garb, he would take up his quarters in some humble tavern or obscure boarding-house, and when he visited Baltimore, he usually attended the market with some vegetables, a load of hay, or sat with a calf, tied by the leg, until it was time to rehearse 'Richard the Third'. His simple Republican deportment, well spiced when occasion served, with 'the jolly dog' and 'the good fellow' who was 'not too proud' to sing a song in a beer-house, or give you a taste of his quality in an oyster-cellar, rendered him most popular with the multitude; a scholar and a linguist, he was an intelligent listener to the pothouse pedant and could 'drink with any tinker in his own language', carefully concealing any advantages he possessed above the capacity of his companions, his acquirements were lauded and admired; for it is the character of the nation, as I have read it, sometimes to allow a foreigner to be equal, but never superior in anything. This probably *accidental* mode of conduct, naturally enough compared with his prototype Kean's arbitrary offences, aided by Booth's undisputed talent, for years caused him to be greatly followed and admired.

"His father, who was a devotee to the doctrines civil and religious which clogged with blood the wings of liberty during the French Revolution, named him Junius Brutus, as a type of the stern Republican character he hoped his son would achieve; and with an excellent education mixed the seeds of those dogmas which, no matter how gilded over by the poetic imaginings of a Voltaire, a Byron, or a Shelley are, to a mind early tutored to admit them and undefended by Christianity, dangerous to the happiness of the social compact, and fatal to the ties with which conscience should bind the intercourse with our fellowmen. . . . Kean's irregularities were coarse and brutal, but their ill effects recoiled exclusively upon himself; Booth's involved the destiny of those nearest and dearest; for years he sheltered himself from their consequences by assuming madness; and the long practice of this periodical 'antic disposition' like Hamlet's ended in its being, I believe, partially the fact. . . .

"A sketch of his numerous eccentricities would alone fill a volume; but, being generally divested of wit or humour and, for the most part, mischievous in their character, an account of them would be painful either to write or read. I don't mean to assert that his having been called after the pattern of severe justice, who assumed the mask of folly in the cause of virtue, had any influence on the conduct of Booth; but baptising children as if to designate their character is a nonsensical custom and ought to be condemned. There are enough good, homely Christian names to satisfy the varied tastes of the most fastidious, and this deviation from the beaten track to please the doting folly of a mother, or the political prejudices of a father, is often, in after time, a positive affliction to the bearer. I feel positively obliged to my godfathers and godmothers for having unostentatiously named me after the amiable, rugged-coated modest Joseph; and the etymology of the designation to have been fortunate enough to prove the appropriateness of my being already the father and grandfather of children in two quarters of the world."

These words were written in 1843. Some point was to be added to them just over twenty years later when John Wilkes Booth assassinated Abraham Lincoln, but Cowell himself, who died in 1863, did not live to know that. At any rate, he was true to his principles by calling his own boy Samuel. Of him he writes at the age of nine:

"Booth was on a visit to my house during his sojourn at

Boston, and while amusing himself with my children, during a leisure morning, made the discovery that my dear boy Samuel was perfect both in the words and music of Crack in *The Turnpike Gate* [this was the part in which Joe Cowell had such a success all over the United States] and could give an excellent imitation of his father in that character. After dinner we had a full rehearsal. The pianoforte was put in requisition, and Hamblen and myself played the off-parts by turns. I confess I thought he was extremely clever—what father would not? Sam's talent furnished food for a chat in my room at the theatre that evening; and Dana, the principal of the committee of management, pertinently said:

"' Now, Cowell, if *you* were to have the profits of your benefit you would let your son play for it.'

"This legitimate Yankee suspicion, of course, I had no better means of removing than by letting Sam perform. He was delighted at the novelty, and no further instructed than by a usual rehearsal he made his first appearance three nights afterwards. Whatever he may be now, he was a very little boy, even for his age in 1829; and he certainly eclipsed anything in the way of juvenile prodigies which I had ever seen—and so an overflowing house said too. But from long experience of the consequences in after life of forcing precocious talent *I never urged him to learn a line.* For some two or three years following he played and sang such parts and comic songs as he thought proper for his own amusement and my emolument; but in the course of that time he never studied more than six characters, and his impression of me *was me*, at the small end of a telescope. He chose, when it was time to choose, the stage for his profession, and is now an admitted favourite at the Edinburgh theatre: no small boast at his age (23) for there the drama is considered one of the mental endowments of that refined and critical portion of Great Britain. And his uncle, William Murray, the manager, who when a mere boy, was entrusted by his sister's husband, Henry Siddons, with the direction of the National Theatre, has been for years universally admitted as the most finished disciplinarian now remaining to uphold the good old school."

Sam Cowell became the most popular singer of comic songs both in Great Britain and America, but he died in 1864 at the age of forty-four. His precocity at nine was to be surpassed by that of his nieces thirty years later at the ages of four and six.

Cowell relates an amusing experience of his which was duplicated in fiction by Mark Twain when the innocents abroad meant to get up and see the sunrise over the Rigi and saw the sunset instead.

"I left Boston in the mail-stage, after a jolly supper, at one in the morning, and arrived at Providence, Rhode Island, in time for rehearsal the same day. The weather was excruciatingly hot, as hot weather always is in high latitudes when it is hot, and after dinner I determined to take my lost share of sleep . . . finding a mattress thrown in a corner of a balcony, where all the air Providence could bestow appeared to flutter, I arranged a *siesta*. When I awoke it was dusk, and I set off for the theatre, all my companions being there, though I only had to play Crack in the last piece. As I passed through the bar I enquired of a servant sweeping it out, 'What is the time?'.

"'About four, sir,' said he.

"About four?" said I, "about eight more likely", and on I walked.

"The shops were all closed, and everything appeared particularly quiet; but the steady habits of Providence I was prepared for by long report, and therefore its appearance was not extraordinary. The carriers hanging the evening papers on the knobs of the doors, or insinuating them underneath, were the only human beings I met with on my way to the theatre, which to my astonishment I found closed and quiet. A thought flashed across my mind—Could it be possible? I made an inquiry of a milkman, and found to my amazement that it was not *tonight* but *tomorrow morning*."

And here is a vignette of Cincinnati:

"Cincinnati in 1829 was a very different place from what it is now, but even then it wore a most imposing appearance; thanks to the clear-headed adventurous Yankees, who, axe in hand, cut through the pathless forests, undismayed by toil and defying danger until they found a spot, rough-hewn and disguised by Nature as the site for future ages to enthrone the pride of the Ohio valley, the 'Queen City of the West'. We put up at the hotel near the landing, kept by Captain Cromwell and in his little way quite as despotic as his namesake, the poor apology for a king; for after dinner—an operation which was performed by his boarders in three minutes at furthest—myself and two acquaintances I had formed on the road drew towards the fire, and commenced smoking our cigars:

" 'You can't smoke here,' said Captain Cromwell. And we instantly 'pleaded ignorance of his rules; though they might be thought a little fastidious after our scramble for dinner, and threw our cigars in the fire.

" 'And you can't sit here,' said Captain Cromwell. 'If you want to sit, you must sit in the bar; and if you want to smoke, you can smoke in the bar.'

"Slapping his hand on the table, after the manner of his ancestor dismissing the Long Parliament; and into the bar we went."

Of that same year 1829 Cowell writes:

"That year I bought a pretty little farm of one hundred acres in Whitewater township, Hamilton County, Ohio, eighteen miles northwest from Cincinnati, and seven due south from the estate of General Harrison at North Bend. He was then clerk of the County Court; a most amiable and kind-hearted neighbour, he then as little dreaming as I did that in ten years from that time he would be the most enthusiastically popular President of the United States ever known *'for a little month'*. He might in all probability have lived for many years but for this over-excitement that was heaped upon him, honoured as the defender of his County in her determination to maintain the position she had achieved, and pointed out in his extreme old age as a model for the American farmer in the peaceful valley of the Miami."

Harrison was inaugurated as President on March 4th and he died on April 4th, 1841, weakened by pneumonia and unable to survive the incessant importunity of office-seekers; he was sixty-eight years old. He was the ninth President of the United States; his grandson, elected in 1888, was the twenty-third. Benjamin Harrison was born in 1833 on his grandfather's farm at North Bend, and if Joseph Cowell could have lived to see that Presidency of the future he would probably have reflected on the advantage of being christened Benjamin.

"To compare small things with large," Cowell goes on.

"I meant and had a right to believe that there I should pass the remainder of my days, making my profession during the winter months a profitable pastime. But it was not to be. When Caldwell built his Dramatic Temple in 1836, I once more joined his standard for the season, and was hailed as New Orleans knows how to welcome back a favourite; but, in the midst of our splendid career, I was unexpectedly laid low on a bed of sickness for four long months. To Doctor Carey who tended my flickering chance of life. . . . I am indebted for being able now to say, I here, for the sake of others, throw a veil of oblivion over my theatrical life, which individually I would wish to lift . . . but I am 'one, in suffering all, that suffers nothing' in *appearance*; an iron constitution has upheld what, in a fragile one, would have been sympathized with as a sensitive mind; and my *uncountable* number of friends in the United States—I shake hands with twenty-five thousand at least every year—will bear me out in the assertion that during the varieties of fortune they have known me to struggle with 'Old Joe Cowell' has always seemed the same. . . . The nature of my task prevents me from giving even a sketch of the beautiful 'Crescent City', as she now is; but to me she must ever be most clear, as the depository of the unlettered tomb which 'I never shall have length of days enough to rain upon remembrance with my eyes'."

This is the only allusion in his book that Cowell makes to his second wife, my great-grandmother, of whom presently.

When he recovered from his illness 'Old Joe Cowell', who was just fifty, played a season in Nashville and in the following winter 1842-3 a season in Mobile, where he made his farewell appearance.

He has a paragraph about the passion of the American public for lectures which does not seem altogether irrelevant a hundred and twenty years later.

"For some time past a horde of locomotive *penny-magazine* men had been scattering their real and pretended knowledge about the country, dignified by the name of lectures, till, like every bubble that fashion indiscriminately inflates, the practice had become most ridiculously distended. Of course, the more inexplicable the subject of dissertation, the more attractive, and therefore every description of mystical humbuggery had been administered and greedily swallowed and followed, though decency might be set at defiance under the influence of *exhilarating gas*, or common sense illustrated by *experimental Mesmerism*. This imbecile mania produced some little good at any rate. It had opened an unexpected path for a few scientific men, with a small share of worldly tact, and expensive families, to find a ready money-market for their hitherto unsaleable philosophical attainments."

Thirty Years Passed Among the Players of England and America, by Joe Cowell, Comedian, concludes at New Orleans:

"On the day that the fanatic, Miller, said the world would end; I took my departure from the Balize—which is more like the last end of it than any place that can be imagined—in the brig *Orchilla*, bound to Baltimore, with her hold full of pork, and a deck-load of molasses and blue-bottle flies."

What has the eighth of me inherited from that great-grandfather? His iron constitution and contempt for worry, and, I fancy, his particular sense of humour passed on through his daughter Sidney Frances Cowell and by my mother. My father's sense of humour inherited from my grandfather Henry Compton was dissimilar from my own. Fortunately, I have not inherited Joe Cowell's temper, or the even more violent temper of my maternal grandfather, Hezekiak Bateman. My own equanimity comes from my grandmother Emmeline Montague. Probably my use of the pen came from Joe Cowell.

THE BATEMANS

A T the time of the French Revolution an émigré family
had rooms in Half Moon Street off Piccadilly. The son
of the house whose name was Sheppard eloped with one of
the daughters to America. A tradition in the family said that
these French émigrés were minor Bourbons, but my mother
and her three sisters were very vague about their great-
grandparents and disapproving as they did of their grand-
parent Joseph Cowell were disinclined to talk about him.
It would seem that Sheppard had lived in what would one
day be the heart of Cincinnati. If that be true he must have
been one of the first pioneers of the Ohio. His only child was
a daughter called Frances who in 1822 became the second
wife of Joseph Cowell. She had one daughter, Sidney Frances,
who was born in New York in March 1823. I have a Book of
Common Prayer inscribed:

> *For Miss Sidney Frances Cowell the infant daughter of*
> *Joseph Cowell. Presented on the day of her christening by*
> *her father's friend*
>
> *John Blake*
>
> *New York May 22nd 1824*

It is clear from this that Joseph Cowell had abandoned the
faith of Midshipman Joseph Leathley Whitshed and attached
himself outwardly to 'The Protestant Episcopal Church' in
the United States of America. The mother of his daughter
died when the latter was very young and was buried in New
Orleans. In those reminiscences of his Joseph Cowell avoids
almost completely any reference to his domestic affairs. He
does not even record the death of his mother, nor his marriage to Frances Sheppard. His granddaughters, who all
disapproved extremely of Joe Cowell, believed that he
behaved badly to his second wife and that the tears he claimed
to have shed over 'her unlettered tomb' were crocodile's

tears. That may be true, or they may have done him an injustice.

My grandmother was brought up on the farm her father had acquired in Ohio, where she taught herself to read and write, and at the age of four was reading Sterne's *Sentimental Journey*; to the end of her days *Tristram Shandy* was her favourite book. Not only did she teach herself to read, but at the same age she could accompany herself on the guitar when she was singing. Junius Brutus Booth was a great friend of her childhood. When her pet canary died the tragedian arranged a funeral procession and read the Burial Service in full over the dead bird. A relic of that friendship remains in the shape of a New Year's card of greeting from Junius Brutus Booth for 1834, when she was not yet eleven years old. I do not know at what age she went on the stage, but when she was sixteen she married a young actor ten years older than herself, Hezekiah Linthicum Bateman.

H. L. Bateman was the youngest son of a Baltimore man, Henry Bateman, who died when my grandfather was young. He himself was brought up by his mother, a formidable Welsh woman called Catherine Evans who alternated between Methodism and Episcopalianism. She must have been in a Methodist mood when she called her youngest son Hezekiah, for which he never forgave her, nor for that matter anybody who ventured to call him by that name. He was educated at a private school in Baltimore and was intended by his mother to be a civil engineer. He had other ideas and left home to go on the stage before he was twenty. He was not successful as an actor, though as John Unit in a play written by his wife called *Self*, which was produced at St Louis, Missouri, in 1857, he made an immediate success. I have never seen a prompt copy either of *Self* or of a tragedy in blank verse called *Geraldine* which was produced at Philadelphia in 1859, but both plays were regularly played in stock all over the United States for many years.

My mother once told me that her father was without religion and never went inside a church. Probably his mother overfed him in youth with her Methodism. In the last year of his life he decided to read Isaiah, which he enjoyed; he then went on to read Jeremiah, whom he found so depressing

6. Ellen Bateman as Richard III

6. Kate Bateman as Macbeth

7. Isabel, Kate and Virginia, 1864

that he abandoned his belated study of the Old Testament,
and did not resume it.

In 1847 he brought his wife and two small daughters Kate
and Ellen, aged four and two, to England and appeared as
Othello at the Surrey Theatre. At that date American actors
were extremely unpopular in England and he was hissed off
the stage. They were penniless and had to return to America
in the steerage of a sailing-ship. The voyage lasted over two
months, and my grandmother nearly died of sea-sickness and
exhaustion. My grandfather saved her life by tapping a barrel
of Guinness's stout in the hold of the ship. Two years later
his fortunes were restored by the fantastic success of those two
eldest daughters who at the age of six and four were drawing
great audiences all over the United States in scenes from
Shakespeare. In 1849 Ellen the younger was presented with
a gold chalice from the virgin gold of California. It was
inscribed 'To Ellen Bateman from the Sierra Nevada, 1849.'
Perhaps that Forty-niner who was the father of Clementine
contributed some dust toward that cup. Walter Lacy, an old
actor who had seen Edmund Kean, used to declare Ellen was
the best Richard III he had seen since.

In 1851 these two children came to England and filled the
St James's Theatre for a hundred nights during the Great
Exhibition. The Duchess of Sutherland, who had lost her own
three daughters as children, took a fancy to the little girls
and invited them to go round the Exhibition with her. Two
relics of that visit were familiar to me in childhood. One was
a wax doll of the little Prince of Wales in a sailor suit, the
other a wax doll of the Princess Royal. I remember being
impressed by the way the waxen faces of the royal children
had turned yellow with the years.

When the Civil War came my grandfather, who was then
living in Washington Avenue, Brooklyn, found himself completely out of sympathy with his position in New York, being
as he was a passionate sympathiser with the South. My
mother used to recall the way the other little girls at their
school were for ever marching about singing *John Brown's Body*
and making faces at herself and her younger sister Isabel as
'rebs'.

By this time Ellen, the younger of the two Bateman children,

had married at the age of fifteen a young Frenchman, Claude
Greppo, who was travelling in America for a big Lyons silk
firm. He introduced another young Frenchman who was
exploiting perhaps the first colour process in photography.
He took pictures of my mother and Isabel who were ten and
eight years old. In one of them they had a shawl draped round
them by their mother.

Some months later in 1863 my grandfather was visiting St
Louis, where he was interested in the theatre, and at the depot he
saw Federal troops arriving and being welcomed by the ladies
of St Louis who were presenting them with boxes of candy
on the outside of which was a coloured picture. My grandfather
looked glumly over his shoulder at a box being examined by
the recipient and saw to his anger and mortification that
sweet Northern girlhood was being represented by his two
youngest daughters, whose shoulders were draped with the
Stars and Stripes into which my grandmother's shawl had
been turned. He returned to New York still in a rage. William
Winter in that copy of Joe Cowell's reminiscences has noted
him as the father-in-law of H. L. Bateman 'whom we used to
call "Chain Lightning".' It was in a chain lightning mood
that he took his two youngest daughters with him to England
that December, refusing to let them stay on at a Northern
school. I have a memento of that voyage across the Atlantic
in a first edition of Kingsley's *Water Babies* inscribed:

> *To Jenny and Bella*
>
> *as a reminiscence of Berth No. 185 on board R.M.S.*
> *Scotia and what was enacted there from their*
> *audience*
>
> *Frank R. Mather*
>
> *January 6th 1864*

The *Scotia* was the last of the Cunard paddle wheels. She
had a tonnage of 3871 and reduced the record of Trans-
atlantic passages to 8 days 22 hours. *The Scotsman* of June 26th,
1861 thus recorded her launching:
"The Scotia is a most magnificent steamer and will be the
largest merchant vessel afloat with the exception of the Great

Eastern. For comfort and elegance the saloons will be unrivalled and will afford ample accommodation for dining 300."

Kate Bateman, after retiring from the stage in 1854 to go to school, returned to it in 1860 when she was seventeen to make her reappearance in a dramatisation by her mother of Longfellow's poem *Evangeline*. Later she was to have a triumphant success in *Leah* both in Britain and the United States, playing the part for nearly twenty years.

Here is a letter from Longfellow to my grandmother about that dramatisation of *Evangeline*:

> *Cambridge*
> *Massachusetts*
> *March* 19, 1860

Dear Madam,

I have had the honour of receiving your letter in reference to your dramatic version of 'Evangeline'. So far as the theatrical representation goes neither I nor my publisher have any objection to make. But we think there would be some objection to printing the play, as thereby our copyright might in some way be put in jeopardy.

Hoping that your dramatic version may have that success which I have no doubts it merits,

> *I remain*
> *Yours truly*
> *Henry W. Longfellow*

It would be surprising today to find a poet so amiable about a dramatisation of one of his notable works without any financial reward. Mr T. S. Eliot is the most amiable of men, but even he would hardly consent to a dramatisation of one of his poems without a suggestion about the monetary side of the business. And even if he were as amiable as his American predecessor, certainly his agent would not be.

Tennyson was more difficult than Longfellow. My grandfather proposed to put on his play *Queen Mary* at the Lyceum and much correspondence and conversation were required before the poet could get into his head that *Queen Mary* as published would play for half an hour longer than *Hamlet*.

Here is one of Tennyson's letters:

F

Farringford
Freshwater
Isle of Wight
Jan. 7, 1876

Dear Mrs Bateman,

By all means let me see the book again. Some of the changes of scene were only jotted down in the moment and might I daresay be improved.
Yours very truly,

A. *Tennyson*

And then a postcript:

Do you think all *the changes good?*

Lord Lytton, as one would expect, was more practical than Tennyson. When my grandfather commissioned W. G. Wills to write a play about *Eugene Aram*, to follow up the success of his *Charles I* at the Lyceum, he was worried whether Lytton might be jealous for his successful novel *Eugene Aram* and wrote to ask him what he felt about the project.

Lytton replied from Torquay on Christmas Eve 1872 in a letter the handwriting of which suggests a sick man; indeed less than a month later he was dead. It is a generous letter.

"In the first place accept for yourself and your gifted daughter my best wishes for the Season. May the New Year add to you all happiness and public prosperity and success. . . . With regard to a play founded on Eugene Aram I should not have the smallest right to object to any dramatist treating it at his will provided he does not take the characters, incidents, situations as well as language invented by myself. If he do so borrow from me, however partially, then I should like to see MS of his drama, not otherwise."

My grandfather was particularly anxious for Irving to have a success as Eugene Aram because in 1864 he had heard him recite Hood's poem in Manchester and made up his mind then that if he were ever given the opportunity he would make Irving a star. The opportunity came when my grandfather acquired a long lease of the Lyceum Theatre in 1871.

In 1873 my grandmother wrote to Lewis Carroll to ask if

he would consider the possibility of her making a dramatic version of *Alice in Wonderland* and *Alice Through the Looking Glass*. Mr C. L. Dodgson wrote back sensibly to say that much as he appreciated the compliment he must dissuade her from entertaining the idea. It is a pity that later he did not dissuade others from entertaining the idea.

On Sunday March 21st, 1875, during the run of *Hamlet*, Irving gave a supper to my grandfather and some other friends at the Pall Mall restaurant in the Haymarket. The proprietor had asked for an extension of the licence but the police had refused him, and he failed to let Irving know this. The result was that, just when the evening was going well, at five minutes to eleven the waiters came in to clear the room. My grandfather lost his temper and went back, sizzling and seething, to Rutland Gate where they were then living, having moved there from Kensington Gore. Next morning when dressed he had a heart attack. He seemed better in the afternoon and my grandmother and Isabel, who was playing Ophelia, went down to the theatre, leaving my mother to sit with him. At ten o'clock in sudden apprehension she touched his hand. It was ice. He must have had angina pectoris for some years but the pain was always ascribed to acute dyspepsia. It was a suitable end for a man who had always battled fiercely with life. I have had a similar contempt for the conventions of authority but fortunately for myself I have always been able to laugh at them, and the power of ridicule puts no strain on the heart of him who can cast it.

The *Annual Register* for 1875 thus records him:

"A native of Maryland, Mr Bateman became celebrated on both sides of the Atlantic . . . the marvellously successful revival of *Hamlet* was the crowning triumph of the 'Old Colonel' as he was familiarly called in theatrical circles, and this had reached its height when he almost suddenly expired in his sixty-third year."

My other grandfather, Henry Compton, was playing the First Gravedigger in that famous revival. He was then in his seventy-first year.

After H. L. Bateman's death my grandmother continued in the management of the Lyceum. It will be more appropriate to tell the story of that in my second octave, when for the first time I met Irving at the age of fifteen. When in 1878 she gave her lease to Irving together with the plays, the scenery, the properties and the wardrobe she decided to rebuild Sadler's Wells, which involved her in heavy financial loss and ended in her death from pneumonia in January 1881 when she was in her fifty-eighth year.

In her old age my mother scribbled some notes about her mother which give a better idea of her than I could who never knew her.

"She went on the stage at sixteen, playing sixteen parts a week in stock. At sixteen, too, she was married. Babies were coming every two years or so and she would be writing plays with one hand while the other was holding the baby. There were times of extreme poverty at first. She never got over the grief of losing her eldest boy when he was two years old, for apparently he was something of a prodigy, already reading. She was herself so clever and capable that she thought everyone else should and could be the same. So she took it for granted that her two eldest daughters could play scenes from Shakespeare in early childhood and saw nothing unusual in it. We were all given books of history to read at absurd ages and expected to know all the plays of Shakespeare. She was strange in a way. She did not like her two sons or myself. There is no other way of putting it. Even when Dick (Richmond), her eldest living son, was burnt at sea in the *Nile* on the way to take up a job as professor of French and German in Japan she did not seem to feel it greatly, though she was glad to hear from one of the only two survivors that Dick had behaved with great gallantry. 'But what else would he do?' she commented. She worshipped Kate, her eldest daughter, and adored Isabel, her youngest. She was fond of Ellen, who was as clever as herself, but only too happy to see her married at fifteen to a Frenchman. She made my father do whatever she wanted but she had no notion that she did, and nor had he. She prevented Kate's marrying the man she really loved. She insisted on Isabel's playing leading parts at sixteen; she played them well up to a point, but she had no great gift like Kate and she disliked acting.

"My mother was in a way a religious woman, but she had a tremendous prejudice against Roman Catholics probably because of her own father's behaviour who had been baptized and brought up as a Catholic. Her own mother, also a Catholic, had died in her infancy. Isabel and I were in the parish of St Luke's in Brooklyn of which Dr Dillon was the Rector, and both of us asked to be confirmed when we were nine and seven years old. And this he persuaded the Bishop of New Jersey to do which was an extraordinarily broadminded thing for an eminent Episcopalian in the year 1862.

"My mother was intensely proud with a strange sort of temper. She was very long-suffering with some people, but she was unjust, unpleasant and impatient with others. I think my own temper is very like hers, only I trust that by the grace of God I have a certain command over myself that she lacked. I don't think I should have tossed the Lyceum lease to Irving as she did, but I *should* probably have bought the lease of old Sadler's Wells as she did and embarked on the foolish project of rebuilding it. By the time the theatre was ready to be opened she was crippled by debt, and although business was always quite good it was not enough to free her from the rash commitments she had undertaken. The last production at Sadler's Wells was *The School for Scandal*, in which I played Lady Teazle. I had played this on tour with the Chippendales and all that was left of the famous old Haymarket Company. So I had the advantage of playing it with those who had inherited the traditions of old English comedy from the days of Sheridan at Drury Lane.

"Business at Sadler's Wells was very good. Then in January 1881 my mother got a chill. It was a bitter winter. We had given up Albany Courtyard and were living now in Taviton Street, Bloomsbury. We used to wait at the corner of Euston Road for the bus to take us along the dreary way to where we got out for Sadler's Wells and then there was a little walk. No more brougham nor even a four-wheel cab. Money troubles forbade either. My mother's chill turned to pneumonia. I nursed her during the day and Isabel at night when I had to be at the theatre. Dear Dr Ringer called in Sir Stephen Paget in consultation, but there was nothing anybody could do except wait. When Isabel offered Sir Stephen his fee he refused to accept it and dear Dr Ringer would never accept a penny from us at any time."

I must interrupt for a moment to say that Dr Sydney Ringer would render me an inestimable service twenty years later, but that must wait for telling until my second octave.

"My mother was delirious until the crisis came. She kept on talking about her baby boy Frank who had died all but forty years ago. 'Oh, what a beautiful young man!' she kept saying. When the fever left her, life went with it. We did not close the theatre because we did not want to put the company out of work. J. L. Toole with his warm heart offered to play without salary in a one-act farce before *The School for Scandal*. Irving did not come to inquire during her illness but he called the day after her death. I happened to open the door to him and made him come up and look at her. I said to him quite simply 'She would have liked you to say good-bye, but you broke her heart.' The room was full of coloured autumn leaves from America which Ellen had gathered and pressed and sent, not dreaming when she did so that they would be buried with her mother. We drove all the way from Taviton Street to Hendon Churchyard in a four-wheeler behind the hearse. My mother had been there one day in the summer and said she should like to be buried there. The churchyard is on a sloping piece of ground, very slippery and difficult in such weather. A few old friends came to the funeral. Charles Warner came, though he was ill with laryngitis. Our acting manager, Chalmers or Chambers, came. He had gone with us from the Lyceum to Sadler's Wells. It was an unfortunate day for him in a worldly way when he did so, but it was done from unselfish devotion, and so who can call it really unfortunate? He taught Isabel to keep all the books, double entry and all that. Our maid Olive drove with us in the four-wheeler. She had come with us from Albany Courtyard to Taviton Street and refused any wages. She was not at all adequate as a maid, but how adequate as a friend, ready to do anything and everything for any of us.

"My mother was a most attractive woman. She was probably a lovely girl, but she thought of herself as impossible to be looked at, which she thought I was. She used to console me with the hope that when I was an old woman I might be worth looking at. She was an utter Bohemian herself, but at the same time, paradoxically, she was determined that we must all be extremely conventional. She had the smallest appetite conceivable. She never drank anything but water until a year or so before her death, when she would take half a glass of sherry. She had a marvellous memory and could recite anything that was asked for. She always wrote my father's speeches and Irving's speeches for them. She was racked with many anxieties before her death. She once said, 'Well was this awful theatre with which I've saddled myself called Sadler's Wells!' Indeed bankruptcy seemed imminent. So she started to write a novel called *Isola*. I remember it began with a very young girl stranded and sitting on one of her boxes on the quay at New Orleans, obviously the memory of an episode in her own life. She had written about half of her book when she became ill and the manuscript like so much else was destroyed at her death. Besides many plays she wrote short stories and articles for papers and magazines and was a frequent contributor to *Harper's*. She was always full of ideas and if my father had followed some of her suggestions he would have been wise, but equally wise if he had *not* followed some of them. She spent hardly anything on herself. When she had any money it was always spent on other people or projects. She desired to help everyone in any way she could. She taught Dion Boucicault's wife—a lovely little Irish girl— to read and write. She used to write her letters for her during a theatrical season when they were together.

"She started the cab shelters in London because her old driver whose name was Witts had so many hours to wait about in the cold. She kept bothering people until at last the secretary of the cab-drivers' company or union came to see her, after which the first cab-shelter was put up in Leicester Square. She wanted the first shelter to be put up where there was a cab-rank outside the stage door of the Lyceum, and she pleaded for another outside the Royal entrance to the theatre.

"She was as I said intensely conventional as far as we were concerned. She made an enemy of Labouchere, and *Truth* was a bad enemy to make, by refusing to allow us to go to a ball given by Henrietta Hodgson. She was living with La-bouchere in the same way as George Eliot was living with Lewes, and everyone accepted it, my mother included. But *we* were supposed to be too young to know about such unions!

She had a sarcastic tongue, and her wit made it all the worse. She did not remember the advice she once gave me as a girl not to be sarcastic because it made one unpopular.

"She had no idea how to dress either herself or us. She only had money given her to keep house with and never anything of her own until after my father's death. Isabel and I were the worst dressed girls imaginable. At last Irving rebelled and told my mother that it was not correct for us to be badly dressed. I remember his suggesting the dressmaker of a friend of his. That was Miss James, a great admirer of his, very plain but extremely well dressed. Irving expected her to leave him her money, but she left it instead to the Dogs' Home at Battersea. However, Miss James did recommend her dressmaker, and so we did have some nice dresses made at last.

"My mother had astonishing health until her last fatal illness. I do not remember her being in bed for a day until then. Her vitality was fantastic. She used to say that, if the transmigration of souls into animals was true, she in a future life would undoubtedly become an old omnibus horse.

"Looking back now in my old age I think that she only had three fairly peaceful and happy years. This was when we were living in Brooklyn in a small semi-detached house in Washington Avenue after Kate's début in *Evangeline* at the Winter Garden, New York. After that she and my father were touring the States and going to England for her first appearance in London. So she had a sort of settled home life, and we had our first dog, a Maltese terrier called Fidèle. Isabel and I had French lessons and German lessons and music lessons. Then came the war about which my father felt bitterly sympathetic with the South. It was the business of the coloured picture of Isabel and myself on the candy boxes which decided my father to bring us over to England at the end of 1863 where Kate was now acting with tremendous success. At this time our grandfather was rather a trial. He was proud of Kate's success and glad to be given some of her earnings; his son, our Uncle Sam, had not been so successful as expected with his American concert hour, but he too had to help his father financially. When our grandfather was over in England in 1848 he had married a disreputable young Cockney whom my mother always called 'poor 'Arriet'. Money was found to let him get back to England where he lived on at Putney until the end of 1863, spending his time in painting. I remember a good portrait of himself he painted as Crack, his favourite part. I believe it is now in some New York club.[1] He was buried in Brompton Cemetery; my father was buried in Kensal Green. A few months after my grandfather died his son Sam died at Blandford in Dorset where friends had hoped he would recover from what was called consumption. I think it was really a consumption of drink. Isabel and I liked him, but we did not care for his wife.[2] who always had a grievance about something and could not understand why her enthusiasm for the war fever in New York enraged my father so much."

I have made use of these rather rambling notes written by my mother when she was over eighty-five because I think I owe more to the American half of myself. What I fortunately did not inherit was the temper of my Baltimore grandfather. My own precocity did not appear at all remarkable to my mother. She took it for granted, so much so that when my younger brother could not read by his fourth birthday she took him to a brain specialist under the impression that he was mentally wanting. I suppose my father had never dared to admit that he was nearly five before he could read.

---

[1] It is in the Players' Club in Grammercy Park.

[2] Her diary, *The Cowells in New York*, was published by the O.U.P. in 1834.

TWO YEARS OLD 1885

I DO not remember my second birthday. After that Christmas of 1884 in Coventry the Compton Comedy Company toured Wales and at the beginning of February crossed the Irish Channel to Waterford. It was as bad as that crossing can be. My mother, who was expecting a baby in May, was so ill that she had to be carried off the boat. I must have been sick too, for I can recall from seventy-seven years ago my new nurse bending over me in the bunk with what seems a bright yellow face. I suppose that was the effect of her face seen through my sea-sick eyes.

We reached Waterford on Sunday morning, too late to catch the train to Cork where the Company was playing for the week. So we had to spend the whole day in Waterford and stay there for the night. It happened to be the third anniversary of the first performance of the C.C.C. at Southport in 1881, and my father invited the members of the Company to supper, with a smoking concert to follow. This was the first of some thirty anniversary suppers every year on February 7th. I must have quickly recovered from my sea-sickness, for my mother told me later that I much enjoyed the concert for as long as I was allowed to stay up, and that I recited some lines from *Lady Godiva* as my contribution to the evening's entertainment. At these anniversary gatherings every member of the Company had to contribute either a song or a recitation.

The next thing I remember is sitting on my nurse's knee in the front of the dress circle of the Cork Opera House on the right-hand side, or as an actor would say, on the prompt side. My father was rehearsing a scene from *The Comedy of Errors* in which he played one of the two Dromios. The stage was empty except for a small house in the middle of it at the door of which Antipholus of Ephesus had to knock. The young man who was playing the part did not walk up the steps and knock in the way my father thought he should knock. And from that distant past comes back his voice. "No, no, my boy. All you have to do is to walk up the steps and knock like

this." Then he would show him what a simple movement it
was. Yet somehow the young man did not seem able to follow
it. My father was always very patient and was hardly ever
irritable with members of the Company. My mother was less
patient. And again from that distant past I see her coming on
to the stage and hear the coldness in her voice as she tries to
show the young man what he has to do. I am told that my
own voice takes this cold tone when I am annoyed, but I am
unaware of deliberately assuming it.

Down in the stalls two or three of the ladies of the Company
looked up and waved to me, smiling and blowing kisses. The
suspicion that they were laughing at me was confirmed when
presently a rehearsal of the minuet in *The School for Scandal*
was called, and from the stage the ladies of the Company
proceeded to wave to me and blow more kisses. I began to
show signs of weeping, and I was then presented with a penny
to buy some sweets; the next thing I remember is sitting in
my perambulator much distressed by the sight of the children
of Cork without shoes or stockings. I remember clearly the
sight of the children but I do not remember offering my
penny, with which I am told I wished to endow them with
shoes and stockings, nor that when Nanny tut-tutted at such
a notion I tried to take off my own shoes and give them to
the children. I say that she tut-tutted, for as I look back on
those earliest years of mine I hear those eternal 'tut-tuts',
inadequate as 'tut-tut' is to express phonetically that disapproving click of the tongue against the roof of the mouth.
She probably put up the hood of the perambulator, for putting
up the hood of the perambulator was the way nurse or nursemaid could always assert grown-up power.

I wonder if many people can recall the sensation of riding
in a 'pram'—that bump down from the pavement into the
roadway and that bump up when the opposite pavement was
reached. One shot forward against the safety-strap as one
bumped down, and backward as one bumped up. And then
those ominous words 'it's coming on to rain', after which the
hated hood was raised and the brass catches—or whatever
they are called—were straightened with a click. The world on
either side of one was excluded and one sat in a melancholy
made more intolerable by the smell that came from the rubbery

hood. Long ago I was once told that margarine used to be made out of old perambulator hoods. I do not suppose that was true, but it was quite credible once upon a time. Thanks to television, the public has at last been persuaded that the 'g' is hard and today the 'marjarine' of the past has become as respectable as butter, thanks to the emotional interviews with margarine eaters we see on Commerical TV. I wish mispronunciations better worth correction could secure attention. Contróversy is the latest juvenile delinquent, and looks like being as popular as 'vittamins' and 'zebbra' crossings. We are too tolerant nowadays. When a guest spoke of a bálcony, as we call it nowadays, instead of a balcóny, Samuel Rogers used to ask him to leave the breakfast-table. I lack the courage to invite a guest of mine who says contróversy to leave my house.

Back to the perambulator. People have questioned my ability to remember pram transport but the power of a smell to stimulate the memory is a commonplace, and it should be borne in mind that the child's response to smell and to colour is much stronger than it will be when he is grown up. I have tried putting my head inside the hood of a perambulator and no longer detect that rubbery smell: it may be that they are made of less olfactory material nowadays. Being strapped in was another grievance. I can recall the slightly resentful emotion of helplessness as nurse or nursemaid treated one as casually as they would have treated a parcel they were tying up. And the rug, that sacrosanct rug on which not the minutest fragment of sugar from a sweet must be allowed to sparkle. Perhaps my anxiety to spend my penny on shoes and stockings for the children of Cork was due to the fuss I knew my old nurse would make about the eating of whatever sweets it had purchased. 'No, no, wait till we get home.' 'Well, one, but only one, mind.' 'You shall have another before you go to bed if you're a good boy'. 'There now, what did I tell you? You're scattering the sugar all over the rug.' 'Tut-tut-tut-tut-tut!' And so on.

My mother used to tell me that when I came back from that pram ride and told her of my distress about the bare feet of the children of Cork she immediately had a vision of me as a great philanthropist in the future, a budding Shaftesbury in petticoats. However, the vision quickly faded as she and my father tried to understand what I meant by saying rapturously 'And then the moogits.' This was my attempt to tell them of seeing for the first time an organ-grinder with a monkey and my pleasure in the music. It may seem strange that a child already able to read nursery rhymes could get no nearer to 'music' than 'moogits'; but all my life the sight of words has been essential; the sounds of words is not enough. I cannot learn a language by ear any more easily than I can learn a tune. I must see the words if it is to be remembered correctly. Once I have a word visually correct I can mimic the pronunciation and accent with a good deal of accuracy, and this applies equally to a foreign language or to the varieties of English accents.

When I told my father about this 'moogits' he asked me to repeat the word in order to understand what I was trying to say. I have been told that when I was asked to repeat an uncomprehended word I would repeat if for the first time with a slightly forced smile to conceal my pessimism about the intelligence of grown-ups. But if I was asked to repeat the word a second time my countenance would darken with rage and the uncomprehended word would be uttered between clenched teeth in as near as a two-year-old can get to a resentful contempt for grown-up imbecility. Thus did my father have to understand what I meant by 'moogits'. Nanny then stepped forward to translate 'moogits' into 'music', delighted no doubt to have an opportunity of reminding my mother that I was not nearly so clever a child as she seemed to think I was.

My parents were already tremendous favourites with Irish audiences, and the many friends they had in Cork probably paid me more attention than Nanny thought good for me. There would have been a lot of sniffing and tut-tutting. I can very vaguely recall Charles Plunket, the R.M., and a little more clearly Jack Cronin, a young wine merchant who had a huge crate made to hold my perambulator and cot and my other things. I used greatly to enjoy superintending, as I supposed, the packing of this crate every week: I was told by my mother, though I find it difficult to believe, that I was able on one occasion to show my father how to put my cot together when my mother was not around. Nanny was completely incompetent over anything like that, and today I should be even more incompetent.

It was called the 'Shakespeare travelling-cot'. There were several wooden rods or poles with brass sockets which had to be put together for the framework and hold the canvas substance of the bed. Then at the head two rods or poles met in a triangle and took two curtains which were laced at the back like stays. When the cot was taken to pieces it was packed into a long canvas bag. This is a most inadequate description and evidently I grasped the complexity of its construction much more clearly when I was two years old than I do now. I can still recall the cosiness of that cot and the sense of security which the curtains at the head of it gave to me. It may account for the fact that to this day I like to sleep in a four-poster bed.

Scotland and Ireland were the two countries in which my father loved best to act, and after a year or two the Compton Comedy Company, after playing through February and March in Edinburgh, Glasgow, Aberdeen, Dundee, Greenock, Paisley, Perth, Stirling, Ayr, Kirkcaldy, Falkirk and sometimes Dumfries, Kilmarnock and Inverness, crossed over to Ireland when Lent was over and always played in the Gaiety Theatre on Easter Monday, with Belfast, Cork, Limerick and sometimes Derry and Waterford to follow. They never played in Wexford, which I always regret when as President of the Wexford Festival I stand upon the stage of the old Wexford theatre to make a speech.

In Cork on one occasion in the late 'eighties my father had what he thought was the happy idea of asking the colonel of some regiment stationed near by to allow its band to play instead of the regular Opera House orchestra. On the opening Monday night the band's performance was loudly applauded and encored by the audience, and after the final curtain my father turned to go to his dressing-room, much pleased with himself. Suddenly there was pandemonium in the theatre, and presently the conductor came to his dressing-room.

"I'm sorry, Mr Compton," he said. "The regimental band will not be able to play tomorrow night."

"But it had a great success," my father protested.

"Did you not hear the shindy when the curtain came down?"

"I did hear a good deal of noise, yes."

"That was *God Save the Queen*, and tomorrow night they'll be here with anything they can lay their hands on to throw at us."

"Must the band play *God Save the Queen?*"

"Mr Compton!"

My father thought for a moment or two.

"Must you play the whole of the national anthem?"

"Well, it might not be necessary to play the whole of it."

"Couldn't you play the first few bars and get back under the stage at once?"

And that was how it was settled to avoid the brickbats or rotten eggs or anything else that was thrown by an audience which, until *God Save the Queen* began, had applauded and encored the regimental band throughout the rest of the evening.

My father used to tell a good story about Limerick at the same period. On the opening night he usually played Davy Garrick. It was the custom of the Limerick audience to greet his return every year by calling for a speech and handing up a harp of Erin or a shillelagh tied with green ribbon or a bouquet of shamrocks for his leading lady, in those days my mother. On this occasion the house was absolutely packed when last year's Mayor of Limerick arrived and greeted John Henry Savile, the business-manager.

"How are you, my dear Savile? I've come to give a welcome to my old friend Compton. Let me have a good seat, will you?"

The ex-Mayor, Mr O'Dea or O'Shea or whatever O' it was, seemed somewhat elated and Savile, a very prudent man with a heavy moustache and a deep voice, afraid lest the ex-Mayor's welcome might be a little too boisterous, said:

"I'm sorry, Mr O'——, I'm afraid there isn't a seat left in the house."

"Nonsense, Savile. I've just left a civic banquet to welcome my old friend Compton back to the city of Limerick. You've got to find me a seat."

"There's one stall left in the front row," the box-office keeper intervened. "It's just been returned."

"The very seat I'd like to have," the ex-Mayor declared.

Savile shook his head, but there was nothing for it. He had

to present the ex-Mayor with a ticket for that stall. In he went and on reaching his seat right in the middle of the front row he sat down and immediately fell fast asleep.

The curtain went up on the first act. After five or six minutes my father made his entrance and was greeted with loud applause. The ex-Mayor slept on. The curtain went up on the second act and the famous drunken scene. At the end of it my father had to take curtain after curtain. The shillelagh or harp of Erin was handed up, and there were calls of 'speech'. My father had a wonderful way in those speeches of his of making any audience in Great Britain and Ireland feel that the particular town or city in which he was playing that week was the one place to which he had been wanting to return since he played there last a year ago. And when he had such a genuine affection as he had for Limerick he was able to convey it with considerable charm. Amid all the applause the ex-Mayor slept on.

The curtain went up on the third act in which Violet Gresham comes to Garrick's house, having discovered that the drunkenness had been assumed to keep a rash promise he had made to her father the Alderman to cure his daughter's infatuation for an actor. Unknown to Garrick and the young woman the Alderman himself is hidden behind a screen and hears Garrick giving his daughter good advice.

"Go back to your father, and if ever in the future you think of the poor actor who crossed your path, think of him kindly. . . . ." And so on, the off break in Garrick's voice taking emotional wickets all over the theatre. Just when the Alderman was preparing to step out from behind the screen to furnish a happy ending to the play the ex-Mayor woke up. In those days the orchestra of the old Limerick theatre was almost under the stage so that when the ex-Mayor rose from his stall and advanced towards it he could stretch a hand over the footlights.

"Welcome, my dear old friend Compton, welcome back to the city of Limerick," he said in rich tones that rang through the house.

Being an Irish audience it was not in the least put out by such an interruption. There were a few murmurs, of 'sit down and don't disturb the man' and the play went peacefully on.

8. Edward Compton

8. Virginia and Isabel Bateman

9. Adelaide Neilson

I have a souvenir of that old Limerick theatre in a note from my mother which an old friend of hers sent me a few years ago.

> *Theatre Royal, Limerick*
>
> *May* 3. '87
>
> *I'm writing this in a wait of 'The Rivals'—such a theatre as this is! a thorough old barn and such a splendid audience—they deserve a good theatre.*"

Thirty-five years later my second sister Ellen Compton was playing in Ireland during the troubles. In Limerick she went to a grocer's shop to order some things and when she gave her name the grocer asked:

"Are you any relation of Edward Compton?"

"I'm his daughter."

"There's nothing to pay," the grocer said.

My father had then been dead four years.

Once upon a time in a Yorkshire town—I think it was Bradford—my father was playing in this third act when a chap in a corner of the gallery called down in a hoarse whisper "Compton!" My father paid no attention, thinking that an attendant would come along and tell the interrupter to be quiet. But he kept on whispering "Compton!". Finally, in despair of getting Garrick's attention, he called out "Compton! The old bugger behind the screen is watching thee. Mind out, lad."

From Cork in 1885 presumably we went on to Dublin and Belfast, These early tours are difficult to date because the regular progress of the C.C.C. had not yet been fixed. At any rate we were in Derry at the very end of February. Why I know this will transpire presently.

I remember being taken to the Bishop's Palace. The Bishop's wife was Mrs Alexander, who wrote some well-known hymns, but I cannot see clearly the face either of her or of Dr Alexander. What I do remember clearly was being told by my old nurse about the siege of Derry, with gruesome details about what the poor besieged had to eat. Yet somehow I was not moved to feel the least sympathy with the besieged. I cannot suppose that this was an early manifestation of my hatred of Dutch

G

William; it was probably due to the boring, self-important way in which Nanny told the tale.

The most vivid memory, however, is of waking in the middle of the night and hearing the tramp-tramp of feet outside past the window. I called out. Nanny did not wake. Soon my mother came in and, lifting me out of the cot, she went with me to the window and pulled back the blind. Down below were soldiers marching and in the middle of them were two priests.

"Oh dear," my mother sighed. "Two poor priests."

I told this story to Tim Healy thirty-nine years later when I was staying with him at Vice-Regal Lodge during the Tailtean Games in 1924.

"They were Father —— and Father ——. That was in February 1885," said Tim Healy.

I stupidly did not make a note of the names at the time and I cannot trace anything about two priests being arrested at that time. Probably they were being transferred from one prison to another, which would not be an item of news.

From Derry we went to Greenock, and I remember being much interested by the process of getting a number of pigs on board. To my immense pleasure one of the dockers put me to ride pig-a-back on a pig, and on it I mounted the gangway. Why that pig was so docile I cannot guess now, but I remember thinking at the time that it was because I was wearing a brown check ulster which had just been bought for me and of which I was proud because it made me feel more grown up than I could feel in petticoats. The great moment of being breeched was still some months away. Somewhere on the way up the Clyde I was distressed by the sight of a wrecked fishing-boat on a rock. My old nurse was constantly dinning into me the need for taking great care of my toys and I observed, no doubt with the intention of impressing on everybody my own respect for toys, that these naughty fishmen had broken their boat.

My mother did not act in Greenock and my Aunt Isabel came up to take her place for a while. She had just finished playing the heroine in the Adelphi melodrama *In the Ranks*, which had run for eighteen months. The Company went on without my mother. She was not at all well and we stayed for a few days at Gourock before going down to the little house in Great Malvern where her baby was expected to be born at the end of April or the beginning of May.

The journey from Scotland was a formidable business. We reached some place on the way in the middle of the night and I can remember walking along a dark platform with my mother to look for our luggage and I can remember going into her room at the hotel next morning to help her take her breakfast in bed.

It must have been about the middle of March when we reached Malvern. The little house was at the Wych and one passed close by through a kind of arch from Worcestershire into Herefordshire.

The mistress of this little house was Mrs Barnes, a tall handsome old woman who wore a mutch. I admired her mutch and asked Nanny why she did not wear a frilly cap round her face like Mrs Barnes; at which she sniffed and tut-tutted. Probably the notion that she could be capable of such a breach of the severe standards of genteel procedure ruled by the butler and the housekeeper annoyed her. A mutch was old-fashioned, and for Nanny old-fashioned was the most pejorative adjective she could summon from her vocabulary. When my face expressed dislike of something it was always scolded as an old-fashioned look. I hated bluebottle flies and I was once heard urging a bluebottle that was buzzing round me to depart as a great big old-fashioned fly.

Tom Barnes, the cat, or Mr Barnes as I preferred to call him, shared my disapproval of bluebottle flies and I welcomed his help in getting rid of them, though I could not help regretting slightly his habit of eating them, when caught, with every sign of tasty enjoyment. Mr Barnes was a very large neuter tabby cat, though he was probably not as large as I see him now with the mind's eye in which he appears the same size as myself. Mr Barnes accompanied me everywhere and liked to rest with me during that hour when the two-year-old was supposed to recover from the exhaustion of the morning and be ready to eat his dinner. Nanny had a ludicrous notion that by resting with me Mr Barnes would draw my breath and so he was always hustled away. However, to my relief he nearly always managed to get back because I could not bear the nursery door to be closed. My mother defeated Nanny on this and insisted that if I wanted the door left ajar left ajar it must be. And how grateful I was when two black-beetles appeared beside my cot and were chased away by Mr Barnes.

That early spring in Malvern was cold and blustery, but I was able to have a great deal of my mother's company and with the help of blocks with the letters on them I mastered the alphabet and could spell any reasonably short word that was asked for.

I used to read to her nursery rhymes and stories. I was particularly fond of Dick Whittington and this story my mother discouraged because I always invited her to gaze with me at a double-page illustration of the rats devouring everything. She told me in later years that she had been afraid the rats might have an effect on the features of the child that was to be born in a few weeks.

I used to read to Mr Barnes when my mother was resting, and he was naturally a sympathetic observer of this picture; he did not mind how often I showed it to him. He also liked another double-page coloured picture of Tom Thumb on the verge of being swallowed by an enormous fish with two rows of savage teeth. As for myself I was so frightened by this picture that it required an effort of courage to turn the page and enjoy the ghastly fascination of it. Mr Barnes used to reassure me. If this horrible fish took it into its head to jump out of the book and try to swallow me he knew how to deal with any fish.

From that time comes back a memory of two hymns— *Once in Royal David's City* and *There is a green hill far away*. The latter still conjures up for me the landscape behind that little house in Malvern. Probably like most children, I thought 'without a city wall' meant that there was no city wall round it and I did not associate it in the least with any proximity to a city. It was just a green hill far away. *Once in Royal David's City* seems to go back still earlier to the dim beginnings of my recollection. So much did it impress itself upon me with some curious polychromatic pattern that even to this day I hardly break up the words into individual significations; I perceive the whole hymn as I might look back at a Persian rug with purple slightly predominating in the colour scheme; even the melody to which it was sung has the same prismatic quality.

I was a long way at this date from the discovery of Rimbaud's famous sonnet about the colours of the five vowels, but I was already affected by the colours of words and the shape of sentences. Thus the grace before meals *For what we are going to receive* always presented itself as an oblong chocolate-brown affair whereas the grace after meals *For what we have received* appeared a round mustard-yellow affair.

The little house in Malvern had a small garden every blade of grass in which I loved passionately. The first daisies smelt marvellously sweet to that nose of childhood whose percipience and power of scent we who have lost it do not always realise. I used to carry small bunches of them around, inviting everybody to sniff them and murmuring 'smell so sweet' as an assurance of reward for their sniff. I recall my anxiety for one small bunch, that seemed to smell particularly sweet, to be sent up to Scotland where my father was acting so that he might enjoy this rich perfume of daisies, which by then would have been imperceptible to his thirty-one-year nose. I was still unable to manage the complicated consonants of Scotland and called it Cottyland.

Toward the end of that April I was taken to London by my cousin Sidney Crowe to stay once more with her old nurse Lizzie Dillon in St John's Wood. Sidney, who was at school in Malvern, was then just fourteen. She celebrated her ninetieth birthday in February 1961. She was the only daughter of my mother's eldest sister Kate and George Crowe, who was one of my godfathers. For some reason I called her Dah, and Dah she remained for many years to myself and younger brother and sisters.

All I remember from that brief visit to London was a large bush of white lilac in the Dillons' garden and wondering why my old nurse could never be as jolly as Lizzie Dillon.

Uncle George and Aunt Katie came back to Malvern with Sidney and myself when the news of my brother's birth on May 4th reached them. George Crowe did not like children and was neither kind to nor patient with his own daughter, but for some reason difficult to understand he took a fancy to me. He was a strange man. He was a son of Eyre Evans Crowe, one of those early Victorian tyrants who insisted on his youngest son's becoming a doctor instead of what he wanted to be, a civil engineer. One of his elder brothers was Eyre Crowe the painter, and another was Sir Jospeh Crowe, the joint author of Crowe and Cavalcaselle's history of painting and father of Sir Eyre Crowe, the outstanding Permanent Under-Secretary of the Foreign Office in this century.

After George Crowe married my aunt he acted as her manager and gave up the practise of medicine. He had a passion for poker work, and indeed for a lot of other ingenious ways of wasting time; he spent a year making a clock out of fish bones—a clock which worked, moreoever!

He was six feet five inches tall with a trim dark beard, and I spent many hours with him in that late spring and summer of 1885. He taught me to recognise every wild flower we found on our walks together. This was sometimes embarrassing for me because when people invited me to admire the pretty buttercup I would have to explain that it was a crow's-foot not a buttercup. In spite of protests from my old nurse he would take me out at night to show me the planets and the constellations. The Great Bear, the Pleiades and Orion became as familiar as the nightlight burning in my nursery. We must have presented an unusual spectacle, that very tall man with a dark beard wandering about on the Malvern hills with a two-year-old child who could point at Orion sloping gradually southward as summer drew on or show where Cassiopeia was in the sky without being able to pronounce her name as clearly as he would have wished.

There was a laburnum in the garden of that little Malvern house and I was much surprised by my uncle's warning me that the seed pods of the laburnum at which I had gazed spellbound by its beauty in blossom, were poisonous. I called them seed-lump-seeds and I can recall the awe with which I stroked those dangerous pods. I still think of them as seed-lump-seeds.

At this date I always spoke of myself in the third person as 'Monty' and when I look back now to myself at two years old I can recapture the objective view of myself all those years ago. Once I came in with a bunch of speedwell and showed the flowers as 'Monty's eyes'. There was no vanity in this; it

was a coldly objective judgment. Nanny at once contradicted
what she, immeasureably stupid, thought was an example of
self-admiration, by reminding me that my hair was mousy.

By now she had her own baby, my brother Frank, an obvious
redhead from the start, and the hostility towards me grew.
I loved being in the garden with Mr Barnes for company.
To play in a garden meant that I would dirty my frock and
I was for ever being dragged away for utterly unnecessary
washings. My mother used to protest, but that old nurse with
her button nose and wrinkles and greying hair parted in the
middle was mulish, and my mother fearful of being accused
of spoiling me always used to end by surrendering to Nanny.

I remember clearly being brought in to see my mother
when we returned from London the day after my brother was
born. Before he arrived she had sometimes talked to me about
the possibility of soon having a baby sister, and though impressed by the sight of a baby brother I was anxious to know
where the baby sister was. Of course the baby brother had
been brought by a stork and I remember thinking that the
stork must be a very stupid bird if it brought a baby brother
when it was expected to bring a baby sister. It was about now
that my Aunt Isabel arrived in Malvern, bringing with her
two fox terrier puppies, a brown and white one called Scamp
for her elder sister Kate, and an all white one called Ranks,
in memory of that run of Adelphi drama. That autumn she
would be playing the heroine in the Drury Lane drama *Human
Nature*.

At this date she had already decided to join a sisterhood
one day and had resolved that she would never marry. Her
mind had been set on paying back some of her mother's debts
and all the money she could spare was spent in this way. In
1899 she would be received into the community of St Mary
the Virgin, Wantage, of which she was one day to become
Mother General.

She was now thirty years old and very much my godmother
as well as my aunt. Never after the silver knife and fork at
my christening did she give me any presents except books in
my childhood and youth. To her I owe Kingsley's *Heroes*,
Scott's *Tales of a Grandfather*, Church's tales from Homer and
Virgil, Lamb's tales from Shakespeare, the two *Alices*, the

Swiss Family Robinson, in fact all those books which were such vital food for the imagination of the young, now, alas, swamped every Christmas by a flood of what with rare exceptions are worthless books for children.

My name for this godmother of mine was Little Auntie, which was handed on to my younger brother and sisters. What I remember most clearly of her arrival in Malvern that summer was my mother's filling the fireplace in the sitting-room with flowers to welcome Isabel. I can see now that flowery fireplace and seem to be sitting again on the hearthrug gazing at it in a rapture, and like an echo from all these years ago I can hear my voice telling Mr Barnes that he must not upset the flowers because Mumma had put the flowers there for Little Auntie.

In a copy of Christina Rossetti's poems which she gave to my mother I recall reading with a kind of glowing thrill her writing under my mother's name:

> For there is no friend like a sister
> In calm or stormy weather;
> To cheer one on the tedious way,
> To fetch one if one goes astray,
> To lift one if one totters down,
> To strengthen whilst one stands.

But I would have been about five before I first read those lines.

I remember going to my brother's christening and standing by the font with a Madonna lily in my hand, which two of the aesthetic ladies of the 'eighties had insisted upon, though I am sure it would have looked more appropriate in the hands of the Blessed Damozel. It was about now that I had my only unpleasant encounter with a flower. Mrs Barnes had a calceolaria in a pot which I much admired, and then one day I thought I would open the mouth of one of the blooms as I was wont to open the mouths of the snapdragons to let them close again of their own accord. The calceolaria betrayed my confidence because when I opened its mouth a small insect came out of it and made my heart beat so fast under the shock of its abrupt appearance that I retained a lifelong prejudice against calceolarias until I was able to grow the little pale mauve calceolaria of New Zealand called *Sinclairi*. And that was not until forty years later, when I was living in the island of Jethou.

My father arrived back from town that June about the same day as my Aunt Isabel, who had been taking my mother's place in his Company, and in spite of Nanny's disapproval I was able to have uproarious games with him. I remember being terribly distressed when my brother Frank was suddenly sick. "Oh, baby brother," I said to him with sympathetic realisation of the rules and regulations for polite behaviour that would irk his future, "oh, baby brother, you will soon have to put up your hand and say 'beg pardon'."

One day my father played cricket with me, and this I greatly enjoyed. I have been told that the next day I wanted another game and asked for 'keek it'. Failing to understand that 'keek it' meant cricket, he tried kicking everything until I became frenzied with rage at what seemed his perverse stupidity. However, at last he grasped what I wanted and cricket was resumed.

Then there was a day of misadventure with water. My father had a malacca cane with a silver top, and on walks I took with him there was a favourite game of trying to catch his cane in the way a kitten tries to catch a piece of string. I can see now that malacca cane eluding my grasp round a sunken water-butt into which I plunged. As I look back on the incident I seem to have fallen into a deep well, and indeed I once related the story as a fall into a well to be corrected by my mother and told that it was a water-butt. I recall being carried home on my father's shoulder and my old nurse's attempt to turn my soaking into an example of wilfulness on my part as she took off my wet clothes and dressed me in my best frock of damson-coloured velvet with a lace collar.

My father, who had probably been rebuked himself for his carelessness, started another game with me in the course of which, sitting on the edge of the bath, I toppled backwards into it. I do not remember what happened after that. Probably Nanny put me to bed.

Another opportunity for my old nurse to spoil sport was my enjoyment in playing with Ranks and Scamp, the two puppies, because in the exuberance of their greeting when I called to the 'baby bow-wows' they usually managed to knock me over and this of course involved the crime of getting my dress rumpled or dirtied.

About now somebody gave me *Hookeybeak the Raven and other tales*, illustrated by Wilhelm Busch. Of the other tales the only one that interested me enough to read it over and over again was *The Worrying Bluebottle and the Gentleman who lost his Temper*. Hookeybeak the Raven enthralled me. It began:

> Here's Tommy Tit, who's gathering berries in the wood;
> Here's Hookeybeak the Raven—that Raven wasn't good.

I suppose my first attempt at meditation was inspired by Hookeybeak. "That Raven wasn't good" I used to murmur to myself over and over again. The mischief in which Hookeybeak delighted was pictured and related in verse for some two dozen pages until on the last page Hookeybeak, in making a mess of Aunt Matilda Tabitha's knitting, managed to hang himself,

> But round his neck, oh horror! was caught the worsted thread,
> And Hookeybeak fell down that day, and hung till stiff and dead.
> And Aunt Matilda Tabitha she said to Tommy Tit
> 'You see, he wasn't good, my dear, and here's the end of it!'

These lines played upon my fancy with an elegiac emotion I should not feel so sharply again for quite a long time. It was to comfort my sorrow that I repeated over and over again 'That Raven wasn't good'. As the ancient Greeks were awed by the emotion of watching the protagonist in a tragedy moving towards his doom without being able to deflect him from his fatal course, so I, reading the story of Hookeybeak, was powerless to prevent his end. 'That Raven wasn't good.' His end was ineluctable.

On the other hand, the bluebottle's end at the hands of the gentleman who lost his temper was welcome. The breakage of china involved before the fly-flap at last brought the bluebottle down to to be crushed under a triumphant foot merely postponed an eagerly awaited end. This was what every bluebottle deserved. To this day if a bluebottle comes into my room I cannot rest until either I or one of my cats has slain him.

Some twenty-five years ago in a broadcast I mentioned Hookeybeak the Raven, and said how much I regretted that my original copy had disappeared like so many nursery favourites read to pieces by a succession of youthful readers. No less then seventeen listeners sent me copies of Hookeybeak the Raven, all to be returned after I had refreshed my memory except one. And that copy I gratefully have beside me as I write these words.

Some of the pictures of Wilhelm Busch have been painted from a nursery box of water colours. Every page is grubby with childish fingers. The preface in this edition published by Routledge contains these observations:

"The old assertion, frequently repeated and devoutly believed for some generations that the Germans have no sense of humour, and were altogether of too saturnine a disposition to enjoy 'fun', has of late years received some rude shocks. Various 'fun books' from the good old 'Struwwelpeter' downwards have proved that German woodcut art—or, as our neighbours delight to call it, Xylography—is appreciated in England. To these 'fun books' comes a new recruit in an English dress popular and well known in Germany. It is hoped that friend 'Hookeybeak' may make for himself a wide circle of acquaintances among our young friends here, though the legend frankly avows that 'that Raven wasn't good'. The indispensable 'moral' will be found in its proper place in each narrative."

All these stories like the stories in *Struwwelpeter* tell of some human being or animal being hurt or teased. There is never a trace of genial humour, and one may speculate how much of the behaviour of the Germans in this century was due to the influence of the books read by them in childhood. That may be an idle speculation because for the Germans to be able to produce such books seems to reveal their national character.

When the time came for my parents to go on tour toward the end of July I had to endure the pangs of parting with my mother and coming under the strict control of my old nurse. The first battles over sago and tapioca and rice puddings began, battles which would continue for some years. Luckily for me George Crowe and his wife remained in Malvern when Sidney's summer holidays began. Nanny was furious when my godfather took me walking with him at night on the Malvern

Hills to look at the stars, but he with his great height and complete contempt for her tantrums was too much for her. The walks went on.

It must have been about the middle of September when Nanny and Frank and I rejoined the C.C.C. at Hastings, whence we went on to Brighton. Here I recall a visit to the aquarium and being appalled by an octopus which I was worried would be able to get out of the tank and enwrap me in its fearful tentacles. As I recall that octopus it seems the size of the one in Victor Hugo's *Travailleurs de la Mer*, but I do not suppose its tentacles were more than a couple of feet long. And I also recall a curious creature swimming about a tank about the size and shape and colour of an Association football with feelers all over it. I see it clearly with my mind's eye, but no such creature can have existed. Whence did this figment project itself into my memory? The explanation may be that, frightened by the octopus, I dreamed of this creature and that it is the memory of a dream which remains in my mind.

At Brighton my father produced a very bad play called *True Love*, to a matinée of which I was taken and at which I was much distressed by my mother's unhappiness in various scenes. When I was being put to bed with my brother Frank, he and I both seated on what in those days were politely known as 'articles,' I said to my mother, "Monty would not like to be a actor," and then after a pause I added with a sympathetic look at Frank, "Baby brother would not like to be a actor."

Whether my determination not to go on the stage dates from that evening in Brighton all those years ago a sapient psychoanalyst of today would no doubt be able to decide.

At Torquay that autumn I went to a matinée of *The Rivals*, the humour of which escaped me and I was doubly distressed by my father as Bob Acres being so frightened in the rehearsal of the duel and still more by the faces Sir Anthony Absolute, played by Lewis Ball and never played as well by any actor since he died, made at Lydia Languish, my mother.

My next memory of that autumn of 1885 is a visit in Bristol from my French uncle Claude Greppo who brought me some toys. I can see him arriving at the top of some steep Bristol street and hear his asthmatic breathing. He was always called

Mr Greppo; not even his wife, my Aunt Ellen, who had married him when she was fifteen, called him Claude.

The Christmas of 1885 was spent in Scarborough. My father and mother stayed with my godfather, John Bolton, Frank and I were in rooms with Nanny. My mother did insist that I should sleep with her on Christmas Eve so that she could have the pleasure of seeing my excitement over the stocking. Among other things there was a drum which I beat with such enthusiasm that my mother told me it was not kind to beat it quite so hard because I should wake Pappa. I can recall the longing to beat that drum and I can recall going to the window and tapping on it with my fingers. I was told many years later that I turned to my mother and asked anxiously, "Was that a kind little noise?"

When Christmas was over, the Company went to Scotland, and for some reason I had to be left behind with Nanny. All that afternoon when the packing was being done I kept putting my beloved rubber ball into the portmanteau, into one of the big hampers, into the travelling bath, and even into my father's leather hat-case. Every time I hopefully put it in it was taken out until the bitter moment of departure came.

THREE YEARS OLD 1886

I SUPPOSE we remained behind in Scarborough only for
about a fortnight, but a fortnight to a two-year-old is an
eternity, Mr Goodricke, the manager of the Spa, used to ask
me to his house where his two boys and his daughter Clara
were very kind to me. My great stand-by, however, was an
old lady. Mrs Delamere had probably been a very handsome
young woman and in her old age she was determined still to
attract attention. She wore a lush black wig and was covered
with jewellery and beads and bangles. Her dresses were richly
coloured silks and velvets and she always wore mittens. Her
caps had wonderful ribbons and I think she must have used
a good deal of rouge because her cheeks as I recall them do
not seem the cheeks of an old lady. Mr Delamere was a good-
looking jolly Irishman who some years before had cut out my
godfather, John Bolton, by marrying Mrs Delamere when
she was a rich widow. So Mr Delamere was never spoken of
by John Bolton, although he remained friends with Mrs
Delamere, whom he still greatly admired. Mrs Delamere later
asked my mother to intercede for poor Mr Delamere; John
Bolton relented and Mr Delamere was allowed to visit his
house.

The next thing I remember is going to Glasgow and staying
for a week with my Aunt Isabel before my mother and father
arrived. She insisted on buying for me a sailor suit which I
was hardly ever allowed to wear because Nanny did not
consider I had reached an age for knickerbockers. This naturally upset me a good deal because those knickerbockers were
a pledge of being grown up. My pride in them was enough, of
course, to make my old nurse disapprove of them.

My next memory is of warm blankets hanging in front of
a fire, of a kettle steaming away, of the smell of hot oil and the
sound of my baby brother struggling for his life with croup.
He did not die; but it was a close thing. In the middle of this
I recall the extremely unpleasant but obviously once upon a
time regular habit of dealing with a small child's constipation

by forcing a spill of tightly rolled greased paper into his unfortunate little behind. This was probably a habit of early Victorian days in which my old nurse was following a fashion. I cannot believe it was her own idiotic idea. She was of course profoundly attached to the barbaric medicine of once upon a time, some of which like Dr Gregory's filthy powder I am astonished to be told is still used today, but I no longer hear of senna tea or castor-oil being given to a wretched child in warm milk. Then there was the grey powder (I do not know from what it was ground) administered in a dessert-spoon and helped down by a tea-spoonful of jam. Ipecacuanha was another disgusting tea-spoonful; licorice powder an equally disgusting glassful. I suppose the idea of making every aperient a foul business was to instil in the child's mind the notion that constipation was something sinful for which a penalty had to be paid. I believe that syrup of squills is an aperient and very rarely that sweet medicine provided a delicious tea-spoonful. But oh, how rarely! The other pleasant medicine which made a sore throat almost welcome was honey and borax, but then Condy's Fluid very soon made it most unwelcome. Nanny had a horror of pills. When one protested against her loathsome medicine she would threaten one with being made to take a pill, and in early childhood I was led to believe that it would be as easy to swallow my beloved rubber ball as a pill.

Holy Week was very late this year and it was spent in West Hartlepool; the first time I had returned to my birthplace since I had arrived there three and a quarter years earlier. By now my mother was expecting a third child, and after the anxious experience of my brother's croup it was felt that life on tour was not the ideal life for small children. So my father went down to find a house in London.

I do not know where the C.C.C. opened on Easter Monday, but it must have been somewhere close to West Hartlepool—probably Newcastle or Middlesborough—because my mother did not have to travel on Easter Sunday and took me to church for the first time. It was a children's service at Christ Church in the afternoon. When the organ started I asked what it was, and on being told that it was the organ I exclaimed in a loud and incredulous voice, "Organ? Organ? Where's the monkey?" Organ grinders with monkeys had been one of my greatest joys since I had seen the first one in Cork over a year earlier. Later on this story was told to somebody who sent it to *Punch*, and so I can fairly claim that I made my debut in print from my birthplace just on seventy-six years ago as I write of it now. The absence of the monkey did not prevent my joining in all the hymns. My mother told me that the words were delivered with complete accuracy in what she described as a deep booming voice quite regardless of any tune.

I was already capable of intense concentration and my favourite game was making words out of alphabet blocks. I was fascinated too by an animal alphabet. I the Ichneumon and W the Wolverine were the two animals over which I pored longest. I can well understand the attraction of the ichneumon:

> I's the ichneumon, a wonderful beast,
> For crocodile's eggs are its favourite feast.

But why the wolverine? I suppose it sounded more ferocious than the wolf in Little Red Riding Hood. I must have been preoccupied with spelling 'ichneumon' one afternoon when my mother was sewing and I was sitting on the hearthrug with my blocks. Presently she dropped a needle and I was asked to pick it up. I did what she asked but it was a tremendous effort to withdraw myself from that word-making to look for a needle. "Oh dear," I sighed as I got to my feet, "Monty has such a lot to do." I was still speaking of myself always in the third person, but I would be repeating that reflection to myself in the first person for the rest of my life, for I cannot recall a moment whether it was work or play when I did not feel I had such a lot to do. If I were asked now what was the secret of a happy life I think I should say that it was the perpetual sense of having such a lot to do, though I should qualify it by adding that with all one had to do it was vital to be more interested in the world of people and places and things than in oneself. I suppose in the jargon of today I am what we call an extravert (which with a sigh for the surrender of the Oxford Dictionary I refuse to spell with an 'o') rather than an introvert. Earnest young intellectuals may often be heard referring to extraverts with condescension, and there is general agreement in such circles that a novelist who becomes his characters is inferior

10. The Author
   Aged 7 months

Aged 11 months

Aged 21 months

Aged 2

11. Aunt Kate and George Crowe

11. C. M. with Sidney Crowe

to the novelist whose characters become him. That opinion
was once summed up in a condescending reference by Charlotte
Brontë to Jane Austen. Poor Miss Brontë really did believe
that she was a greater novelist than Jane Austen.

Early in May we were in Birmingham. I know this because
I was presented with a Tennyson birthday book by T. Edgar
Pemberton, who was a brass-founder there with great skill as
a playwright. He was a most lovable man and to him and his
family I owe some of the best hours of my youth. Of them in
another octave.

At the beginning of June we were in Chester, where I was
taken to see Thomas Hughes, who was then a County Court
Judge. He presented me with the sixth edition of *Tom Brown's
School Days*, which had been published in the previous year
with a new preface. It is inscribed 'Edward Montague Compton
from the author with all good wishes. Chester. June 1886.' It
may be noted that he does not sign his name. He held always
to the original 'By An Old Boy'. My copy is bound in leather
with gilt edges and beautifully marbled endpapers. I imagine
Macmillans must have given him a few presentation copies.
I wish publishers could bind their presentation copies in
leather today. His Honour wrote his name in my birthday
book, the first entry after my father's. Under his date, October
19, one of the quotations from Tennyson says:

> Let never maiden think, however fair,
> She is not fairer in new clothes than old.

Against this is '*oh!*' from Tom Hughes. And against his
signature '*Ths Hughes*' he wrote in his small exquisitely clear
handwriting '*But enters his protest against the new clothes doctrine
(see opposite page)*'.

I can just remember this occasion, but the picture is not
clear. I was probably too much concerned with handing the
birthday book to him and making my request for his signature
to register the great man's appearance. I wonder if there is
anybody else alive in 1962 with a signed copy of this book
first published a hundred and five years ago.

Some years were to pass before I read *Tom Brown's School
Days*, but let me record here that when I did read it, in spite
of its remoteness from the present of my own school, I was

H

aware of a life comprehensible to me which Dean Farrar could not convey with *Eric or Little by Little* published a year or two after *Tom Brown's School Days*.

The house in London chosen by my father was 54 Avonmore Road, West Kensington. At this date West Kensington had recently been carved out of Fulham and attached nominally to Kensington; South Kensington had established a precedent for this prolongation of the old Court Suburb by extricating itself from Brompton, and North Kensington had managed to detach itself socially from Notting Hill. The dream held out to my father as the reward for spending £1000 on buying the 99 years' lease of 54 Avonmore Road was that one day, and that day not far off, a bridge was to link Avonmore Road with West Cromwell Road. When this happened, 54 Avonmore Road would be worth three times as much as it was worth in 1886.

This project was inspired by Frank Braine, who had been a young organist at Christ Church, Kensington in my father's youth, and who was now the organist at St Matthias, Earl's Court, at the south end of Warwick Road. St Matthias was destroyed in the Second World War by enemy action; I shall have more to say about it in my next octave.

As things were when Braine acquired 64 Avonmore Road he had to walk to the Hammersmith Road and by Addison Bridge over the railway and then along the extension of Kensington High Street to Warwick Road, up the whole length of which he had to walk to reach St Matthias. Brisk walker as he was, this must have taken him at least twenty minutes and probably more. If the bridge was made he would be able to reach his church in five minutes, and in this dream he lived for some years.

Frank Braine was a passionate devotee of Charles Dickens and was himself a figure out of Dickens. I was to describe him many years later in a novel of mine called *Our Street* under the name of Lockett.

"Thackeray is too cynical for me," he used to proclaim. "He hasn't the humanity of Dickens. Head is not enough. We must have heart as well."

Whether it was that Frank Braine by reading so much Dickens had turned into a Dickensian character himself or

whether he enjoyed Dickens because he was born a Dickensian
character it would have been hard to decide. Some think that
people who love certain animals grow like them, others that
people love certain animals on account of a natural affinity.
My own belief is in the second theory. I believe that Frank
Braine must have been a Dickensian baby in his cradle. He
was a short man with a florid face and protruding eyes, and
he wore curly mutton-chop whiskers of what must once have
been an exceptionally vivid carroty hue, though by the time
I first remember him a considerable number of grey hairs had
toned down the colour. He was a noted singing-master, and
it was always said that he could have been a teacher of the
piano second to none if he would.

"But there's a point," Frank Braine used to declare in that
resonant metallic voice of his, "at which a man may become
a miserable slave, and that point is reached with the first
lesson he gives on the piano."

I have run ahead of my age, but I wanted to introduce him
as what my mother used to call a fatal influence over my
father. In other words, she thought the purchase of 54 Avonmore Road a mistake. She herself, having once lived in
Kensington Gore, felt that West Kensington was a piece of pre-
tentiousness. She was right. When my father bought 1 Nevern
Square in 1901 the lease of 54 Avonmore Road was sold for
£600 instead of the £3000 which Braine had prophesied.

The Avonmore Road of 1886 would look strange indeed
to the Avonmore Road of today. As one turned out of the
Hammersmith Road, Avonmore Mansions proclaimed themselves proudly on the left. These were among the first and may
indeed have been the very first flats in London erected as such.
They are still standing today, but whether they yet have a
lift I do not know. On the opposite side of the road began a
row of detached Regency houses separated from Hammersmith Road by large long gardens in front of them. Those
gardens would be buried early in the 'nineties beneath the
ugly bulk of Glyn Mansions and other blocks of flats.

The continuation of Avonmore Road just built in 1886
was a row of tall thin red-brick houses with even numbers
facing a stretch of waste ground on the far side of which were
the backs of the grey houses in Lisgar Terrace. In a year or

two the waste ground would be covered by the odd numbers of Avonmore Road, architecturally slightly less monotonous. There was a longish stretch of waste ground where the even numbers stopped, and here were the remains of the country in the shape of half a dozen elms and an old hawthorn tree.

At the back of Avonmore Road was the railway along which went the trains between Addison Road Station and Clapham Junction and also trains bound for the north-west of London which, as far as we were concerned, were travelling to places as remote and wild as Oregon would once have seemed to New Yorkers. Beyond the railway was a large area in which a number of coal merchants kept huge stacks of coal. Beyond this again was Warwick Road.

In the area of every house in Avonmore Road except ours and the Braines' at 64 was a lime tree and at the end of every garden at the back except ours and the Braines' were three poplars. Under Frank Braine's influence a plane tree was planted in our area and at the back a plane tree separated the two poplars.

Seaforth House, as my father out of piety to the memory of my grandfather called 54 Avonmore Road (we always called it just 54), was a thin house four storeys high above a basement. A wide flight of stone steps led up to the front-door, the upper part of which in the fashion of the time had two panels of stained glass in the kind of design favoured by the calendars one gets at Christmas time. I need hardly add that in my childhood I much admired those panels of stained glass. Moreover, that front door had a kind of sanctity about it, for it was never used when my parents were away on tour. On the right of the entrance hall was the dining-room and at the end of it the drawing-room. Under the staircase was a door with panels of ground glass through which one descended to the basement. Here in front, looking out on the area, was the morning-room behind which were the kitchen, the pantry and the scullery with another area from which steps led up into the tiny garden, as from the balcony outside the drawing-room they led down into it. Opposite the bottom of the basement stairs was a door leading down into the coal cellar and on the left was the area door, which was the only one used in the absence of my parents.

On the first floor was my parents' bedroom with a dressing-room attached, out of which one could walk on to a balcony. Behind this bedroom was my father's library and at the end of the landing the housemaid's closet and the lavatory. On the second floor was the spare-room with its dressing-room in front and at the back the night-nursery and bathroom. On the top floor was the day-nursery with a large recess and a dormer window, and at the back of this was the servants' bedroom and the cistern-cupboard. The top landing was lighted from above by a skylight.

Presumably it was the middle of June when we moved into 54 Avonmore Road, but I have only the dimmest memory of the business. I can hear with a momentary affright the first train going by with what in memory seems an almost appalling roar, which was so soon to shrink to no more than a reassuring rumble in hours of solitude to let one know that people did still exist. The railed bed in which I was presently to sleep in the night-nursery had presumably not yet been installed beside Nanny's bed in which she would sleep, my brother in the Shakespeare cot on the other side of her. Anyway, for two or three nights I slept with Nellie, the house-parlourmaid, in a double bed in the spare-room. Within a year that double bed would be for a long time a purgatory of terror for me. Yet my first memory of it is a pleasant one, I was asleep and woke suddenly to see Nellie undressing in the gaslight shining from a globed bracket beside the fireplace, which was immediately opposite the foot of the bed. She was a fair girl with a straw-berries and cream complexion, and as she pulled the chemise over her head and bent down to pick up and don her night-dress I paid the first compliment I can remember paying to the female form. If I were in tune with the repressions, frustra-tions and inhibitions of the Freudian school, I should be able to produce all sorts of emotional complications from this incident. Instead of which I can look back into the distant part of my life with the satisfaction of knowing that my first sexual response was natural if perhaps rather precocious. For the psycho-analyst I am a wash-out.

Very soon after moving into Avonmore Road we went to Southsea for the summer, Nellie and Cook, remaining in London. I cannot remember that first cook; she has been swallowed up by Mrs Frith, a figure out of Rabelais who came to us later. The Crowes had gone to live in Southsea, and that autumn my aunt would make her last provincial tour with *Leah*. I have a programme of the Lyceum, Edinburgh, for the week beginning October 25th, 1886, and something which nobody would ever read today in a Lyceum programme:

Thursday being the Sacramental Fast-Day
the Royal Lyceum Theatre will remain
CLOSED

In the previous year Robert Dolling had come to take over St Agatha's Landport from Dr Linklater, the Winchester College missioner. Dolling was an Ulsterman, the son of a High Sheriff of Londonderry who married a niece of Lord Caledon. He had been educated at Harrow and Trinity College, Cambridge, and inherited early considerable private means. Yet he was a fervid home ruler, a supporter of dis-establishment, a socialist and an Anglo-Catholic, or what then would be called an 'advanced ritualist'. Moreover, he was as near as anybody I have ever known to the saintliness of a Francis of Assisi. As a young man he had worked at St Alban's Holborn, with Father Stanton and Father Mackonochie. Then he had formed a guild of postmen by whom he was known as Brother Bob, and had worked among the poor in Southwark. He was not ordained until 1883 when he was thirty-two years of age. He had helped my mother and my Aunt Isabel during those difficult days of Sadler's Wells, and one of his sisters Josephine lived with my aunt Mrs Crowe when she became a widow in 1890. Working with him at Landport were two more of his sisters, Geraldine and Elise, and also a fourth sister Adelaide who was a nurse.

I had heard much about Bobbie Dolling before we went to Southsea, and I imagined him as a small boy with whom I should have wonderful games. When I met for the first time an immensely corpulent man I burst into tears of disappoint-ment, to his benevolent amusement. I do not remember much about St Agatha'a Mission Church at this date and shall say no more now about Robert Dolling who became for me 'Uncle' Robert and whose sisters all became 'aunts'.

My father and I used to go for walks on Southsea Common,

where he used to fall into holes about a foot deep from which he would pretend he could not extricate himself without my help. When with the utmost difficulty I succeeded in rescuing him I used to beg him when we came to another hole not to fall into it, and of course he always did. I wonder what the other frequenters of Southsea Common thought my father was playing at. He was completely unselfconscious about behaviour like this and by such behaviour would often acutely embarrass my brother and myself when we were older. Another picture of Southsea Common is the pageantry of a great review like the grand review at Rochester in *The Pickwick Papers*.

Portsmouth as I look back to it in those days seems crowded with soldiers and sailors. I recall the enchantment of sitting by a window and watching the march past of regiments to Church Parade on Sunday mornings, and after the scarlet of some line regiment the Royal Artillery in a uniform that owing to the heightened colour sense of the small child seems to be a glowing ultramarine instead of the very dark blue it really was. I recall, too, being puzzled by the rounded spikes of their helmets and asking Nanny why they were round like that instead of sharp. No doubt the answer I would have received from Nanny was 'because they are.' Those maddening replies of nurses and nursemaids!

"No, I can't play any more."

"Why?"

"Because I've got a bone in my leg."

"Tell me a story."

> I'll tell you a story about Jack a 'Nory
> And now my story's begun.
> I'll tell you another about Jack and his brother,
> And now my story's done.

I remember sitting on the knee of an old pensioner who told me what he did at Waterloo, but, alas, I have forgotten what it was exactly, though I know that horses came into it. And I am almost sure that I was patted on the head by a veteran of Trafalgar, but I cannot be absolutely certain about this. A powder-monkey at Trafalgar would have been in his mid-nineties by 1886.

A vivid memory of that summer is walking beside my brother's perambulator and seeing a chained gang of convicts who were working in Portsmouth harbour. The warders are running around and barking orders at the unfortunate men. They all had trim beards and peaked caps and carried carbines, and as I see them with the mind's eye their uniforms appear a much richer blue than they certainly were.

At the far end of the gang was a tall gaunt man who seemed to lift his fettered leg with difficulty as he walked and whose expression was one of utter agony. Were I able to draw I could draw his features with complete accuracy. It was a finely cut profile and his eyes seemed to be staring at despair. I felt a great sorrow for those convicts, probably all of whom have been mercifully at rest for many years. I do not think I am being either fanciful or sentimental if I say that the sight of those convicts affected my view of human nature because it gave me my first glimpse of man's inhumanity to man.

"Don't stand there staring at those poor men," said my old nurse sharply.

Turning quickly, my cheek struck one of the pointed bricks in the wall of the lately built Portsmouth Barracks, and like the big slow drops of rain that herald a thunderstorm the big slow drops of blood fell on the pavement beside the perambulator. I was hurriedly taken to a chemist's shop, where the cut was patched; the scar is still there.

The Compton Comedy Company did not go on tour that autumn because my father was doing a season at the Strand Theatre. He opened with *Davy Garrick* by William Muskerry. Charles Wyndham, who was playing Robertson's version of the French play from which both the English plays were taken, tried to get an injunction against Muskerry's version. The case was contemptuously dismissed with costs against Wyndham. *Garrick* was followed by *The Rivals* and *The School for Scandal*. The actor who was to play Old Rowley fell ill and my father told me that I would have to play the part. I took this quite seriously, and amused by this he rehearsed me. I can see him now as I enter the room after the sale of the family portraits and hear him as he says:

"Ha! old Rowley! egad, you are just come in time to take leave of some old acquaintances."

And I can hear myself replying with a very solemn sigh:

"Yes, I heard they were a-going. But I wonder you can have such spirits under so many distresses."

When the time came for my parents to go down to the theatre for the first night of *The School for Scandal* I was ready to accompany them, and fell into a passion of weeping when I was told that I was not really going to play Old Rowley. Finally, in spite of the usual protests from Nanny about spoiling, they took me with them, and I can recall Trip, played by my cousin Harry Morell (Mackenzie) standing in the wings with me on his shoulder to watch the party at table and hear my father sing '*Here's to the maiden of bashful fifteen*'. I recall, too, the actor who played Old Rowley coming up to me and saying that the reason why I had not been able to play the part was the difficulty of getting his costume altered to fit me in time. Being an extremely reasonable child, I saw the soundness of this argument and ceased to repine.

My godfather, John Bolton, 'Godpapa' to me (my other godfather preferred to be Uncle George) came to London and took me to see the Lord Mayor's Show, the magic of which has never been spoiled by seeing another. It must have been unusually attractive to children that year because the streets along which the Show passed were lined with troops, the Socialists having threatened to break up the procession. There had been serious rioting earlier in the year. I have a vague memory of an elephant in the procession ridden by Britannia with her trident.

When I got home and tried to tell my old nurse about the marvels I had seen she refused to listen. She was furious that she and my brother Frank, now nineteen months old, had not been taken.

By now I was always in a sailor suit. The hated petticoats had gone for ever some months before, but my knickerbockers instead of being kept up by braces were buttoned to a sort of red flannel corset. This was a source of grief to me and I longed for braces.

On a gloomy November day I was sitting by the dining-room window, wishing that Christmas was not such an endless time away when along the road opposite came a boy in a ragged pair of breeches without a coat. He was rattling a stick along the rickety fence that still bounded the waste ground between Avonmore Road and the back of Lisgar Terrace. As he drew nearer, whistling as he walked, I saw with admiring envy that he was wearing braces fastened by one button at the back and two buttons in front. His shirt was torn and grubby. What did it matter? This enviable boy was wearing braces and he was free. Over me came a fervid wish for freedom, and to myself I promised that once the intolerable handicap of childhood had been overcome I too would always be free. Of course, I did not express the emotion I felt in those words, but with the words of age I recall that emotion, and I think I can claim that freedom has been the guiding principle by which I have lived my own life and desired it for the lives of others. Later on that November day, when Nanny sent down a nursemaid whose name I have forgotten to fetch me up to bed, I longed to be outside somewhere in the darkness with that ragged boy.

"Come along, come along like a good boy," the nursemaid urged, and as we went up the first flight of stairs she put me in front of her and with her knee urged my ascent. On the first landing I could hear Nanny's fussy voice as she leaned over the balusters of the second landing:

"Bed, bed, bed. Time for bed, time for bed," and then suddenly the pain of bed was sweetly alleviated by the thought that in bed I should be able to suck my thumb. And I recall that this thought gave me the same physical response as I had given to the sight of Nellie in the gas-light pulling off her chemise and bending down to pick up her nightdress. Yet I must insist to eager Freudians that the physical response was a momentary feeling and that this was the only occasion on which I recall its happening. In any case, thumb-sucking was soon a pleasure of which I was deprived because when I went to bed my hands were tied up in bags. I think that deprivation of thumb-sucking was what aggravated the bad habit of biting my nails.

Waking in the morning, the first thing that always caught my eye was that squat red crescent of my old nurse's bustle hanging at the end of her bed. The paper of the night-nursery was an ugly dark olive-green with a pattern of improbable vegetation. The night-nursery oppressed my spirit, and it was a relief when some weeks after the birth of my sister Viola I was put to sleep by myself in the big double-bed of the spare-room next door. That was when my hands were put into bags to stop the thumb-sucking.

My sister Viola was born on November 26th, 1886, and I have a picture in the mind's eye of my father taking me down-stairs from the day-nursery to be shown the baby sister beside my mother. She must have been born in the afternoon because I remember the friendly gas-light from the bracket on the landing outside the door of my parents' bedroom and dressing-room. The globes of convoluted rose-pink glass shed a becoming radiance that I much admired. I can see my mother's exquisite complexion against the pillow and I can see a bundle beside her; clearer than either I see a jar of French plums on the table beside the bed.

Another memory of that autumn is the shape of Olympia with a half-finished roof which looked as if a great chunk had been bitten out of it, I can see this shape against the sky, and this must have been from the window of the day-nursery; it may have been my leaning out of that dormer window in the roof that prompted the immediate institution of safety bars.

Olympia was opened and finished by the end of the year. I have found a contemporary advertisement:

OLYMPIA
The National Agricultural Hall

OLYMPIA is at Addison Road Station and also within a few minutes walk of West Kensington Station and High Street, Kensington. The most accessible place from every point. The trains of all the railways and 126 omnibuses set down visitors at the very doors of Olympia.

OYLMPIA is the Largest Hall in the Kingdom. Accommoda-tion for 9000 visitors. Comfortably warm throughout. Brilliantly illuminated by Electric Light. Dining, Refreshment and Grill Rooms.

THE HIPPODROME is an altogether high-class and instructive 'Show', devoid of one single element of vulgarity. Such a Show has never been seen in London.

Two performances daily, 2 and 7.30 p.m. Admission—

Private Boxes £2, 2s. and £1, 1s.; Stalls and First Promenade, 5s.; Grand Circle and Second Promenade 2s. 6d.; Amphitheatre, 1s. Railway entrance opposite Addison-road Station.

Royal approval of the 'National Agricultural Hall' was shown a month or two later when the Queen attended a private performance of that 'instructive Show, devoid of one single element of vulgarity'.

Queen Victoria in her bonnet and bustle sitting all alone except for one or two attendants in that huge building must have been a remarkable sight.

I was given a rocking-horse that Christmas. It had brown fur and was stuffed. The usual rocking-horse of the period was all wood and much bigger than mine. Sometime in the early 'eighties the *Illustrated London News* issued a large chromolithograph with its Christmas number entitled *Yoicks! Tally-ho!* This represented a boy in a jockey-cap with his sister behind riding one of those big rocking-horses. This was to be seen framed on the walls of many nurseries; we had it in our day-nursery, and I was a little disappointed to find my rocking-horse small compared with the splendid steed in the picture. However, the real horsehair was a compensation. Brownie's stable was in the bay-window of the morning-room; for some reason, Nanny objected to his presence up in the nursery. She probably thought Frank would clamber up and fall off it to get a third scar on his forehead. One, as I seem to remember, was made by the coal scuttle when he was indulging himself in the curious habit of eating coal and the other may have been made when he got his head into a tin of golden syrup he was trying to empty. So when I wanted a ride on Brownie I had to ask Nanny's permission to rock myself up and down in the morning-room.

One of my memories of that autumn of 1886 is of bus-rides to the city with my father. Tales of his boyhood as we drove along Kensington High Street; in Knightsbridge that Highlander outside a tobacconist; the huge candles in the window of Tucker's candle-shop; Mills' Buildings pointed out as a dangerous slum which policemen would only enter in pairs; the house in that beautiful row just after the Barracks where he had had rooms when he first acted in London; the china cockatoo sitting on a circular perch which hung in the bow-window of Lady Burdett-Coutts' house at the corner of Stratton Street on a level with the top of the passing omnibus.

But there was one disappointment the first time I drove in an omnibus along Piccadilly.

"We shall be at the Circus in a minute or two," said my father.

My heart beat with excitement.

"Here we are at the Circus," said my father as the omnibus stopped.

"Circus?" I exclaimed. "Circus? I don't see the clowns. Where are the clowns?"

I had never been to a circus then, but I had seen pictures of clowns in a circus.

However, I saw my first clown some weeks later when I went to see *The Forty Thieves*. That was my first pantomime, and my first visit to Drury Lane, a few days before my fourth birthday. I remember well that long journey by District Railway from West Kensington to the Temple, the fresh air of the Embankment when we emerged from the choking fumes of the underground, the adventurous crossing of the Strand, the rather frightening walk through narrow thronged streets round Drury Lane, long since cleared away. Nanny must have been carrying Frank, who was now four months away from two. No doubt she was determined that he should go to this matinée. regardless of any fatigue to herself. I remember too the orange-girls with big baskets of oranges standing outside in the colonnade and crying their wares as they had been crying them since the days of Nell Gwynn. I wonder if there are any orange-girls round Drury Lane today? Then came the sight of that crowded auditorium from a box in the dress-circle tier on the O.P. side—that is on the left as you look at the stage— the unforgettable pantomime smell of the past, a mixture of gas, oranges, human beings and dust, the noise of excited children and grown-ups in the gallery and upper boxes (as the upper circle was called then), in pit and stalls and dress-circle, and in private boxes too.

Of the pantomime itself I can remember nothing except one incident so vivid that probably it took possession of my memory at the expense of Ali Baba, Morgiana, and the Harlequinade.

That incident was when Charles Lauri, as a donkey, and Paul Martinetti, as a monkey, climbed up from the stage to the boxes on the prompt side and ran all the way round the plush-covered parapet of the dress circle, raising shrieks from all the children in the first rows. When the two animals reached our box Frank let out a yell so loud, and continued to yell so loudly, that Nanny had to take him out of the box; I was left alone, a rather apprehensive child, for the rest of the scene.

On my fourth birthday I was given a Lancer's uniform with breastplate, helmet, sabretache and sword, and I recall the excitement with which I was allowed to cut them free from the shiny sheet of cardboard to which they were attached. Nanny, of course, had to deprive me of the sword almost at once, because she was sure I might endanger with it if not the life at least the skin of my brother Frank. I still have a photograph of myself in this uniform in which the sword is buckled on. My mournful expression may be due less to the trial of being photographed than to the thought that this photograph was being taken for my mother to have when she was away. The Strand season was coming to an end. The Compton Comedy Company was soon going on tour again and I should be left at Avonmore Road with Nanny, the ordeal of life with whom for four years was about to begin. I can still recall the misery with which the thought of being separated from Pappa and Mumma oppressed me.

The Company was playing *She Stoops to Conquer* that January. My mother was acting again, playing Kate Hardcastle; my father was playing Young Marlowe. A young actor called Sydney Valentine was playing Tony Lumpkin. Then Valentine fell ill, and my father finding it easier to get a good Young Marlowe than a good Tony Lumpkin played Tony himself, after which he went on to play it always with the C.C.C.

I remember my father's taking me with him when he went to visit Valentine on his sick-bed. I can see now the bunch of grapes my father put beside his bed, and as my father sits talking to the invalid I am looking out of the window at the barges going up and down the Thames. I think Valentine had rooms at Greenwich, but it may have been Woolwich. No matter. What remains of that visit is the sight of the river under a grey January sky.

The parting with my mother was faintly but only faintly alleviated by Grandmama's arrival to stay at 54. I recall her bringing with her three large volumes of Shakespeare (which I still have) illustrated by engravings of various actors in their famous parts. There was one of my grandfather as Launcelot Gobbo in *The Two Gentlemen of Verona* with his dog, and this led her into telling stories about her late husband. He seemed so marvellous in them that for a time I took it into my head that he was my guardian angel. That my guardian angel should be dressed like Touchstone or Dogberry did not strike me as at all out of keeping with the usual representation of guardian angels.

IN looking through the *Annual Register* to check if possible incidents I remember it occurred to me that some extracts from the *Chronicle of Events in 1887* might entertain and instruct the reader of seventy-five years on. Alas, the *Annual Register* of today will be useless to the social historian of the future and I commend to the present editors that chronicle of events which makes the *Annual Register* of once upon a time invaluable. I continue to buy it every year but the editors seem preoccupied with dreary statistics about new born States, and for me the *Annual Register* in spite of its bright red binding is a white elephant.

January

3. At the Jardin des Plantes, Paris, a hippopotamus suddenly went mad and attacked its keeper as he was in the act of cleaning the cage. The keeper shouted for help, but was dead before he could be rescued.

10. An Austrian named Winkelmeier, 21 years of age, and measuring 8 ft. 9 ins. in height, appeared in London. He showed no extraordinary development until the age of fourteen, when he began to grow rapidly. In the opinion of Dr Virchow, he would not attain his full growth until he had completed his twenty-fifth year. He died in the course of the summer.

11. At Rossmanagher, Limerick, where the police had been sent to support the eviction of a tenant who owed four years' rent, amounting to 700 L, they found the house barricaded and the parish-priest bound with a chain to the doorpost, daring the police to enter. A scuffle ensued, but eventually the tenant agreed to purchase the holding at 45s. per acre and at eighteen years' purchase.

15. Father McGlynn inhibited and deprived by his diocesan, Archibshop Corrigan of New York, for having taken part in Mr Henry George's labour movement. Father McGlynn was subsequently summoned to Rome to defend before the Propaganda his Socialistic views, but took no notice of the invitation.

20. 'Old London', a reproduction of a street in the fifteenth century, which had formed one of the principal attractions of the annual exhibition of South Kensington since 1883, and cost 15,000 L to erect, sold by auction for 160 L. [This was always called the Earl's Court Exhibition by the following year.]

27. A young woman of good family at Chicago had declared her intention of marrying Spiess, the Anarchist lying under sentence of death in the city gaol. As the authorities would not permit the ceremony to take place in prison, Spiess prepared a written document, in virtue of which his brother acted as his proxy, and the marriage was celebrated.

February

1. Mr Justice Kekewich gave judgment for the defendant in the case of Allcard *v.* Skinner. The former, during her membership of a Church of England sisterhood had given 6000 L to promote its work, but on joining the Church of Rome she desired to be reimbursed the amount.

The King of the Belgians, from his palace at Brussels, carried on a long conversation by telephone with M. Grévy at the Elysée in Paris, and in the course of the evening the Queen of the Belgians 'assisted' by telephone at the performance of an entire act of Gounod's 'Faust' performed at the Paris Opéra.

7. The subscription to Allsopp's Brewery Company, amounted to over 100,000,000 L—or about forty times the capital required by the new Company.

10. According to a Parliamentary return, the proportion of illiterates to the total number of voters at the general election of 1886 was:

England Wales 2,416,272 voters of whom 38,587 were illiterate

Scotland	358,155	,,	,,	,,	4,830	,,	,,
Ireland	194,934	,,	,,	,,	36,722	,,	,,

14. A fire, which lasted upwards of eight-and-forty hours, broke out on the premises of Messrs Draper, firewood merchants at Battersea. The adjoining premises, occupied by the Earl of Shrewsbury's cab-horses, being in danger, the horses were cast

I

loose, and over 300 galloped about the neighbouring streets throughout the night.

March

15. For some hours of the morning London was covered, high up above the houses, with a black fog which rendered the streets perfectly dark. A snowstorm, which was general over the United Kingdom, began during the night, and lasted the greater part of the day. The snow round London averaged six inches in depth.

21. At Melbourne, in a cricket-match between the Smokers and Non-Smokers, chosen from the English and Australian teams, the latter (ten strong) scored 803 runs in their first innings, against 350 made by the former, who in their second innings had scored 135 for five wickets when time was called.

[And this was in the days when the pipe and the cigar were the mainstays of smoking. I was tempted to omit this excerpt, but honesty prevailed.]

April

8. The Metropolitan volunteers commenced a series of operations in the field. One section was marched against Dover by way of Canterbury . . . the scouting was done in great measure by 'cyclists' of whom a company, consisting of about 100 men, were found able to traverse ground unfit for cavalry.

15. In the House of Commons . . . Colonel Saunderson's assertion that certain members of the Home Rule party had associated themselves knowingly with murderers produced a 'scene', in the course of which Mr Healy was suspended from the service of the House, by 118 to 52, for refusing to withdraw the expression that Colonel Saunderson was a liar.

19. An outbreak of rabies among the deer in Richmond Park led to a large number of the animals being slaughtered.

20. Two officials—one a quartermaster-sergeant, and the other a civilian—dismissed from the Royal Arsenal, Woolwich, for giving information to a foreign Government concerning the secrets of the Ordnance Department.

23. The Queen, accompanied by the Prince and Princess Henry of Battenberg, visited the monastery of the Grande Chartreuse; the rule forbidding the entry of women, except

reigning sovereigns, to the precincts being relaxed by the Pope.

27. Maharajah Dhuleep Singh and Mrs Patrick Carey, travelling together in Russia, bitterly denouncing the British Government, made the object of many attentions on the part of the Panslavist party at Moscow.

May

5. Rev. J. Bell Cox, of St Margaret's, Liverpool, arrested under a warrant of Lord Penzance, for contumacy in the matter of conducting Divine Service, and removed to Walton Gaol.

12. In the House of Commons, the motion to reduce the cost of preparing Westminster Abbey for the Jubilee Service, viz, 17,000 L to 2000 L, negatived by 208 to 84.

13. Three per cent consols were sold at $103\frac{1}{4}$ the highest price recorded since their creation in 1751.

The Regency of Gwalior having decided to place its savings in the hands of the Indian Government, an agent of the financial department was sent to receive the treasure, which was found to be buried in large pits, covered with earth and pavement. Pit after pit was opened, and rupees to the value of five millions sterling were disinterred and shovelled into bags for conveyance to Calcutta.

18. The *London Gazette* announced the issue of the 'Jubilee Coinage' to be marked by a modification of the Queen's profile, and by the introduction of a new coin—the double florin.

31. The Sikh priests of the golden temple at Umritshur, having learned that the Maharajah Dhuleep Singh had openly lent himself to Russian intrigues, discontinued to offer the customary prayers for his welfare.

June

13. A large body of the Kentish Constabulary suddenly called upon to preserve order at Chatham, where riotous demonstrations had broken out against the Jezreelites, a religious sect founded about two years previously by James White, a private soldier. Before his death the control of the body had been assumed by his widow, who styled herself Queen Esther. Dissension had, however, occurred among the

body, and vague charges of fraud were made by those dis-
affected to the governing body. The populace of Chatham,
siding with the seceders, attacked a Jezreelite procession, broke
its instruments of music, and sacked a building in construction
which was destined to contain 14,000 persons.

14. The temperature rose somewhat suddenly to a remarkable height, attaining 79° in the shade and 139° in the sunshine
at Greenwich Observatory.

21. The Queen, accompanied by her children and grand
children, and attended by a number of foreign sovereigns or
their representatives, went in state from Buckingham Palace
to Westminster Abbey, where a special Jubilee Service was
held.

July

1. Cambridge won all eight events at the Henley Regatta
of which Trinity Hall won five.

10. Archibishop Corrigan of New York pronounced sentence
of major excommunication against Father M'Glynn for
refusing to submit himself to the summons of the Pope.

August

13. Mdlle Drouin, a French lady, attended by her maid,
arrived at the Marine Hotel, Cowes, where she had engaged
rooms in advance. Shortly after her arrival the police paid
her a visit and took her into custody on discovering, in her
luggage, three small cakes of supposed dynamite. After a few
days she was released with many expressions of apology, and
50 L was offered to her as compensation for the annoyance
to which she had been subjected.

September

28. The 'Hoang Ho, or Yellow River, which, according to
Chinese records, had already changed its course nine times
in 2,500 years, burst its artificial embankments. . . . The loss
of life was estimated at from one to two millions.

30. By the decision of the Jockey Club, the Marquess of
Ailesbury, the owner of the horse Everitt, and Taylor, the
trainer, warned off Newmarket Heath and all race-courses
for life, in consequence of orders given to Martin, the jockey,

not to win the race for the Harewood Plate at the York August Meeting.

October

2. Shortly after midnight, the Rev. W. M. Farley, vicar of Cretingham, Suffolk, was murdered by his curate, the Rev. A. Gilbert Cooper, an inmate of the house. He forced his way into the vicar's bedroom, and whilst talking to him in the presence of Mrs Farley, he suddenly stooped down and cut the vicar's throat from ear to ear.

17. The 'unemployed' who throughout the previous week had assembled in Trafalgar Square, met in somewhat larger numbers, and a deputation marched to the Mansion House to see the Lord Mayor. The members returning to the mass of demonstrators in Trafalgar Square with no satisfactory assurance, a serious disturbance took place, which the police had great difficulty in repressing. On the next day the 'unemployed' . . . met in Hyde Park, where they did much damage.

19. The 'unemployed' after holding a meeting in Hyde Park, suddenly turned into May Fair through Grosvenor Street and Smith Street. . . . In Dover Street, Piccadilly, a collision between the mob and police took place, where after a few casualties on either side the former were thoroughly dispersed.

23. Having met in large numbers at Clerkenwell Green, a number of Socialists and others marched in procession to Westminster Abbey, where they behaved in a disgraceful manner, talking and smoking in the building during the service.

November

12. The horse and bicycle contest at the Agricultural Hall, to test their relative value for postal purposes, terminated in favour of the horsemen, Broncho Charley and Beadsley (cowboys of the Wild West Show) covering in the 48 hours (eight hours a day) 814 miles 4 laps, while the champion cyclists were about two miles behind. The horsemen employed thirty horses, and gained much by the agility with which they changed horses.

13. The Metropolitan Radical Association having called a meeting in Trafalgar Square to demand the release of Mr

William O'Brien, M.P., Sir Charles Warren issued a notice prohibiting the meeting as well as the approach of any organised procession. The square was occupied by the police from an early hour and in the afternoon organised processions approached from every quarter. A series of struggles ensued with the police in various places on the way, in Shaftesbury Avenue, Parliament Street, Pall Mall, and the Strand, and serious conflicts took place. A little before 5 p.m. the Foot Guards were brought up to relieve the police, and a little later the Life Guards arrived, and in both cases the troops were accompanied by magistrates. A large number of arrests were made, chiefly for assaulting the police, including Mr Cunninghame Graham, M.P., and Mr Burns, and upwards of 100 persons, and constables were more or less hurt, two of the police being stabbed.

15. The Election for the Lord Rectorship of the Glasgow University resulted in each candidate having a majority in two of the four 'nations', thus giving the casting vote to the Chancellor (Earl of Stair); but the votes recorded were—Lord Rosebery 867, Lord Lytton 845. After some days' delay the Chancellor gave his vote in favour of Lord Lytton.

26. *The Times* announced that Mr C. S. Parnell, M.P., whose whereabouts had so long been a mystery, had for a long time been residing in one of the London suburbs under the assumed name of Preston.

December

15. The Home Secretary and President of the Local Government board received a deputation of East London work people who desired to prevent the unrestricted immigration of pauper aliens. It was stated that since 1880 there had been a reduction of 50 per cent in the tailoring wages on account of the influx of Polish Jews induced to come over by the 'sweaters' who had command of the labour market.

18. The Pope received at the Vatican with great ceremonial the Duke of Norfolk, accredited as special envoy from the Queen to congratulate his Holiness on his jubilee. The last occasion on which an accredited envoy had been sent from England to the Papal See was in 1687, when Lord Castlemaine represented James II.

William Linnell, who had died in Charing Cross Hospital in consequence of injuries received during the disturbances in Trafalgar Square, conveyed from Trafalgar Square to Bow Common Cemetery, followed by a large procession. Throughout the long line of march order was preserved but in the darkness which had set in before the grave was reached the cemetery became the scene of confusion and uproar.

19. A prize fight for the Champion's belt and 1,000 L between Jem Smith, an Englishman, and Jake Kilrain, an American, took place on a small island in the Seine, near Rouen. The men fought 106 rounds, lasting 2½ hours, when an adjournment, on account of the increasing darkness, and on the journey home 'a draw' was agreed to with the approval of all concerned. About 100 people, chiefly English and American, witnessed the fight.

26. The first display of wintry weather throughout Great Britain marked by several ice and snow incidents, including thirteen deaths.

Those excerpts from the year of Queen Victoria's Golden Jubilee help me to realise what a long time I have been allowed to live. The telephone is still such a novelty that a conversation between Belgium and France is considered worth chronicling as an event, and when the Queen of the Belgians listens in over the telephone to an operatic performance in Paris I recall that one of the attractions of the Earl's Court Exhibition (the hope of calling it the South Kensington Exhibition was destroyed by the common sense of the public) was paying sixpence to listen by means of this marvellous invention to five crackling minutes of some play. The exploit of those two cowboys in holding the horse's own against the new safety bicycle was some compensation for that company of 'cyclists' (note the significance of the inverted commas for this new word) which during the military operations of the volunteers against Dover was able to 'traverse ground unfit for cavalry'. That could not have been said of the old penny-farthing bicycle. Yet the velocipede was not extinct, and in this year or more probably in the following year I recall the thrill of being given a lift on a penny-farthing. One stood on the mounting-step and clung to the rider. No doubt this was forbidden by prudent nurses or governesses for the very young. The safety cycle with solid tyres would be displaced by the bicycle with cushion tyres, and cushion tyres in another year or two by pneumatic tyres. The solid-tyred safety bicycle which was so much admired in 1887 as a notable advance in human transport would be called a 'boneshaker' by the time I went to school in 1891.

I may have been presented to Broncho Bill and Beadsley, those two cowboys who defeated the bicycle at the Agricultural Hall in Islington. At any rate, I was presented to Buffalo Bill himself and can look back at him with all the awe I must have felt when this tremendous figure of boyhood's fancy bent down to pat me on the shoulder. I expect he shook hands with young Winston Churchill who also visited him that summer. After all, Sir Winston Churchill had by then reached the mature age of thirteen.

Those of us like myself who enjoy on television the attack on a coach by Indians in the Wild West of once upon a time cannot get the thrill out of it that we who saw an attack in the arena at Earl's Court got. For one thing the cowboys galloping to the rescue are in black and white. At Earl's Court their romantic appearance was much enhanced by the colours of their shirts. That gave me a chance for a favourite colour and when, as many of us were, we were given it that Christmas of 1887 a box of lead cowboys and Indians, instead of the usual toy soldiers, every one of us was the cowboy whose shirt he most admired. Yes, much as I enjoy television Westerns I must assure my co-fans that they are far from being able to provide the excitement of the coach galloping round the arena at Earl's Court with whooping Indians in pursuit and those multi-coloured cowboys charging in to the rescue after the coach had made two breath-takings rounds of the arena.

And I can still see—was it Annie Get Your Gun?—a young woman tossing glass balls into the air and shattering every one of them with that unerring weapon of hers, being mounted on a horse for the feat.

Probably my eldest Bateman aunt knew Colonel Cody and commended me to him. Otherwise I cannot guess why Buffalo Bill should have gone out of his way to be so kind to a four-year-old boy. And 'Annie Get Your Gun' was just as kind,

taking me into various wigwams and presenting me to whatever Red Indian chief it was sitting outside his wigwam and
smoking a long pipe. It was a pang to be dragged away from
that enchanting Wild West world by my old nurse sniffing and
muttering 'Time to go home, time to go home.' However, on
this occasion I did not burst into tears; I hope I kept them back
in an effort to emulate the stoicism of the dignified Red Indians
by whom I was surrounded.

It is noteworthy that the Chronicle of 1887 refers to the
Socialists as the contemporary *Annual Register* might refer to
the Communists. Labour as a political party had not yet
appeared. The abundance of capital illustrated by a bank-rate
of 2 per cent and an over-subscription to the Allsopp's issue
of well over ninety million pounds is a shocking contrast to
the treatment of the 'unemployed', whose grievances are
suggested to be imaginary by the use of inverted commas.
And treatment of Ireland by Lord Salisbury's Conservative
government is bewildering in its revelation of the depths of
stupidity into which human beings are capable of diving. It
is sad, too, to find the Vatican still obstinately obscurantist in
its approach to social reform.

It is refreshing, however, to find the military authorities
possessing enough common sense to be content with sacking
a couple of officials at Woolwich Arsenal for giving information
to a foreign government about the Ordnance Department.
Today such offenders would probably receive sentences of
fantastic severity.

It is time that I came back to my own life in 1887.

When my parents went off on tour in February my sister
Viola was hardly three months old and she must already have
been weaned. Certainly there was no wet nurse. My grandmother staying at 54 that spring slept in my parents' room and
I was moved from the railed-in bed in the night-nursery to
the big bed in the spare room. I do not recall any night terrors
yet; they were a torment to come. Before my parents came
back for Holy Week my grandmother went to live in St
Leonard's, where she had rooms in Warrior Square.

Easter was fairly early this year. I recall sitting in the bay
window of the dining-room watching for the four-wheel cab
to turn the corner and bring back my much-missed father and

mother. That four-wheeler coming round the corner on Palm
Sunday would be for me an annual moment of ecstasy for the
next four long years. The luggage on top consisted of a theatrical
hamper, a large leather portmanteau, a large luncheon-basket,
and a travelling bath into which a lot was packed. Inside the
cab was a large leather dressing-bag, my father's hat-case, and
his two desks in leather cases; one of these in which he kept
his personal correspondence, writing paper and equipment
was older than the other in which were kept the business papers
connected with his Company. When the desks were opened
they provided a slanting blotter on which to write. The two
always stood side by side on a table in the window of the
sitting-room in whatever theatrical lodgings my father was
staying. He had a horror of hotels and if he was compelled to
stay in an hotel because there were no suitable lodgings available, that place and its theatre with two exceptions were never
revisited; the exceptions were Douglas and Llandudno. To
many of his theatrical rooms my father returned every year for
over twenty years, and I can still feel the warmth of welcome
he received from so many landladies all over Great Britain
and Ireland.

These Holy Weeks so precious to me were not kept as
religiously as my mother would have liked. For my father
they were a holiday and he was disinclined to spend any time
in church. He went every night to the theatre except on Good
Friday, and my mother always went with him because she
was sensible enough to realise that any insistence by her on
religious observation would prejudice him against religion.
My father always thoroughly enjoyed seeing the plays running
in London, and for an actor he was extraordinarily enthusiastic
about the merits of other actors' performances. He was completely without jealousy. My mother was a great deal more critical of the plays themselves, and her taste was much more reliable
than my father's; he thought it was a good play if it gave the
performers an opportunity to shine, regardless of what my
mother thought was the nonsense in which they were shining.

I think it must have been in that spring of 1887 that I was
taken to see *Dorothy* at the Lyric Theatre. Lurcher, the leading
comic part, was played by Percy Compton, a younger brother
of my father's. Soon after this he married a ward in Chancery

and was sentenced to six weeks for contempt of court. Aunt Constance was a beautiful heiress, and was certainly worth six weeks' imprisonment.

Naturally what I remember best of *Dorothy* is the pack of hounds. The operetta ran for nearly three years and Dorothy became an immensely popular name for girls.

On May Day I saw what may have been the last Jack-in-the-green celebrating an occasion as old as the Maypole. Why the London chimney sweeps should have preserved this ancient rite so long is a mystery. There was a procession of sweeps with whistles and drum led by a woman, or a man dressed as a woman, in a motley dress covered with spangles and behind her was a chimney sweep in a wicker cage covered with greenery. I regret to say that I was extremely frightened by these revels because I thought I was going to be stolen and made to climb up chimneys. I had read a good deal about the adventures and misadventures of boys in the power of chimney sweeps. I was equally frightened when a caravan of chair-mending gypsies used to solicit custom, having a vision of being stolen, stripped of my clothes, stained with walnut juice, and then sent out to beg in rags for my kidnappers. I remember telling this once to the late J. M. N. Jeffries, that most admirable of war correspondents, and he told me that his sister really had been stolen by gypsies. So my childish apprehension was not so silly as it sounds.

I was for a long time under the impression that I had seen the Prince of Wales open the new Hammersmith Suspension Bridge this June, but I discovered that this ceremony was performed by Prince Albert Victor of Wales who a year or two later would be created Duke of Clarence and Avondale. At this date he was twenty-three years old and a captain in the 10th Hussars. I remember very clearly arriving with my old nurse at the end of the road that leads from Hammersmith Broadway to the Thames. She was wheeling the perambulator with my young brother and baby sister in it and in the crowd of people gathered round the entrance of the bridge to watch the ceremony I did not stand a chance of seeing anything of it. Then a policeman picked me up and seated me on—what is the beginning of a suspension bridge called? Buttress? Anyway, it was on the left-hand side looking towards Barnes. There I had a splendid view of the proceedings. I used to think I could recall somebody in a red coat and a cocked hat walking his horse up to the ribbon tied across the entrance to the bridge, but if it was Prince Albert Victor he must have been in the uniform of a Hussar. I am sure, however, that there was somebody about in a general's uniform. The Prince's horse that was taking him to lean over and cut the ribbon turned round as soon as he brought his royal rider up to it, and this he did some half dozen times before the Prince could manage to cut the ribbon and declare Hammersmith Suspension Bridge open.

A week or two later in that June I had an adventure. Nanny had brought us to Kensington Gardens, and I was looking at the flower-beds in front of Kensington Palace with the absorption I always gave to flowers, when on turning round I saw to my alarm that Nanny and the perambulator had vanished. I can feel now the beating of my heart when I found myself alone. I ran to the Broad Walk. There was no sign of the perambulator. I ran back to the front of the Palace. I was still alone. There was only one thing to be done; I must appeal to the police. With thudding heart I ran as fast as I could go to the gate leading out of the Gardens into High Street and then I ran along the narrow pavement, still narrow today, toward Church Street. As I look at myself running I do not see complete people in my mind's eye but only many pairs of legs round which I hurry, panting. At last I reach the dangerous crossing of Church Street and see the blue lamp over the door of the police station on the opposite side. A blue omnibus coming from Earl's Court Road stops to take on a third horse so that the omnibus will not have to be walked up Campden Hill, at the top of which the extra horse will be released to walk back to St Mary Abbot's. That third horse, called the cock-horse, was always ridden by a boy, and how one envied him! On this morning, however, I was too much overwhelmed by the problem of being lost to think about that lucky boy. As I stood there waiting for the traffic to be clear of the crossing I considered what I should say when I entered the police-station. Then I crossed, went into it and announced:

"My name is Edward Montague Compton Mackenzie. I live at 54 Avonmore Road, and I'm lost. Will you take me home, please."

One of the policemen picked me up and seated me on the charge counter, and as I looked round I saw to my surprise that the policemen were all without their tunics; it had not occurred to me before that policemen ever undressed. It may have been that fourteenth of June when the temperature suddenly shot up to 79° in the shade. At that date we were not using the 'Mackenzie' in our name. Indeed, I did not become 'Mackenzie' till 1894 when I went to St Paul's. Nevertheless, whenever I was asked my name I always gave it with the strictest accuracy. That previous autumn when my father had sometimes taken me into Barker's I was often put up on the counter and asked my name, presumably for the fun of hearing me rattle it off. The late Sir John Barker had known my father in his boyhood and he used to advise him about his cigars.

Those Kensington policemen, the youngest of whom if he be still alive would be ninety-six today, were most kind and friendly, and finally that youngest policeman was told to take me back to Avonmore Road. He was tall with fair, curly hair, and riding on his shoulder down the shopping side of High Street, Kensington, I felt pleased that I had been lost. As we went along he kept pointing out the Jubilee decorations in the houses of those dignified terraces in Upper Phillimore Gardens, Lower Phillimore Gardens and the rest which today have vanished under the megahyaline concrete ant-hills and bee-hives of the swarming present. I see the V.R.'s and profiles of the Queen in multitudinous gas-jets which would be lighted after dusk to celebrate her Golden Jubilee.

The main thought that preoccupied me, however, was the importance of giving the policeman who had brought me home half a crown. This coin represented for me the zenith of human wealth as the tip one was given by old friends of the family and uncles. I am glad to remember that half a crown was produced by Nanny and accepted with a grin. I recall how flustered she was, but I did not realise the reason then. Gin was her secret joy, and she must have gone off with the peram-bulator to have one at a public-house which used to stand close by Palace Gardens gate and was frequented by various members of the domestic staffs of Millionaires' Row. She did not scold me; she did not even reproach me. The incident was dismissed. No doubt she wanted to make it seem of such little importance that I would not mention it when my parents came back from tour a few days later. But I think the most important result of that declaration of my name and address and predicament in Kensington Police Station was that thence onwards I ceased to speak of myself in the third person and the weight of self-consciousness that oppresses the child and even more heavily the youth as he wrestles with adolescence first made itself felt.

From that week or two of that sunny June before we went to Cromer for my parents' summer holiday a picture stays in my mind of a clean-shaven man with reddish hair sitting in the bay window of the dining-room and busily writing. This was Charles Terry, a brother of Ellen, who was at this date my father's business manager. Earlier in the year he had parted with J. H. Savile from the Compton Comedy Company in order that the latter might act as business manager to the Company my father had started for Isabel Bateman to play on tour dramas like *Jane Shore*, *Green Bushes* and *East Lynne*.

Charles Terry was the father of Minnie Terry, who had a great success as a child actress. She was about two years older than I was, and my first love, but I did not meet her till some time in the following year.

The first memory I have of that summer in Cromer is of the difficulty my mother had in persuading me to paddle. I do not know why I should have been so frightened of the sea, but frightened of it I was. However, as my chief object in life then was to please my mother I at last summoned up courage to paddle, and having once felt the water round my ankles loved it, after which existence seemed to have been created for human beings to paddle, and at Cromer there was no hostile shingle. We stayed in a small detached redbrick house called Prospect Villa which looked out over a large field; it has probably long been built on. In a corner of this field was a notice board inscribed:

Trespassers will be Prosecuted. (By Order)
Benjamin B. Bond Cabell.

Squire Cabell's minatory notice boards were all over the place in the Cromer of seventy-five years ago, and along every field path in which I was walking I would welcome the road again and so escape from being suddenly attacked by Mr Benjamin Bond Cabell. 'Prosecuted' suggested 'executed'; and having been recently reading about the execution of Mary Queen of Scots I was anxious.

Benjamin Bond Cabell sounded as sinister a figure as tall Agrippa in *Shock-headed Peter*. When I asked my father about the meaning of 'prosecute' he told me it meant being taken before the magistrate. I thought he said 'magistree'. I was probably confusing 'magistrate' with 'majesty'. Of course my father ever afterwards spoke of the magistree, and used to tease me by getting over the fence into the field in front of Prospect Villa. "Come out, come out," I used to cry in despair. "Come out before the magistree catches you."

Perhaps on account of the self-consciousness that developed after I gave up the third person I was more sensitive to my father's teasing now. He used to embarrass me greatly by singing with exaggerated passion a song from which I recall the last four lines:

> Will you be my hollyhock?
> Will you be my rose?
> Will you let me kiss the two lips
> Just underneath your nose?

"No, no, no," I would cry and struggle to avoid the embarrassment of being kissed with a smack of my father's lips.

My Aunt Ellen Greppo, whom I met for the first time, came with her younger daughter Ellen, who was now a very beautiful girl of about eighteen, and took another house in Cromer. My Aunt Isabel stayed with her, and her youngest son Bob, who had just gone on the stage, calling himself Robert Greville, came to Cromer for a while. Mr Greppo was in France.

We stayed at Prospect Villa in June and July 1887 and again in 1891 and for a third time we were in Cromer for our school holidays in 1895 in a jolly house called Holly Lodge. Yet I remember the third time less vividly than the first two. I shall be telling about the second visit in the last chapter of this First Octave, but a confusion in my mind about those first two visits must be corrected now because I have told the following story in a broadcast and in a book of mine *Sublime Tobacco* inaccurately. Here is the authentic narrative:

One morning I found myself sitting on the beach near a beautiful lady dressed in a beige-coloured dress of some light silky looking material. I am hopeless about getting the material of women's dresses correct and have been much chaffed by some of my women friends about my attempts to describe their clothes in various books of mine. I recall too what I think I am right in calling the leg o' mutton sleeves of that beige dress.

This tall and beautiful lady had heavily plaited dark hair and was not wearing a hat; she had a notebook on her knee in which after looking out to sea for several moments she would write a few words and then gaze out to sea again before writing any more. Presently she said something to me, but what it was I cannot remember. Then suddenly the clock in the tower of St Peter and St Paul's Church struck one, and she said something about being late for lunch as she rose and walked toward the ramp up from the beach. As she reached it everybody on the beach turned round to stare at her; she opened a small parasol of café-au-lait lace and held it up on the right side of her face to hide it as she walked up the ramp. Then somebody asked me, "What did the Empress of Austria say to you?" I remember feeling astonished and disappointed that she was not wearing a crown. Then somebody said "And she smokes". This impressed me because I had just smoked my first cigarette, of which more anon.

Now, when I told this story in a broadcast and in an article or two I decided that this incident must have taken place in 1891 and that my being disappointed by her not wearing a crown was imagination since by the time I was eight I should not have expected an empress to be wearing her crown on a beach. I could not believe that a picture so clear in detail could have been retained by a child of four. In 1891 I had my arm in a sling after a bad accident to my hand and I began to fancy that the Empress must have asked why my arm was in a sling and given the reminiscence accordingly.

Some months ago I was telling Edward Crankshaw this story and he, who was writing a book about that period in Austria, said he would check up on the dates. He wrote to tell me that the Empress was not in Cromer in 1891; she was

12. Brother Frank

12. Sister Viola

13. Isabel as Ophelia

13. Aunt Isabel

there in 1887. So I realised that my emotion of disappointment over the crown was an accurate memory because a four-year-old might easily have supposed that empresses and queens walked about in crowns as they did in fairy-tale illustrations.

Now for that cigarette. Bob Greppo, my tall fair-haired American cousin, used to come and sit on the lawn of Prospect Villa in order to avoid going for walks with his sister and extremely energetic mother. In the middle of the lawn was a circular flower-bed round which I used to stalk the sparrows with a funnel-shaped packet of salt in the hope of catching one of them by putting some of that salt on its tail. My old nurse had told me that one could always catch birds by putting salt on their tails. At last, tired and discouraged by my lack of success under the hot sun of that Golden Jubilee summer, I sat down on the grass beside my cousin, who was lolling in a deck-chair and as usual rolling a cigarette with an air of what seemed almost magical insouciance.

"Would you like to try one?" he drawled.

I accepted his offer with alacrity, and put the cigarette between my lips as I had put many a chocolate cigarette. Do children still smoke chocolate cigarettes, and chocolate cigars with tips of fondant to represent ash and stained with cochineal at the very end to stimulate the glow of a lighted cigar?

There was to be no simulation now. Bob struck a wax vesta which, as he applied the flame to the end of the cigarette, seemed in its majesty to dim the very sun.

"Suck it in slowly and puff it out again."

The first attempt was not slow enough, and the smoke made me splutter.

"Not so fast. Gently. Watch me."

I watched him; after a couple more attempts I was able to smoke like this much-admired American cousin.

It was meet that I, with a long American ancestry back to the time of the first colonisation of Maryland, should be granted by an American cousin my first experience of the most precious gift that the New World gave to the Old. I like to imagine that my immunity from any of the ill-effects which in moral tales always accompany childhood's first experiments with tobacco may have been an inheritance from some Red

K

Indian ancestress of three centuries ago. Anyway, I smoked that first cigarette with enjoyment and without a qualm.

"Now, don't go bragging about being able to smoke," Bob warned me. "Your mother might be angry. I hear them coming back from their walk, though why people want to walk about in this heat I can't understand."

Poor Bob Greppo, or Greville as he called himself when without much justification he went on the stage. He was in my father's Company for two or three years but never rose above 'seond walking gentleman', that is to say Careless in *The School for Scandal*, Fag in *The Rivals* and the rest. Then he became too fond of brandy and with its help died in his early forties.

I owe him a tribute he paid me when I was about seven. "Monty is very much improved. You wouldn't think now that he knew anything."

He must have suffered probably from my asking him whether he had read this book or that, not, let me add in self-defence, out of any desire to show off but because I was genuinely anxious to know what other people thought about the books I had read. And Bob was not a reader.

One memory that comes back to me from that Cromer summer of seventy-five years ago is my first encounter with ox-eyed daises in a mass; in Malvern I had never seen more than two or three at a time. They seem as big as chrysanthemums when I look back at my first sight of those myriads in the field beyond the dividing hedge. I longed to wander among them, but there was the notice:

Trespassers will be prosecuted. (By Order)
Benjamin B. Bond Cabell

That field was as unattainable as a field of asphodels in Elysium.

The greatest delight of all was my mother's company, which Nanny's pre-occupation with Frank, just two, and Viola, only eight months old, allowed me to enjoy. I can see her now working away at embroidering with silk flowers a coat my father would wear for many years as Charles Surface, and which indeed I myself would wear on a March night twenty years on when he lost his voice, and I having learnt the part on a Sunday night played it with one rehearsal on Monday at the Lyceum Theatre, Edinburgh, where my first play was to be produced three nights later.

While my mother was occupied with her embroidery I used to play Punch and Judy by arranging a towel-horse as the show box and turn knitted handkerchiefs into the puppets. My early frights by Punch and Judy had long been forgotten, and that Christmas I would be given a miniature Punch and Judy show with Punch, Judy, the dog Toby, the Clown and the Hangman, with a squeaker for Punch's voice.

The only shadow upon that golden summer long ago was the shadow of bed. In the matter of bed Nanny was inexorable. Six o'clock and not a moment's grace. I had a device for retaining my mother's presence as long as possible after she had kissed me good-night by asking for one more kiss but much much the longest kiss in all the world. Nanny had a maddening way of turning the simplest request into a treat, and so when I asked my mother if I might do this or that or have this or that I used to ask for it as much the greatest treat in all the world, to which if it happened to be on a Sunday I would add "and because it's Sunday".

When I was left to sleep I used to lie awake for a long time in the summer gloaming, and lying there I would hear the voices of the grown-ups returning from their walk before supper and think how fortunate they were still to be up and not intolerably cribbed, cabined and confined by bed. Oh, to be grown-up and free from this endless purgatory of childhood, which, brightened though many moments were by beloved figures like my mother, above all my mother, presented the perpetual threat of being left with my old nurse to spend with her an endless time of unreasonableness ahead and winter on the way.

Probably I was so much distressed at the prospect of being parted from my mother that in spite of being accused of spoiling me, as she always was by Nanny, I was taken with them when the summer holiday of my parents was over and the C.C.C. met at Scarborough to rehearse for a week before the new tour began in August. Percy Marshall, the father of Herbert Marshall, with whom I made great friends, was with them, playing Sir Lucius O'Trigger among other parts. Lewis

Ball, who joined my father when he started the Company in 1881, was still with him and would remain with him for almost another twenty years. He was by far the best Sir Anthony Absolute, Sir Peter Teazle and Hardcastle I have ever seen. For the last forty years the actors and actresses of the British stage have grown steadily more remote from any glimmering notion of how Sheridan and Goldsmith ought to be played.

At Scarborough I stayed for the first time in the house of my godfather, John Bolton. He was a portly man with grey mutton-chop whiskers whom I cannot recall seeing dressed in anything but a frock-coat. He was a man of considerable wealth, much of it in Scarborough house property, the rents of which he always collected himself. I seem to remember his house was called Bolton Lodge. It was a spacious house with four large bow-windows standing in about an acre of ground with a drive up to the front door. The only guest allowed to smoke in it was my father, and I can recall the faint smell of one of those heavy Victorian dinners as one entered the big hall from which a very wide staircase went up in a curve to the first landing. Other guests of John Bolton had to retire to smoke in a kind of small temple in the garden, where smoking-jackets and smoking-caps were provided for them, so that when they returned from their much disapproved of after-dinner cigars they would not contaminate the inside of the house with a hint of the hated tobacco.

The wall of the big main staircase was hung with Royal Academy pictures, every picture telling a story, but none of them a pre-Raphaelite story. There was a four-post bed in every bedroom, and toilet sets of the finest china. In every room was a striking clock, and even now the echo of those clocks all striking the hour simultaneously still sounds in my mind's ears. He had never used the big drawing-room on the right of the front hall opposite the dining-room since his wife had died young, many years back. The umbrella-stand in the entrance-lobby still held her umbrellas, parasols, and favourite cane. That favourite cane was a very slim malacca with a silver handle fashioned as a hand with a pistol and loaded with lead. That cane fascinated me even then, and one day nine years later would destroy any hopes my father may have had of my being remembered in my godfather's will when I let it fall down through the grating of a drain in trying to rescue some schoolboy's treasure.

John Bolton's own sitting-room was on the first floor, full of curios and rare china, and for me holding the most admired object in the house, a large musical-box with all sorts of instruments including a set of drums; I have never seen such an elaborate musical-box since. There was one bathroom, the window of which was covered with ferns, pasted on the glass. They must have been artificial ferns because they were always green. It was in my godfather's house that I first became frightened at night, sleeping alone as I did in one of those great four-posters.

John Bolton was looked after by a working housekeeper called, I think, Mary. She had a curiously sallow complexion which to the eyes of childhood appeared yellow, and as her face comes back to me from the past it seems as yellow as a banana. Mary was always kind to me and I was fond of her, but not fond enough to hear with equanimity that my parents proposed to leave me behind with my godfather for a week while the C.C.C. was playing at Whitby. I think it must have been the prospect of sleeping in that big four-poster and waking in the middle of the night to the knowledge that Pappa and Mumma were out of reach that made me so apprehensive of being left behind. Anyway, when the moment came for departure I fell into a paroxysm of despairing tears. My mother, determined not to be accused by John Bolton of spoiling me, drove on to the railway station with the luggage; my father remained behind in an effort to persuade me that no greater treat could be imagined than staying with Godpapa; I continued to sob and cling to him; in the end he weakened and brought me with him to the station. The train was just about to start when we arrived, and I can still hear the coldness in my mother's voice and feel the longing to be kissed and forgiven as I sit beside her in the railway-carriage, while no doubt my father was apologising for his weakness in having surrendered to my clamant sobs. He at any rate should not be able to say that she spoilt me, and I was worried by hearing her reproach him for not having insisted on my remaining in Scarborough instead of coming to Whitby.

I have not been to Whitby since, but I seem to see the Abbey with the sea below it. In writing these recollections of early childhood I am deliberately not looking up places in books because I do not want to give any chance for my present self to embroider the past. I learned my lesson when I imagined what the Empress of Austria might have talked to me about when I thought it was 1891 with my arm in a sling instead of being 1887 as it was in fact. So maybe Whitby Abbey is not visible from the sea-front except in the recess of my memory.

One morning at breakfast that week my father and mother were arguing with each other about something, and I had never heard either speak irritably to the other until my mother had been cross with my father for surrendering to me over being left behind with John Bolton.

I became extremely anxious because my belief about marriage was being disturbed. Marriage as I understood it was the result of two people loving one another, and when one loved somebody else one did not argue with that other person. The development to thinking of myself as 'I' from thinking of myself as 'Monty' demanded that all my beliefs should be supported by the fact of truth. As my parents continued their argument my perplexity grew. Was my belief that marriage was an expression of mutual love a mere fancy of my own? I must be reassured, and putting down the spoon with which I was eating my bread and milk I said:

"I thought people are married because they love each other."

I can see the expression on my mother's face as she turned to my father and said: "You're perfectly right, Edward."

Some years later when I was thirteen something I said to her, which will be told in my Second Octave, made her ask me whether I remembered this question about marriage. She added that she never again argued with my father at breakfast, or even at any time in front of me.

"And now you have given me a second lesson I shall never forget."

I had never forgotten the incident, but thus related it sounds as if my remark was intended as an oblique reproof, and in self-defence I must insist that it was inspired only by my own perplexity and the need for reassurance. I just wanted to know that something I believed was true.

I do not remember how I went back to London toward the end of that August. I suppose I was put in charge of a guard and met by my old nurse.

I recall from that early autumn of 1887 the melancholy that filled me for the summer that was going and the winter that was coming as the lavender-girls in their grey shawls and big hats passed along Avonmore Road crying 'Lavender, sweet lavender! Who will buy my lavender?'

As time crept slowly on toward Christmas the gloom was lightened by my grandmother's coming up from St Leonard's for a few days and taking me back to stay with her in Warrior Square. I do not remember the number, but the house where she had rooms was about a third of the way along on the right-hand side of the Square as it went sloping gently up from the Marina. My grandmother was a great friend of Mrs Clarke Travers, the wife of the vicar of St Mary Magdalen's church near Warrior Square. In the care of Mr and Mrs Travers was the fourth Lord Ellenborough, who at this date was thirty-one years old and had been looked after by them since he was a child and brought up with their only daughter Maud. Maud was very kind but she was also plain and most eccentric, which was not surprising because Lord Ellenborough was a mongol.

My first introduction to him was a little alarming. My grandmother had taken me up to the Vicarage and presently Towry, as he was always called, came in to the drawing-room.

"Now, Towry, be a good boy," said Mrs Travers, "and say how d'ye do nicely to Monty."

Towry's response was to hurry off in the opposite direction and make his way right round the room by touching one piece of furniture after another, and looking behind him all the time as if he was being pursued. At last, having made a circuit of the room like this, he suddenly rushed with hand outthrust and lower jaw shooting backwards and forwards to touch my hand, muttering, "How d'ye do, Master Monty? Thank you very much." After which he rushed back to the protection of the various pieces of furniture as he returned the way he had come, touching one piece after another and after a pause scuttling on to the next. However, after this first slightly alarming meeting Towry and I became good friends.

Mrs Travers and my grandmother much enjoyed playing

whist after tea, and if they failed to obtain a fourth Maud was not allowed to play. Instead Towry and I were two dummies, I seated on a hassock to make me high enough in my chair to lay out the cards face upwards in front of me, and Towry opposite Mrs Travers, laying out his cards face upwards.

I can hear the two old ladies now. At this date ladies over sixty-five seemed very old indeed.

"The Queen of Hearts, Monty. That's right."

"The Ten of Clubs, Towry. No, no, Towry, that's the Ten of Spades. That's right. Good boy."

After church on Sunday we dined in the middle of the day at the Vicarage. I remember well the first occasion. Mr Clarke Travers had a tremendous squint and when he was saying grace I could not feel sure that he was saying grace for our table or for another table. So to put matters right up above I repeated as soon as Mr Travers had finished "May the Lord make us truly thankful." I remember, too, being puzzled whether Mr Travers was inviting me to have a helping of whatever it was or somebody else at the table. It certainly was a tremendous squint.

The butler's name was Snelson. He can hardly have been much over five feet tall because I remember that when he was helping me to some dish his face was on a level with mine.

On fine days we used to drive in the Ellenborough carriage and pair along the Marina, Towry and I sitting opposite Mrs Travers and my grandmother with our backs to Snelson and the coachman.

Some years after this October of 1887 I remember going to see the Travers family when the Compton Comedy Company was playing at Hastings and hearing Snelson say as he came into the room, "His Lordship's been a very naughty boy this morning, madam. He's dressed himself in his tails and thrown his other clothes out of the window."

The explanation of this was that he had been taken to see *She Stoops to Conquer* the previous night and had so much enjoyed Tony Lumpkin's pink hunting-coat that he wanted to see that pink coat again and decided that the surest way of getting to the theatre was to put on his tails again. I never saw Towry after this, but he lived until 1902 when the barony passed to a cousin. He is for me a most affectionate memory.

I remember nothing of Christmas this year except the Punch and Judy Show with which I was presented. We were probably at Southport, where about now my father started to spend at least a fortnight every year, in the course of which he rehearsed the revival of an old comedy and sometimes a new play as well. Unfortunately I have no records to show in which year these revivals happened and mistakes in chronology will be inevitable. I shall not anticipate clearer memories of Southport in other years by trying to recollect them now.

Another handicap for these early years is having used memories of my own childhood for writing *Sinister Street* but applying them to an imaginary story, and therefore, un-hampered by exact chronology or exact details, building on the foundations of a remembered incident a narrative to suit the key of that imaginary story. I have avoided re-reading *Sinister Street* while writing this Octave because there is always the risk of letting fancy become fact. The Empress of Austria story as I had told it before was a warning. So now on to 1888.

FIVE YEARS OLD 1888

THE Drury Lane pantomime in January 1888 was *Puss in Boots*, and for me it was a tragedy because just as Letty Lind, the principal girl, came on in a coach and Charles Lauri, as the enterprising cat, was crying that his master the Marquis of Carabas was drowning, my old nurse abruptly decided that it was time to go home. We were in a circle box on the prompt side opposite to where we had been the previous year at *The Forty Thieves*. Sybil Braine, who I suppose was about three years older than myself, was with us and Sybil, outwardly a stolid child, showed no sign of being disappointed at having to leave the pantomime before it was finished. Not so myself. I can hear now from long ago the echoes of my sobbing as I was led from the theatre, and I can see now through the glass doors of the dress circle lobby with a last despairing backward glance the glittering silver of Letty Lind's coach.

Looking back now at my old nurse's behaviour it is easy for me to realise that she had been overtaken by a sudden uncontrollable craving for gin, and that this hasty exit from Drury Lane was due to that craving, as six months before it had been responsible for her leaving me alone in Kensington Gardens.

I was still sobbing when we reached the Temple Station, and as we walked from West Kensington Station to Avonmore Road that silver scene of which I never saw the end was still a poignant regret. Indeed I retain a grudge against that old nurse of mine, as from the past that obstinate wrinkled face of hers, with its long upper-lip and small squashed nose, denies me the pleasure of knowing how Puss in Boots rescued his master from the delicate predicament of having nothing on when the princess arrived beside the river in her silver coach.

It may have been at tea on that blighted afternoon that I thought of a way to exasperate Nanny by telling her that I preferred my bread without butter. I was tired of the way she always transformed butter into scrape, of the way in which, if a dab of butter was happily caught in one of the holes of a slice of the real bread we had in those days, she would excavate it with the knife and turn it into another bit of scrape. I was tired of the way she would mutter that too much butter was not good for me and, as it seemed to me, obviously enjoyed depriving me of it. If I told her that I preferred my bread without butter she would be deprived of the pleasure of depriving me. So whether it was on this particular afternoon or not I cannot be sure, but it was about this time that I declined butter on my bread, and to this very day I never eat bread and butter unless urgent politeness to an anxious hostess compels me to accept a single slice.

One 'treat' we were allowed occasionally was dripping on our bread, which often led to sharp competition between Frank and myself for the slice that had more gravy on it. The too frequent result of such squabbles was that I was deprived of my bread and honey. Yes, honey was what my old nurse insisted on calling dripping. She must have considered 'dripping' vulgar. Presumably it was her disapproval of vulgarity which made her substitute for the usual nursery euphemism 'pee-pee' or 'wee-wee' her own euphemism of 'tee-tee'. This to my fancy was spelt 'teety' and I was baffled by the failure of Webster to include the verb in his dictionary. Looking up words in Webster's dictionary, a relic of my American grandmother, was a passion of mine by now. The pusher, a small piece of crust which one was always being adjured to use more carefully to assist the cut up meat on to one's fork, was never associated in my mind with the verb 'to push' but in my fancy was spelt 'poosha', which like 'teety' Webster had carelessly failed to record in his dictionary.

It must have been at the very beginning of 1888 that I first went to Kindergarten. The School and Kindergarten kept by the Misses Allen at Mornington House was the grey brick corner house where Lisgar Terrace started to run parallel with the prolongation of Avonmore Road, and although the Misses Allen's school was in Avonmore Road it seemed to belong to Lisgar Terrace. I fall back on *Sinister Street* for a description of Miss Allen and her sister. Miss Allen's base was a black bell on which was set a black cushion, above which was Miss Allen's round beetroot-coloured face. Miss Josephine was like a green curtain through the folds of which seemed to have burst a red face like her sister's, but thinner. Miss Josephine was pleasanter than Miss Allen and never shouted, perhaps because she was hardly ever without a cold in the head.

Miss Chalders, the mistress of the Kindergarten, was lame and used a single crutch. She was always dressed in one of those loose gowns that the aesthetic ladies of the 'eighties used to wear. They were usually smocked, with a conventional flowery pattern above the smocking. Probably their dresses looked floppier than they really were against the tight waists and bustles of less artistic women. Miss Chalders was immensely kind and infinitely patient with her small charges. From her I learnt to write pothooks and hangers and very soon to pass from pothooks and hangers to real letters. I learnt also to sew alternate lines of red and blue wool upon a small piece of cardboard. I learnt to plait chequered mats and bookmarkers out of shiny slips of chocolate and yellow paper. I learnt to print texts and to revere the tidiness of my pencil-box.

And then I had my first lessons on the piano. There was a small dreary room at the back of the ground floor of Mornington House where as well as learning five-finger exercises from a young woman with a skinny neck and blue hands, I had to play the treble in a series of duets known as Diabelli's exercises. My mistress used to correct me irritably whenever, in the course of our joint effort, my left hand collided with her right. I felt that I had reason to be more aggrieved than she was because I disliked extremely coming into contact with that blue clammy hand of hers.

As I remember, the treble parts in those earlier exercises were written for minims and semibreves and entirely devoted to the space notes F, A, C, and E. The minim used to present itself to my fancy as a face, a curious, fat humpty-dumpty kind of face which was afraid of being attacked by those black goblins of crotchets and quavers that I could see over my left shoulder in the bass being played by my blue-fingered music mistress. I remember hearing somebody described as crotchety and having a vision of a horrible little black woman jumping about like a quaver in the bass. The treble compared with the bass seemed to me an extraordinarily safe part of the world, and I could not understand why it should have such a complicated and vicious-looking shell to indicate it, and why the menacing and unimaginably difficult bass should have a C, which being my favourite letter of the alphabet struck me as unsuitable for such an evil part of the world as the bass.

As well as being like faces, I used to think of these minims and semibreves which I played so laboriously as pieces of silver money, and I remember hearing a person speak of somebody's silvery treble and wondering how that person had known what I thought was my own secret discovery that minims and semibreves were like silver pieces of money.

Then came the fatal day when the mistress told me I must begin the bass clef. I was frightened, but it occurs to me now that this fear may have been connected with the penalties involved in doing things with my left hand. To a left-hander the bass clef should have been a welcome relief, but I suppose I had been made nervous by early difficulties over holding one's spoon or fork in the left hand when it ought to be held in the right and turning over the pages of a book with my left hand when for some unreasonable reason they had to be turned with the right hand. Simultaneously with being introduced to the bass clef I was introduced to the crotchet, and the real misery of learning the piano began. I left behind me the friendly E G B D F which always reminded me of a boy's name and the equally friendly F A C E and was compelled to wrestle with the demon G B D F E and that queer poisonous nut A C E G. I suppose the association was with nutmeg.

If only, with my natural left-handedness, I could have been tactfully introduced to that accursed bass clef, I might have enjoyed music long before I did; but for years the bass clef was to be my bane, and though in due course I was able to read at sight quite complicated passages in the treble I was never able to read the bass at sight.

I have run ahead with my music-lessons. I must have reached that bass clef much later in the year.

In February there arrived in Avonmore Road a large volume which had been presented to my father by a friend in Limerick. The date suggests that it must have been given after the annual supper he held to commemorate the founding of the Compton Comedy Company. That volume was *Don Quixote* illustrated by Doré. It was my companion every day until later in that frightening autumn of 1888 of which I shall be telling presently. Then one afternoon I fell asleep while turning its spell-binding pages and was unfortunately discovered by Nanny asleep with half the pages folded beneath my head and shoulders. Forthwith, to the accompaniment of a machine-gun fire of 'tut-tuts', the volume was put away at the top of a cupboard out of my reach. I still have that volume, and the crease left on those folded pages seventy-four years ago, as I write of it, has not been ironed out even yet by time; indeed it will long outlive the small boy that made it.

The deprivation of *Don Quixote* was to take away from me my greatest solace. I was convinced that when Don Quixote charged the windmills he really was attacking Pentapolin of the Naked Arm, and that, when he was jeered at for his delusions, those who jeered were deluded, not he. No doubt Doré's illustrations were responsible for my belief in the reality of the Knight's visions. I hesitate to assert it, and yet I cannot help feeling that this preoccupation with the story of Don Quixote when I was five years old was at any rate partly responsible for my being all my life a natural minority man, unable to accept majority opinion as necessarily the right opinion to hold. Readers of *Sinister Street* will by now have recognised the origin of various incidents, but I express again the hope that they will not allow my autobiographical narrative to be prejudiced by my fictional narrative. For instance, in *Sinister Street* Michael Fane is made to enjoy being read to by his old nurse. In fact, I always read to myself and if my old nurse had tried to read to me I should have disliked it extremely. However, she never did.

Nevertheless, from time to time I did use fact unadorned from my own life for the life of Michael Fane. One of those unadorned facts was Nanny's perversity in taking me to church at St Mary's in Hammersmith Road, almost next door to St Paul's School. She used often to talk about the beautiful services in St Alban's, Holborn and elsewhere, with their incense and candles and music. Yet every Sunday morning I had to accompany her to an endless service at St Mary's where the vicar preached long sermons in a black gown and the litany never seemed to end. St Mary's was destroyed by a bomb during the Second World War and I confess to having beheld the wreck of it with a glow of pleasure. The last time I went along Hammersmith Road I noticed that St Mary's had been rebuilt in ultramodern style, and I feel sure that contemporary childhood will not have to endure what I had to endure in that Calvinistic crematorium of souls from a Hell-obsessed vicar.

In the afternoon Nanny sent me with Ellen the nursemaid to the Children's Service at St Andrew's which was situated just where Fulham reasserted itself over the child that called itself West Kensington because it was ashamed of its parent. Why, if it was necessary to drag me to church on Sunday morning could not Ellen have taken me to St Andrew's? This was not High Church, but it was far from being Low Church. Mercifully those Sundays in the sixth and seventh years of my life were the only times when I have had practical experience of Calvinistic worship, and in a way I am glad I did have the experience because it has helped me to understand what so many children have had to endure, all too often to fill them with a lifelong revulsion against religious observance.

During those first months of 1888 our old nurse had taken to alluding to my sister Viola as Cissie, and I can see now the expression of distaste on my mother's face and hear now the very tone of her voice as she forbade Frank and myself ever to refer to our young sister by anything except her own name. And difficult indeed was it at first for me to call her Viola, because when I did so she changed into a different creature. Words had such a tremendous significance for me that the name of an object or of a person was in a way more real than the object or person it described. It was as if I had to translate Cissie into Viola in my mind before I could recognise my young sister.

We had travelled up to Blackpool with Nanny and Ellen to spend Holy Week and Easter with my parents, who did not come down to London that year. It would turn out a longer stay than was expected because immediately after Easter, which was very early that year, my mother went down with measles to be followed in turn by myself, Frank and Viola. However, before this happened I had my first love-affair, or rather I fell in love for the first time, but as she was at least

two years older than myself I was much more in love with
Minnie Terry than she was with me. She had come up to
Blackpool to stay with her father Charles Terry, who was
still with the C.C.C. as business manager.

I regret to say I remember much more distinctly than the
face of my first love, who would one day marry that lovable
actor, Edmund Gwenn, the appearance of the first phonograph
I ever saw. It lived under a glass case in the window of the
private parlour in the house where we were lodging. Its owner
used to lift the glass case (like the glass cases that stood over
so many clocks in those days) and reverently turn the handle
for the wax cylinder to crackle out music or song.

I must have been much impressed by that prehistoric phonograph to remember anything about it just before I succumbed
to measles. I do not recall anything about my own illness but
I see my brother and sister with their red hair, red faces and
red flannel jackets, and I can remember that when Frank was
recovering he got hold of a jar of French plums and ate the
lot, the result of which was an abrupt halt to his convalescence.

Some time after we returned to London I went to see *Little
Lord Fauntleroy* at the Prince of Wales's Theatre; I expect I
enjoyed it, having no foreboding that before the year was out
I would be given a party dress of black velvet and Vandyke
collar like many other unfortunate small boys whose mothers
and governesses and nurses had enjoyed what must have been
an intolerably sentimental play.

In June when my parents came back to London my father
took me with him to look at a farmhouse at Eridge, on the
Kent and Sussex border, to see if it was a suitable holiday
house for the latter part of June and the first three weeks of
July. At Hyde Park Corner we alighted from the red omnibus
and crossed the road from St George's Hospital to take a
hansom for Victoria Station from the stand opposite, by the
wall of the grounds of Buckingham Palace. In those days there
was always a tout by every cabstand, who would fuss around
a fare in the hope of extracting a penny from him. It had been
raining earlier in the morning, indeed there was hardly a
fine day all through that wet summer of 1888, and as the cabby
whipped up his horse the tout called after him to be careful
as the road was slippery. Then suddenly the left wheel of the

14. Mrs Edward Compton as Viola in *Twelfth Night*

15. My father as Charles Surface

hansom came off and as we crashed I could see it bowling ahead on its own along Grosvenor Gardens like a hoop. How neither my father nor I was hurt I do not know. The cabby was pitched on to the pavement, and as he got up with a lump on his forehead the tout came along to sympathise.

"I told the Guv'ner that wheel weren't to be trusted. I told him as like as not it would come off. I told him. . . ."

"What the blurry hell does it matter what you blurry well told him?" said the driver angrily, his hand feeling the bruise upon his forehead.

We took another hansom and left our first driver and the tout to argue over the Guv'ner's undue optimism about that wheel.

When we reached the booking-office at Victoria, where my father was getting a return ticket and a half to Tunbridge Wells, I saw what I thought was a bright new farthing on the ground in front of me.

"Pappa," I called, "there's a golden farthing on the ground." My father looked round.

"Put your foot on it, you little duffer," he said sharply.

This I did, and when he had got the tickets my father bent down and picked up half a sovereign.

"Don't shout out like that when you find a piece of gold. Anybody hearing you might have claimed that he had just dropped it."

This within my recollection is the first piece of purely worldly advice I ever received.

I recall from that summer the serious adventure of having to cross the farm yard without being chased by the turkey-cock who ruled with his dictatorial gobbles those mild wives of his. I use the word 'dictatorial' with deliberation because it was a favourite word of Nanny's for me if ever I urged my young brother to do the simplest thing against his will.

"Don't be so dictatorial."

And I used to think that dictatorial was a much more suitable description of that gobbler's behaviour than of my own. Even when Frank discovered that by letting out the catch of his sister's high chair he could bring it down with a crash and make her thump the tray in front of her with yells of fright I was called 'dictatorial' for remonstrating with him.

L

I remember visits to the Pantiles in Tunbridge Wells, and thinking that the steps down to the road from the pavement on our side reminded me of the steps down from the pavement of the Brompton Road on the opposite side from Harrods. And that makes me wonder whether a grocer's shop with an ironmonger's shop next door to which I was taken once or twice either in 1886 or 1887 was the original Harrods opposite to the huge affair it was to become. I do not remember with whom I went to that shop but with the mind's nose smell the bundles of faggots hanging on one side of the entrance.

I recall being put to sleep with Ellen, who would have been about sixteen, probably because my bed was wanted for a night or two for some visitor. Waking in the middle of the night I started to explore the sleeping Ellen in the course of which I was astonished to find myself like Dante once upon a time in a *selva oscura* which I searched in vain for my own little appendage, and being greatly puzzled by not finding it anywhere. I leave the explanation of such behaviour to Freudian theorists with the warning that this behaviour was inspired by curiosity without the least sexual stimulation. Of this I am absolutely positive, discouraging though such certitude will be.

Before we went to Eridge I had been told that one of the delights of that summer in the country would be picnics. For me a picnic became something to look forward to as once the Israelites looked forward to the land of Canaan flowing with milk and honey. And every day it rained.

"Oh, when will we have a picnic?" I used to ask.

"The first fine day," I would be promised.

But the fine day never came, and my disappointment at never being able to enjoy the experience of that wonderful thing called a picnic became so acute that at last my mother declared that whatever the weather tomorrow there should be a picnic. She may have been finally moved to make this promise because I had been taken out to tea somewhere by Nanny a day or two before and when my mother came to kiss me good-night I had suddenly burst into tears. The trouble was that to ask for something at table was strictly forbidden: the mere fact of asking entailed a refusal by Nanny because one had not waited to be asked. At this tea-party there had been what looked a particularly delicious chocolate cake; I had waited to be asked if I would like a slice of it. And nobody had asked me.

"What's the matter? Why are you crying?"

"Nobody asked me if I would like a piece of that brown cake," I had sobbed.

So the picnic fixed for tomorrow was held. It was not raining heavily, but in a drizzle we set out to walk along a field path toward one of the entrances to Eridge Park. I recall the vision of Abergavenny Castle on the other side of its swan-haunted lake appearing through the drizzle like a castle in a much admired volume of mine called *The Old French Fairy Book*, of which my favourite was the tale of the White Cat.

In due course mackintosh sheets were spread under an elm-tree and efforts were made to light a fire without success. At last somebody suggested that we should go on into the Park and picnic in the cave where the guns took their lunch during a pheasant shoot. So we walked up a sloping path that wound round under the trees to reach this cave, in which were a few garden chairs, and here we had our picnic; apprehensively because at any moment a keeper was expected to come along and say that picnicking in the Park was strictly forbidden. A day or two after that picnic there was a 'rain of frogs'. A lane ran from the farm to the main road, and this was completely covered with tiny frogs so thickly that much to my distress it was impossible to take a step without squashing a dozen of them; the hedges too on either side were covered thick with frogs to the top. I have never read anywhere a convincing explanation of this phenomenon, which I count myself fortunate to have seen, even although I was only five years old when I saw it. Just after I wrote that reminiscence of Eridge in 1888 I read in some paper that a prominent psychologist denied the possibility of checking the accuracy of very early memories and seemed inclined to suggest that they were usually the result of adult imagination at work. In 1950 in the course of a tour I was making all over Great Britain to look at the properties of the National Trust I found myself in Tunbridge Wells in the company of the Area Agent, and as we were walking along I said,

"The Pantiles are round there, aren't they?"

He nodded casually.

"Well, I haven't been in Tunbridge Wells since the year 1888," I went on. "So I'm rather pleased with myself for remembering the right turning."

Then I went on to describe the farm house and the path through the fields to Eridge Park and the lane that led to the main road.

"But I know the farm you mean," he said. "It's still exactly as you describe it."

So I think I may claim that my reminiscence of Eridge has not been worked upon by adult imagination during the sixty-two years which had gone by since I last saw it.

That autumn of 1888 began the most difficult time of my childhood because it was then that the nightly fears and fantasies became acute. I recall the gathering dread as the lamplighter came round in the dusk with his glimmering rod to light the street lamps. Night was coming and those gas lamps of long ago with their feeble rays only made the darkness between them more terrifying.

It was Jack the Ripper who first made the prospect of going to bed almost unendurable. I had already had to worry about mice, ever since Ellen told me of a boy who went to sleep with his mouth open and woke up to find a mouse inside him, and on top of that of a mouse which had brought up a family of mice at the bottom of a bed. But the fear of mice's behaviour shrank to nothing beside the activities of Jack the Ripper. It would have been bad enough if I had only heard the talk about him. Nanny with her usual perversity had to maintain that Jack the Ripper's activities had been easily eclipsed by those of Charles Peace, and I was relieved to hear that Charles Peace had paid the penalty for his crimes before I was born, so that the hook he used instead of a hand was not likely to appear round the door of my bedroom.

Talk about Jack the Ripper was small talk compared with the hoarse voices of men selling editions of the *Star* or *Echo* as half a dozen of them, with posters flapping in front of them like aprons, would come shouting along the street the news of another murder in Whitechapel. 'Murder! Murder! Another horrible murder in Whitechapel. Another woman cut up to pieces in Whitechapel!'

Whitechapel became a word of dread, and I can recall the horror of reading 'Whitechapel' at the bottom of the list of fares at the far end inside an omnibus. Suppose the omnibus should refuse to stop at Kensington High Street and go on with its passengers to Whitechapel? What could that Eminent Q.C. in his wig, who was telling bearded Mr Lamplough what a wonderful medicine his Pyretic Saline was, do to save everybody inside that omnibus from being cut up by the knife of Jack the Ripper?

I have written of these nightly fears and fantasies in *Sinister Street* and there is no point in writing about them again. However, I think it may be worth while to reprint *The Child's Epic of the Night* which I wrote when I was twenty-one and dedicated to Logan Pearsall Smith:

THE CHILD'S EPIC OF THE NIGHT

Up the curved stairs went Lancelot,
Where every doorway held a fear—
A cave whence bearded dwarfs might trot,
Or noisy skeletons appear.
From the dim basement far below,
Where all the clocks ticked very loud,
And creeping things went to and fro
Across the kitchen-table's shroud
Of silent whiteness, he had climbed,
Thankful to see the hall alight,
And as the dining-room clock chimed
Eight strokes, he gained the second flight.
Half-way he turned against his will
To know (a sudden breath had fanned
His neck) if all the sticks were still
Safe prisoned in their china stand.
The baluster had never been
So insecure a resting-place,
So apt a loop-hole for a lean
Enchantress, or a witch's face.
Yet how much worse the narrow stairs
Where corners held such quiet things:
Past those inevitable lairs
Accoutred with nocturnal wings,
Wings of a shadowless nightmare,
With swooning heart a boy might sweep

Downwards for ever through the air,
The vast, uneasy air of sleep:
For on the landing farther round
He knew his brother, safe in bed
Two hours ago, had rashly crowned
A baluster's smooth hairless head
With manufactured paper hood—
He knew 'twas gone—but some ill chance
Might lend what in the day was wood,
At night a twisted countenance.
At last he reached his chamber-door;
The rumble of a distant train
Told him that night would come—nay more,
That somewhere people talked again:
A minute, and the noise had fled
And all the merry people gone,
While with immeasurable tread
Silence crept on him all alone.
Worse fear than silence numbed the heart
Of Lancelot, when down the street
Of rain-blurred lamp-posts wide apart
Came sound of cries and shuffling feet,
And men in husky accents told
The news of a dead woman, found
Because, though hidden deep in mould,
Her fingers stuck above the ground.
The cries surged louder, louder, till
The window shook; to Lancelot
The sprouting bulbs upon the sill
Were like dead fingers in a pot.
It was not any use to know
That deeds like this were farther off
Than farthest omnibus could go,
That at such fears his nurse would scoff.
Then fainter grew the murder-cries,
Fainter and fainter down the street,
Till silence lapped him round with eyes,
And filled the room with quiet feet.
But soon the boy looked timidly
Towards the fast closed door, and thought
What in the passage he might see,
As fear and fascination fought.
Quickly he opened wide the door

And waited trembling for a foe—
The clocks ticked louder than before:
The hall-lamp flickered far below:
The house was like a monstrous toy
Whirling with automatic breath,
And all these clocks dismayed the boy,
Ticking and ticking loud with death.
Then craftily without he crept,
And peered between the balusters,
Knowing a face might intercept
His view, half hoped it would be hers,
That woman's who had died and whose
White fingers shimmered in the gloom:
Then shuddering tore off his shoes,
And stole in silence to his room.
He dared not shut the door again
In case, if presently he heard
White fingers tap the window pane,
And saw them, where the rain had blurred
The glass, make pictures of the deed,
A fast-closed door should prove a snare,
And people would not hear nor heed
His voice, nor angels help his prayer.
So he must leave the door ajar
And with the greater speed undress—
The fear of fingers from afar,
If it were open, would be less;
As Lancelot went by the glass,
Desire was strangely mixed with dread
Lest it should tell him he must pass
A huddled figure on the bed;
And yet, when turning round again,
Only a crinkled counterpane.

It always had been hard to leap
Upon the bed, and quickly fling
His clothes into a tangled heap—
How close the stockings always cling!
And now to step upon the floor
Might be to touch white fingers there,
Which, like dead starfish on the shore,
Are damp when children's feet are bare.
Yet he must hide the clothes from sight,

For often he had waked to find
That they were given life at night,
And nodded at him like a blind
And hunchbacked dwarf with meagre hands,
Or writhed and coiled around the chairs,
Like snakes from unfamiliar lands.
This done, he said his evening prayers
In haste, and threw his nightgown on,
Nor dared to breathe until his head
Had through the stifling whiteness gone,
And he had safely reached the bed.
So safe beneath the sheets he lay,
Safe from the viewless window-pane.
Safe from the gaping door, till day
Should come to mock the night again.
The gas-jet was a crocus in
The gardens where he used to linger,
But sometimes it grew pale and thin,
And strangely like a shining finger.
The ceiling held a misty moon,
Where shadows played a pantomime,
And draughts made clown and pantaloon
Caper, while he devised the rhyme.
Mistier then became the moon,
And larger loomed the figures there
To Lancelot, who very soon
Would join that flickering windy fair;
And now his bended knees have made
Fantastic mountains of the sheets,
A black ravine, an ambuscade,
Then waves o'ersailed by fairy fleets.
At last he faded into sleep,
And found that fancies which by day
Lurk in the unexplored and deep
Recesses of a lonely way,
Rose up with more terrific shape,
And so bewitched him of all motion
That he was powerless to escape,
Palsied by some nocturnal potion.
And he was lost within a town,
Empty of lamps, not populous,
With streets that sloped for ever down
Into dim courtyards cavernous.

No staunch policeman wandered here
With comfortable steps and slow,
No friendly postman could appear
To save him from a hiding foe.
And so he moved with beating heart
Along this sinister, unknown,
Deserted street, where never cart
Rattled; and he remained alone.
Alone, he heard a scratching sound
Deep-hidden in the tallest house,
And swift he flew above the ground
And left this city ominous.
While as he sped the lamps grew bright,
And all his way was lit by gold,
And at pale windows faces white
Gibbered until his blood ran cold.
At last he tried to fall once more,
But found that he must sink and sink
Until he reached a corridor,
Through which he swam towards the brink
Of a vast gloomy precipice,
Yawning before him as a grave.
He leaped within it in a trice
And wandered through a golden cave,
Where with small hammers tiny folk
Scratched massive rocks that glinted red,
Scratched louder, louder till he woke,
And, listening found himself in bed.
The bed-posts glittered evilly:
His heart beat like a hammer then:
He listened in an agony,
But like the noise of a quill-pen,
Alas! he heard the scratching still,
And closer drew the friendly clothes,
And wondered if a mouse could fill
A room with eager-working foes.
He asked himself the time, and thought
Of those white flower-ghosts so kind,
Dead dandelions elfin-wrought,
Whose hours are blown away by wind.
Suddenly up in bed he sat,
And listened breathless to the noise,
And even prayed to see a rat

Move stealthily among his toys,
Rather than see the carpet twitch,
And shining fingers crawling through
Yet no dead fingers could unstitch
A gaudy carpet woven true.
The scratching did not cease, the sight
He dreaded did not yet appear.
Oh the long terror of this night!
And was the morning still not near?
The roses on the walls took form
To run a terrifying race,
And seemed to thrill before the storm
Of shadows sweeping o'er their face.
The pillow was a fortress now
For Lancelot to hide his head,
And 'scape the flowery shadow-show,
Or dull the scratching of the dead.
Hope only lived in that thin streak
Of glass not covered by the blind.
At length he saw the greyness seek
To force an entry, yet behind
The fingers made a slow advance:
But suddenly the scratching ceased,
The jalousies began to dance
Like sunlit water, while the East
Told that the day was on the wing—
He heard the sparrows twittering.

Those London sparrows of long ago! No nightingale nor lark nor thrush ever won such gratitude from my heart as the twittering of those London sparrows for whose departure the bloated pigeons of Trafalgar Square are no compensation.

I was very much the prey of bad dreams and nightmares for about two years, and there was one dream, evidently the effect of a bilious attack, which I dreamt in that gloomy autumn of 1888 and never forgot. This was of finding myself alone in a small sailing-boat upon a greenish sea of vomit.

Why I ever had bilious attacks is difficult to say, for the loathsome remedy of castor-oil in warm milk and water did not encourage me to be bilious. Nor did the diet my old nurse believed to be good for children encourage biliousness, bread and heavily watered milk alternating with porridge and heavily watered milk. Eggs were rigorously forbidden, and the top of one's father's or mother's boiled egg in which we were indulged when we were with them exceeded in luxurious tastiness any caviar or *paté de foie gras* of the future. No jam was allowed except raspberry and currant, and that was spread so thinly that it seemed merely to add sweetish seeds to the bread. Keiller's Dundee marmalade was a treat for Sunday's breakfast, but again spread very thinly. The most rewarding sweetness was golden syrup, which it was difficult to spread thinly because it kindly soaked into the bread. For dinner boiled mutton twice a week, and I have never been able to eat it since; boiled beef which we enjoyed on account of the dumplings; and on Sunday roast mutton. If biliousness was my enemy, why was I compelled to eat the fat of boiled mutton which would make a cannibal feel queasy? And those vegetables! Cabbage, which I cannot bear to this day. Spinach, which cooked for grown-up people I can enjoy but which cooked as it was for us makes me shudder to think of it. Curly kale. Ugh! Turnip-tops, Ugh! Ugh! Cauliflower would have been enjoyed if one had not been compelled to eat the 'cauli' as well as the 'flower'. And that was even more true of broccoli. The carrots and worse still turnips, and worst of all that revolting root of the parsnip! I can just manage to eat very young carrots today, but turnips and parsnips are still as distasteful to me as they would be to a cat.

The Israelites could not have welcomed their manna more gratefully than we welcomed the arrival of broad beans. Alas, how brief was the stay of broad beans and how brief the delight of green peas! Scarlet runners would have been all right if Nanny had not gone out of her way to choose the stringiest and toughest she could find at the greengrocer's.

And finally that damnable alternation of rice, sago and tapioca pudding, the last being the most damnable.

Weak tea much diluted by milk, and never more than one lump of sugar. And of course no coffee. To hear Nanny speak of coffee you would have supposed it to be only a little less deadly than arsenic. If ever some uncle or aunt presented us with a box of chocolates the chocolates were immediately impounded by Nanny and doled out one at a time on Sunday as the usual 'treat'. The only sweets with which she was inclined to be comparatively generous were acid drops. I recall seeing what I thought was an acid drop on the mantelpiece of my bedroom and popping it quickly into my mouth only to find that it was a piece of camphor.

I had forgotten roly-poly pudding with treacle. This was Sunday's pudding and extolled by Nanny as the treat of treats. I liked dumplings soaked in the gravy of the boiled beef, but I hated suet and treacle in combination. Oh yes, and then that foul mess known as batter pudding, and that dreary reliquary called bread pudding.

Yet one thing we had which very few children of today are given, however they be indulged, and that was real white bread. Contemporary bread eaters deserve what they get because a genuine baker is no longer given enough support by the public to maintain his product against the competition of the mass-article, which seems to have been baked of some substance more like ground tombstones than flour. The very shape of the loaf of bread we knew is no longer to be seen. We always hoped to be given a slice from the small ball on top, and that of course gave Nanny another 'treat' to be denied for the asking. There was, however, one superlative 'treat' for me and that was to be allowed to sit up to enjoy a dish of sprats, to which once or twice in November it was the custom of Nanny to invite two or three of her friends; usually my bedtime was still six o'clock. It was a very formal occasion and looking back on it I imagine that the guests were housekeepers or cooks who had been in service with my old nurse before she came to us. I seem to hear a jingle of beads and bangles as the visitors arrived and see a doffing of black bonnets and a donning of caps with gay ribbons. I knew that Nanny's surname was Curry, but I had never heard her addressed as Miss Curry until those sprat feasts. The drink was always stout, and I remember that after I had been dismissed to bed these elderly cronies sipped the sweetened London gin of once upon a time. As for me I was allowed the 'treat' of a bottle of fizzy lemonade, which in those days cost a penny.

Less agreeable to look back upon than sitting up for an hour to eat sprats is a memory of rocking myself on my beloved rocking-horse in the bay window of the morning-room and seeing to my horror a party of boys coming down the area-steps with a guy. Their faces were painted and they all made hideous grimaces at me. I was so overcome by fright that I fell backwards off the rocking-horse and got a large bump on the back of my head. My lifelong prejudice against celebrating the Fifth of November instead of Hallowe'en may have started on that November afternoon in 1888.

This year was the tercentenary of the defeat of the Spanish Armada and the occasion was celebrated by producing as the Drury Lane melodrama for that autumn *The Armada*. My old nurse and I went to a matinée and sat in the front row of the stalls. I recall vaguely a young woman about to be burned as a heretic being rescued by British sailors. I recall much more vividly the sea-fight, and can see as if it were yesterday Harry Nicholls, that splendid comedian, standing in the prow of a vessel on the prompt side. Alas, the sea-fight led to one of Nanny's exits before the play was over because the theatre became so full of the fumes of gunpowder that she declared we should all be choked if we did not get out into the air. I suppose, with hindsight, that the fumes of gunpowder gave her a yearning to assuage them with gin.

There was a more poignant premature exit for me that autumn from the Savoy Theatre where, again in the front of the stalls, Nanny and I went to a matinée of *The Yeomen of the Guard*. Just when it seemed that nothing could save Jack Point from the scaffold, and when I was praying that at the last moment he would be reprieved, Nanny muttered that it was time to go home. If we had been in a box I should probably have burst into tears. As it was, the embarrassment of having to walk over other people's feet made me choke back my sobs, but I was woebegone as we waited on the platform of the smoke-filled Temple station for the train to West Kensington. The trains went alternately to Richmond and to Ealing at ten-minute intervals, and I can remember reflecting bitterly that we could still have caught the same train if we had waited to see what happened to Jack Point. The Temple station, always the gloomiest on the District Railway, was gloomier than ever that afternoon. At intervals during the previous year my old nurse had expended many 'tut-tuts' over the vulgarity of calling an opera *Ruddigore*; perhaps she justified to herself not waiting until the final curtain of *The Yeomen of the Guard* by the vulgar name of the earlier opera.

I was moved up out of the Kindergarten some time that autumn and got as far in Latin as the first conjugation with the singular of *mensa* a table, *mensa* O table, *mensam* a table, *mensae* of a table, *mensae* to or for a table, *mensā* by, with or from a table. I remember being puzzled to know why anybody should want to address a table as 'O table'.

We went to Southport for Christmas, and Southport was without rival as a place in which to spend Christmas. Nowhere else in Great Britain was such a street as Lord Street to make one feel the spirit of Christmas. In these days of a commercialised Christmas, when competition demands that every shopping street in every town shall bedeck itself, and that every big store shall have a frowsy Father Christmas hanging around from November onwards, the Lord Street of 1888 might not seem such a wonder as it seemed then. Then it was unique. Strings of fairy lamps were suspended along the length of it, and let it be remembered that fairy lamps in those days were not simultaneously lighted up by electricity. The nightlight in each one had to be lighted separately and every day the nightlights of the day before had to be taken out and replaced with new nightlights. As I write about nightlights I wonder how many contemporary readers under sixty know what I am writing about. As I remember, one could get nightlights that burned for eight or for six hours; I suppose they must have been mostly wax.

The Winter Garden was a paradise for children. I look back to it with gratitude for the delights it provided, perhaps the most cherished of all being a large bran tub into which one made lucky dips to extract treasures. The bran tub as I recall it was even better than the large Christmas tree hung with presents.

But the warmth and glow of Christmas in Southport was all too soon in the past for another long long year until Christmas came again.

Back to Avonmore Road; and those endless frightening winter nights. I do not exaggerate when I say that the sound of the clock striking six was a knell. My bedroom was quite a cheerful room with flowery wall-paper of pale blues and pinks. The bed looked toward the fireplace between the door on the left and the windows with green Venetian blinds on the right. The washstand was between the fireplace and the window. The wardrobe, which had an infernal habit of creaking sometimes in the night, was against the wall beyond the door. On either side of the fireplace was a gas-bracket, only one of which by the washstand was ever lit while I occupied this room. On the other side of the fireplace was an armchair-bed which I do not remember ever being pulled out to make a bed. This was covered with some red and blue material kept in place by many buttons. Against the wall was a dressing-table with nothing on it except my brush and comb, a pin-cushion without any pins, and a little china tree in a saucer, the twigs of which were meant for rings to be hung on them. Above the chimneypiece was a jolly engraving of Louis Wain's cats enjoying themselves round a giant-stride. Above the washstand was a chromolithograph of a little girl sitting on her door-step and eating a slice of bread-and-butter, while she was being watched by a fox-terrier. Underneath was 'Give me a piece, please.'

I was allowed to have the door ajar, which meant I could have the reassurance of hearing an occasional train rumble past on the other side of the house. The gas-jet was not extinguished but left to burn through the night in the shape of a very small crocus with a blue base. The bed was intolerably wide and to this day I dislike sleeping in a wide bed. My protective fantasy was to build myself an impenetrable room which began with a covering of thin wood to which was added a covering of steel to which was added a covering of thick wood to which was added a covering of bricks to which was added a covering of stone. Inside this I could imagine myself safe from murderers, fire, and even earthquakes. An earthquake was a new terror started by reading a book about a black rising of slaves in Jamaica where white planters were murdered and there was an earthquake.

I have alluded to the rumbling reassurance of the trains that people still existed in the desert of night. Another comforting sound was the jingle of a passing hansom-cab, though this was sadly rare. The most consoling sound of all was a tapping behind the fireplace. I was terrified the first time I heard it but when I was told by Laurie Robins who lived next door that this was the sound of an elder brother knocking out his pipe against the side of the grate those taps faintly heard were a benison.

Laurie Robins, a plump freckled boy with a genial grin, was always held up to me by Nanny as a form of perfection in boyhood to which I should aspire. I never had the remotest wish to copy anybody else and I was not prepared to go around smiling when there did not seem any reason to smile. It might be true that smiling was an advantage but I could not bring myself to act off the stage. Although I had no ambition to be an actor when I grew up, it would never have entered my head that I could not play any part if I was called upon to do so. I enjoyed going to the theatre, so much indeed that I once announced my intention of writing a play in eighteen acts when I grew up. A play of five acts seemed regrettably short.

I cannot recall any of the Robins family except Laurie's sister Lily, who had long golden hair. I have a vision in the mind's eye of her walking up Avonmore Road and thinking how beautiful she was. Lily Robins did go on the stage finally, and under the name of Lettice Fairfax was very successful.

I enjoyed it when Laurie Robins came to tea with us because Nanny was so anxious to feed him well that she had to let me have more jam or golden syrup on my bread than usual, and in pressing more slices of cake on Laurie she was bound to let me have more cake than usual. I recall the Robins' morning-room was extraordinarily cosy and untidy compared with ours and I can remember being puzzled to know why Nanny should approve of such untidiness in another house when she was so severe on it in our own.

By now the odd numbers of the prolongation of Avonmore Road were built and occupied. We no longer looked out across waste ground to the back of Lisgar Terrace. The G.P.O. sorting-office which covered another piece of waste ground, had begun to function and Hope-Pinker the sculptor had built his house (Norman Shaw?) which was so much more attractive than the monotony of the rest of our side of the road. Between his house and the sorting-office was his big studio with a great marble lion in it, that marble lion which used to live in his garden before those old-fashioned houses with long gardens in front stretching to Hammersmith Road were obliterated by ugly flats.

SIX YEARS OLD 1889

EARLY in 1889 I left the Miss Allen's school because my mother thought a French governess at home would be more useful. However, I went twice a week to the dancing-class, and this involved me in having to make a gesture. That confounded Little Lord Fauntleroy craze which had led to my being given as a party dress the Little Lord Fauntleroy costume of black velvet and Vandyke collar was a curse. The other boys at the dancing-class were all in white tops. Does this require explanation as a white top to one's sailor-suit instead of the blue of daily use or the pale blue of summer?

Naturally the other boys were inclined to giggle at my black velvet, and after protesting in vain against being made to wear it I decided to make it unwearable by flinging myself down in the gutter on the way to the dancing-class and cutting the breeches, and incidentally severely grazing my own knees. I also managed to tear the Vandyke collar. Thus not only did I avoid the dancing-class, but I also avoided being photographed in that infernal get-up, for a sitting to Faulkner in Baker Street had been arranged. Not even the prospect of visiting the Chamber of Horrors and being shown Charles Peace by Nanny could compensate for having to travel by the Metropolitan Railway to Baker Street, which was much fuller of fumes than the Temple, though not so full of them as Portland Road or worst of all Gower Street.

The pantomime at Drury Lane this year was *The Babes in the Wood*. We sat in a box on the O.P. side of the dress-circle. I am under the impression that this was the year when the pantomime began in the domain of the Demon King and that the famous song about the bogyman was first sung:

> Hush, hush, hush,
> Here comes the bogyman.
> Be on your best behaviour,
> For he'll catch you if he can.

Fizzing blue limes illuminated the scene while he proclaimed his villainous projects until the Fairy Queen entered from the prompt side and, standing in the holy circle cast by a fizzing white lime, vowed she would thwart his villainy. I have tried to trace the year of the Bogyman song without success. It was certainly not sung in front of *Puss in Boots*, but it may have been the prologue of *The Forty Thieves* two years earlier.

The Babes in the Wood was the first Drury Lane pantomime in which the immortal Dan Leno appeared. I can see him now as the Baroness, wheeling a huge perambulator in which side by side were seated the Babes—Herbert Campbell and Harry Nicholls, from which they got out to do a dance together. I also remember Charles Lauri as a lovable poodle, and Robin Hood, the principal boy.

I think it was this year that we saw *Jack the Giant Killer* at the Surrey Theatre, sitting in a box on the prompt side. Of this I remember the Giant Blunderbore putting his head into our box and I can hear the yells of my brother Frank when that huge red face came champing at us. It may, however, have been *Valentine and Orson*, in which there was a terrific fight between the two brothers when so much red paint blood was spilt that the stage looked like the floor of a slaughter-house. Nowadays the psychosis ramp would attribute the most fearful consequences to a childhood exposed to such horrors, but I have not discovered any psychosis in myself as a result.

Those visits to the Surrey Theatre in Blackfriars Road under the management of George Conquest were an adventure, because they meant walking across the bridge from the under-ground station and here the Thames seemed so much broader than it seemed when crossing Hammersmith Bridge or Putney Bridge.

The first French governess was a withered and extremely disagreeable Mademoiselle who lasted a very short time. She was succeeded by Madame 'Flauve', whose portrait I drew in *Sinister Street*. I have forgotten her real name. She was a fat young Frenchwoman with a bilious complexion, little pig's eyes and a dowdy black mantle. She had the thick voice of one who was always swallowing jujubes. I spent the morning learning French and history and geography with her, and in

the afternoon she took me for a walk. The walk was always
to secondhand furniture shops near Hammersmith Broadway,
where she would go on arguing endlessly about the price of
whatever had caught her fancy while I, ineffably bored, waited
outside the shop. She had recently been married and would
bore me by talking in French about her husband, for whom
she was busy furnishing a small house they had taken somewhere in Chiswick.

Madame 'Flauve' was unable to take me for walks in the
afternoon, probably being too much occupied with her own
household arrangements. Nanny was accustomed to take
Frank and Viola out in the morning and to go for a walk by
herself in the afternoon. So Madame 'Flauve's' lack of consideration for her plans was much resented. However, she was
determined to have some of the afternoon to herself and used
to send me out alone to walk up Avonmore Road into the
Hammersmith Road and then turn right to cross Addison
Bridge and walk along the Kensington Road as far as Earl's
Court Road. Presumably Nanny herself found the private bar
of some public-house in the other direction.

I believe I could still take that walk blindfold. First of all
up the prolongation of Avonmore Road past two lamp-posts,
thinking that the newer odd numbers looked more interesting
houses than the stiff line of even numbers where we lived.
However, none of the odd numbers was anything like as
interesting as the house of Hope-Pinker the sculptor, and if
the studio door was open I would have a glimpse of that great
marble lion; then came a brief look at the sorting-office always
in a bustle, it seemed, with postmen hurrying in and emptying
bags of letters and with rows of clerks stamping those letters
with postmarks. By the sorting-office Avonmore Road made
an abrupt rectangular turn past a tumble-down tarred fence
through gaps in which could be seen a large shadowy garden
covered with pale grass under trees with trunks as black as
coal. Beyond the garden was a large decayed house with big
bare windows glinting among the ivy that covered it. After
this Avonmore Road continued on the right in the same
direction as the prolongation. The houses were smaller now
and the bricks of which they were built were a deeper red
than those of 54 Avonmore Road and its neighbours. They

had no basements and one could see into their dining-rooms, so close were they to the pavement. Opposite were the odd number houses, also without basements.

When 2 Avonmore Road was reached there was a stretch of narrow waste-ground in which was a tall advertisement hoarding, the pictures on which were sometimes of great interest. On the other side of the road was the forbidding back of a large board-school, or what today we call a council school. Beyond the board-school were Avonmore Mansions seeming tall and majestic with their yellowish bricks. I knew that these were flats and I had heard them spoken of in our kitchen as a novel and unnatural way of living. However, I was impressed by the uniformed porter sitting on a chair in the entrance hall and I thought he must be a great protection against burglars; I used to wish that we lived in the safety of a flat.

Now turning to the right came a row of about half a dozen shops, one a tobacconist, one a second-hand book shop, one an ice-cream shop with a barber's saloon at the back, and one an umbrella shop which displayed in the window a row of thick club-headed sticks called Night Companions. They were priced at a shilling each. I longed dearly for one of these Night Companions to sleep beside me, and to my joy one afternoon Nanny, having stayed out longer than usual on her walk, arrived with two of these Night Companions, one of which she presented to me and the other to my brother Frank, who was not yet four years old. Frank's Night Companion looked much fiercer than mine; its club-head was more gnarled and it was stained a darker hue than the stem. My Night Companion looked mild and clean-shaven beside it. When Nanny bought the sticks I was stupid enough to show my preference for the fiercer-looking one, and that of course was fatal to any chance I had of being given it as my protector.

Beyond the shops was the Hand and Flower Hotel, which looked very new and yellowish; no doubt some picturesque old inn had been pulled down to make way for it. The Hand and Flower is one of the few remaining features of the Kensington Road of my youth, and though it is no longer yellowish it is just as ugly a piece of late-Victorian architecture as ever, and if it were pulled down and turned into a chromium-plated neon-lighted monstrosity of today it would be no loss to beauty or sentiment.

The next turning to the right beyond Avonmore Road was a queer *cul de sac* called, I think, Portland Place. Coleridge lived here in 1810, and today it is called Addison Bridge Place. This was a quiet terrace without any traffic which overlooked the railway, beyond a row of large elm-trees. Nothing and nobody ever turned down here except an occasional dog or cat; no maid-servants stood gossiping by area-gates, and at the end of it loomed that large decayed house whose melancholy garden I could look at through the tarred fence at right angles to the sorting-office.

Beyond Portland Place one crossed Addison Bridge, above the parapet of which was a hoarding with a huge poster DAILY TELEGRAPH 500,000 DAILY LARGEST CIRCULATION IN THE WORLD printed in white lettering on a blue background. I may be anticipating that poster in 1889, but it was certainly there in the early 'nineties until the *Daily Mail* destroyed its claim to be the largest circulation in the world.

On the other side of the railway bridge was a line of iron railings with pineapples on top of each of them. These were bounded at either end by gates that were marked 'Private. No thoroughfare'; behind them was a stretch of shrubbery, and beyond the drive a terrace of solid mid-Victorian houses the name of which I have forgotten. By the first gate was an old stone milestone with a rounded top, on one side of which was 'London 4 miles' and on the other side 'Hounslow 7 miles'. Hounslow always gave me a sense of adventure, because Hounslow Heath was the favourite resort of highwaymen. After the second gate into the drive of that terrace came my first crossing. This was Warwick Road. I used to stand on the kerb, looking to right and left for any traffic before crossing, and I would think how glad I was that I was not going to walk up Holland Road. Holland Road, which may still be seen in all its pristine monotony, was Nanny's favourite promenade when Frank and I were accompanying Viola in her perambulator. It was the longest, straightest, dullest street we ever walked along; Uxbridge Road at the other end of it seemed farther away than the moon must seem to a contemporary astronaut. The only building that broke its dreadful monotony was St John the Baptist's Church, because St John the Baptist's had lights and vestments and incense, and going to church there might have made even Holland Road a tolerable thoroughfare. I never drive along it now in a car or a taxi without wondering how it could have seemed quite so long, even to childish legs, once upon a time.

There was a much wider crossing after Warwick Road, and this was Warwick Gardens, the houses of which spread into a kind of circle. Today the charm of its shape has been defaced by odds and ends of megahyaline concrete buildings, though some of the original houses still survive. I cannot claim that I ever saw a schoolboy with a richly ugly face bursting out of an Eton collar. I put forward this guess at what G. K. Chesterton looked like in 1889 because that was what his brother Cecil, who was a great friend of mine, looked like in 1895.

After the wide Warwick Gardens crossing came a sort of no man's land which would one day be built over with studios. Here I would sometimes see with slight apprehension a gypsy caravan. I did not really think it was possible for the gypsies to carry me off in full view of the Kensington Road. Nevertheless, I was always glad to find myself beside Butt's big fruiterer's and greengrocer's shop. Outside this I used to ponder for awhile a variety of fruit and vegetables and wish that Nanny would shop here where neither turnips nor turnip-tops were to be seen, at any rate in the window. Beyond Butt's was a stationer whose name I have forgotten. Here there was always a display of cabinet photographs—Mr Gladstone, Lord Salisbury, Mrs Langtry and many others, from bewigged judges and barristers to bewigged actors and actresses. In those days the cabinet photograph of the celebrity or notoriety, taken by Elliot and Fry or Bassano or Russell and displayed in stationers' windows, was the only way in which he or she became a familiar face to the public. Even in the *Illustrated London News* and *Graphic* the faces of the celebrated and notorious were much more often reproduced from drawings than from photographs. These cabinet photographs cost two shillings each, and people used to keep them in boxes with padded tops. I do not know why they were called cabinet photographs. I have just looked them up in the *Concise Oxford*

Dictionary, which says they were a larger size than carte-de-visite photographs. That does not help much because carte-de-visite photographs have been extinct for many years. However, on looking up carte-de-visites I find that they measured $3\frac{1}{2}$ by $2\frac{1}{2}$ inches. I wish they could be reintroduced and with them the photograph album, for they are much the most convenient way of commemorating one's friends. The studio portrait of today is a clumsy and expensive affair which clutters up drawers and is only occasionally worth framing.

Beyond Butt's and those cabinet photographs was Edwardes Terrace, which is mercifully still there. Then came the first turning down into Edwardes Square, with the Regency lodge at the corner. An elderly maiden lady, a friend of my mother's, whose name I have disgracefully forgotten, lived in Edwardes Square, and from time to time we would call at her little house and be given the key to what was one of the greatest pleasures of my early childhood. Unlike most London squares, Edwardes Square was not levelled when it was acquired and laid out by those French émigrés of the Revolution. Therefore the lawns undulated in a way that made me able to suppose I was in the country, and with the oppression of London crushing the years at this date I thought of the country as paradise. There were no tennis-lawns to spoil Edwardes Square; its gravel paths meandered between shrubs edged all the way with flowers. True, the keeper was a figure of ogrish ferocity, but at this date I was not old enough to do things that keepers objected to, and when we were older a fierce keeper added to the zest of mischief.

On the other side of the Kensington Road, Holland House and its park were still in their full glory; when in a taxi I pass what is left of them today I avert my head. Immediately opposite Earl's Court Road, where my prescribed journey finished, was Holland Walk, which I used to enjoy visiting when Ellen the nursemaid was in charge. I recall sitting on a bench one day and gazing with awe at one of the aged trees that grew in a line along the middle of it while Ellen and another nursemaid indulged in a long gossip about 'boys' in whom they were interested. It was for me an astonishing revelation that any 'boy' could possibly be interested either in Ellen or her friend. Indeed, I think I could claim that in

Holland Walk I first became aware of the unpredictable eccentricities of female affection by which I am often as much puzzled on the edge of eighty as I was at the age of six.

In those days where now stands a cinema at the corner of Earl's Court Road stood a row of about half a dozen mid-Victorian houses, called Earl's Terrace, I think. One day when I was turning round after touching the kerb I saw a coffin being carried out from one of the doors on the shoulders of the undertaker's men. Of course I had read about coffins, but this was the first time I had ever seen one, and the sight of it paralysed me with an emotion of horror for a moment. Then I ran as fast as I could away from that coffin.

How I hated those solitary walks! There were other things to frighten me besides gypsies and coffins. In those days deformed beggars were frequent in London; the external signs of bitter poverty were a commonplace. I can see now a man and his wife with half a dozen half-naked children hurrying along, I suppose, from one festering slum to another. The most respectable neighbourhoods would have these slums. There was one almost opposite St Mary's Church in the Hammersmith Road. It was a *cul de sac* entered by a narrow passage. Three or four years later when I was at Colet Court we used to hear that a policeman would not go by himself along that passage into the slum. So I persuaded a friend of mine to undertake the adventure of looking at it. It was a brief look, but I can see now that square of houses with patched and broken windows and blousy women shrieking at one another from them, with rotten vegetables and muck of every kind strewn all over the place, with children sitting in the gutters and with hulking men slouching around, every one of them a Bill Sikes to my fancy. Then some of the kids started to shout at us derisively, and turning quickly we hurried back along the narrow passage to the main road.

I used to worry about poverty and ask myself continuously why some people had to be poor. It was not a question I could pose to anybody else; I knew I should get the unsatisfactory answer of 'because they are'. But that and the question why people in Asia and Africa should let themselves be ruled by a comparative handful of white people, were the two main riddles of my first meditations on the state of the world.

Probably lots of other little boys at this date were puzzled by these two riddles, they without knowing it at the time having outlived the mid-Victorian point of view.

To keep up my spirits on these long lonely walks I used to hum a song which began 'White wings, they never grow weary, they carry me cheerily over the sea.' This was reinforced by 'Hi-tiddly-hi-ti,' one of the pantomime songs and 'Get your hair cut, get your hair cut. There's a barber round the corner and he's waiting for the order, and I'll meet you when the sun goes down.' I have not seen the words of that inspiring song for over seventy years. So I may be misquoting them.

There were only two pleasant encounters on those walks. One was with the pavement-artist who used to display his art on the stretch of road between the two turnings down to Edwardes Square, and he to my disappointment was often not at work. Pavement-artists depended on the weather. It would be useless to cover the paving-stones with colour if it was likely to be washed out by rain. Gradually, it seems to me looking back, the pavement-artists gave up their original method and took to propping half a dozen pictures on canvas against a wall or set of railings. These could be wrapped up if the weather broke. Yet by surrendering to canvas the pavement-artist lost his real hold on the passing public, and I cannot believe he earned as many pennies in that cap placed upside down beside him on the pavement.

The other pleasant encounter was with an old man with a red waistcoat, a long shabby tail-coat and round moleskin cap. He had a small blunt nose, a pair of very blue rather watery eyes, and his chin was covered with a silvery stubble. However, it was not his appearance that held my fancy; it was the fact that he was covered with white rats and white mice which were for sale. I used to beg Nanny to let me buy two white mice if I could not be allowed a pair of white rats, but she would only pucker up her obstinate face and sniff her refusal. I did at last persuade her to let me have a canary who was called Bob, being short for Bob Acres in *The Rivals*. The singing of this canary was a joy, but a much greater joy was the discovery that I could communicate with birds and obtain their perfect confidence. Bob was lost about a year later when my old nurse, with her usual unreasonable obstinacy, insisted on opening the window when he was loose in the room and declaring he would not fly out.

Do not let it be supposed that I am presenting myself in the pathetic light of the misunderstood child. My old nurse's attitude was indeed a valuable insight into human unreasonableness and was much better preparation for my future than would have been the fondness of those devoted Nannies to whom quite a few people look back with the same kind of sentimental regret as they look back to the happiest days of their life at school; that means they were good at games and enjoyed in consequence a fleeting superiority over their fellows which they would lose when a quick brain became more valuable than a quick wrist. Moreover, the rigorous denial of indulgence and the transformation of the simplest desires of a child into 'treats' undoubtedly trained me not to expect that life when grown-up would be entirely easy. At the same time, I was convinced that life when I was grown-up would be a great deal easier than it was for a six-year-old boy.

I have expressed in *Sinister Street* my own feelings about the Ten Commandments, which I was wearily made to repeat every Sunday, after the protracted mental agony of that Sunday letter which had to be written every week to my father and mother, for there never seemed to be anything worth writing about. Those Ten Commandments! *Thou shalt have none other gods than me.* But for me one God was more than enough as I pictured Him old and irritable among clouds. I felt that the Children of Israel must have been strange people to want other gods. *Make to thyself no graven image.* Apart from the toil of learning that very long second commandment I felt that even if I had wanted to make a graven image I should not have known how to set about it. *Thou shalt not take the name of the Lord thy God in vain.* I could not believe that if I ejaculated 'Oh, bother!' God was going to suppose it was a personal affront to Himself as my old nurse used to suggest that it was. *Remember thou keep holy the Sabbath Day.* Besides having to repeat that long fourth commandment, what chance had I of forgetting to keep holy the Sabbath Day? After that service at St Mary's with its endless litany and endless sermon, there was the catechism to repeat in the afternoon, the letter to write to my parents, and the taboo on even looking at one's favourite toys. Occasionally there was a children's service at St Andrew's when hymn 337 which began 'There's a Friend for little children' had a comforting tune whatever doubts one may have had about being included by God in that friendship, and there was another hymn 396 which had a reassuring verse:

> Comfort every sufferer
> Watching late in pain;
> Those who plan some evil
> From their sin restrain.

That seemed to put God on one's side against burglars, and it might relieve ear-ache, from which I suffered badly from time to time.

The only good thing that could be said for Sunday was that sometimes one had apricot jam for tea instead of that continual raspberry and currant. *Honour thy father and thy mother.* That was an easy commandment to keep except for those Sunday letters which were attached to the obligations of the fifth commandment. *Thou shalt do no murder.* Except when I was playing with my Punch and Judy, murder was outside the range of temptation for me, and anyway Punch and Judy was only let's pretend. *Thou shalt not commit adultery.* This was always hastily dismissed as marrying somebody else's wife, an improbability which to me at the age of six did not seem worth forbidding. I believed that people got married because they loved one another, and though that belief had been shaken for a moment, as already related, by hearing my father and mother arguing with one another about something at breakfast, the belief in love as the foundation of marriage had not been disturbed since. *Thou shalt not steal.* I associated stealing with thefts from shops, and indeed when I was taking those solitary walks I was always careful not to linger too long looking into a shop window in case a policeman suddenly appeared and accused me of stealing. However, in the Catechism stealing was associated with picking, to keep my hands from which was part of my duty towards my neighbour. My old nurse was for ever accusing me of picking, by which she meant the abstraction of even so much as a single currant from the jar in which they stood on a shelf in the larder. So thanks to Nanny's downer on picking I realised that God would be much annoyed if I picked an unlawful currant or sultana, and that confirmed my belief in His irritability. *Thou shalt not bear false witness.* This was explained as a warning against telling lies, in which was included any attempt to avoid a direct lie by prevarication, a long and difficult word for a long and difficult process. I could not bring myself to believe that a lie was a serious offence. After all, it was merely a device to avoid punishment, and anybody at the mercy of unreasonable rules for the behaviour of children made by grown-ups was entitled to protect himself. *Thou shalt not covet thy neighbour's house.* I carefully avoided any hint of covetousness because I had long learnt by now that the merest suggestion of liking something or wanting something made Nanny hostile to what one liked or wanted.

I had learnt all these commandments and the rest of the Catechism by heart before I was six years old, and, except for the Apostles' Creed and the Lord's Prayer, not one word of it has had the faintest influence upon my thought or behaviour. That catechism even corrupts the two commandments of Our Lord by making the love of God include fear of Him and making the love of one's neighbour a duty which includes submission to authority.

Fortunately for my mental food, my birthday presents had included *The Heroes* of Charles Kingsley, given to me by my Aunt Isabel, and Marryat's *Children of the New Forest.* Of the former I have written in my own book *Greece in My Life* and it is enough here to acknowledge the stimulus it was to my imagination and to my love of words. Marryat's book inspired me with a hatred for Roundheads which I retain to this day. I think it is a valuable influence on the minds of the young to hate certain historical figures because I believe it makes them less liable to hate the people with whom they come into contact through life. I can affirm that I have never hated any individuals who were still alive except Hitler and the pus of humanity he gathered. My hatred expends itself on figures of the past like Henry VII and Henry VIII, Good Queen Bess, John Knox, Oliver Cromwell, William of Orange, George I, the Butcher Cumberland, Frederick the Great and Disraeli.

Beside these two books given to me as presents I read *Oliver*

Twist with horrified absorption and *Dombey and Son* with slight anxiety about the length of my own life, such a close link did I fancy between Paul Dombey and his old nurse with Nanny and myself.

I did suffer a good deal of pain about this time. Eczema returned, which meant cod-liver oil to be taken in raisin wine, and for a while in ginger wine which I was foolish enough to say I liked better than raisin wine; so of course I was put back on raisin wine. Ear-ache was a dreaded agony and that warm oil poured into the ear; the pain was so great that I could lie awake with ear-ache and forget to be frightened of fire or burglars or anything else in the night. I also used to wake up with cramp in one or other of my legs, a foretaste of pain in the future from the sciatic nerve. Whooping-cough came some time in that winter. It may have been the reason for taking me away from Miss Allen's school and entrusting my education to Madame 'Flauve'.

Easter was late in 1889, but at last my father and mother came back for Holy Week, and in that magical moment when the four-wheeler piled with that familiar luggage came round the corner all the gloom of winter vanished. This may have been the time when I was worried by the exhausted look on the face of the 'runner' who had followed the cab all the way to West Kensington from Euston or St Pancras or King's Cross. When he took off his coat and stood in the hall before carrying the heavy luggage upstairs on his back I could see through a big hole in his shirt his ribs sticking out from a pale thin body. The recognised reward to a 'runner' for following a cab four miles and more in order to handle the heavy luggage at the end of the drive was one shilling, and I was so much distressed by his appearance that I begged my father to give the 'runner' two shillings. I can see the quizzical expression on his face as he asked me if I thought my poor father was made of money. And I regret to say he did not give that extra shilling. No doubt at this date it would have been considered setting a bad example. Probably he would have included his American wife in the need to avoid a suggestion of extravagance. This is not to suggest any meanness of my father, but the puritan stock in him was there to preach frugality and self-discipline. In those days he would never travel first-class; never take a hansom if an omnibus was available; never smoke until after dinner, and dinner for him was always 3 p.m. Then he allowed himself one cigar before going to the theatre. When he came back he would have a very light supper and allow himself two cigars and one pipe (which he never learnt to fill properly) and retire to bed on the stroke of one. He allowed himself two glasses of claret at dinner and one whisky and soda after supper.

When he was over fifty he drank champagne instead of claret, but he did not buy himself a car until he was fifty-five. For years he put himself down in the salary list of the Compton Comedy Company at £10 a week and my mother at £5. Out of this their weekly bill for lodgings and the maintenance of 54 Avonmore Road had to be paid. Whatever he made above this was saved. For him, as for his father before him, the stage was a sacred profession, but that fundamental puritanism of his never extended to the least interest in religion, which was always a grief to my mother who had no desire to celebrate Holy Week by accompanying my father to the plays running in London. I was to realise much later that she had had to make the decision between remaining on tour as her husband's leading lady and remaining at home with her children. With so many examples of theatrical marriages coming to grief she chose to remain on tour and continue acting; I suppose, to put it crudely, because she did not feel that my father's great attraction for women should be made too easy a temptation.

This Holy Week of 1889 was to bring her a difficult test. They would be travelling on Easter Sunday in order to open at some theatre on Easter Monday. I do not know if my father had yet made the Gaiety Theatre, Dublin, his regular venue for Easter Monday, but Ireland may well have been where they were going. For the last night of that precious week it had been promised that we children should be allowed to sit up to the incredible hour of eight o'clock. Some time before seven there was the sound of two hansom-cabs coming along Avonmore Road. They stopped before our door and presently appeared a Mr Coward and a Lady Cregeen to say that they had brought a second hansom in order to take my father and mother out to dinner at the Hotel Victoria in Northumberland Avenue. At this date, apart from the Savoy and the Grand

Hotel, the Victoria was the only place where people dined out at what was then considered the late hour of half-past seven.

"Oh, I don't think we *can* come," said my mother. "It's the children's last night."

But Coward was insistent.

"I'll put that right," he declared.

Then my father said to my mother that he thought they ought to go. I have supposed later that Coward, a wealthy man, was one of my father's backers for his ambition to lease a London theatre for a season, and that he did not feel he could well refuse his invitation. I can recall as if it were yesterday the agony of apprehension in which I listened to this conversation and heard my mother at last surrender. I can see her now walking upstairs to her room to divest herself of the tea-gown she was wearing, that much loved garment symbolic of her intention to be at home.

As they were going out of the front door Coward turned to me to put it right by pressing into my hand half a sovereign.

The door closed. The jingle of the hansom-cabs and trot of the horses' hooves grew less and less audible until silence fell. Then I went up to my bedroom and as I climbed the stairs I thought, not in so many words exactly of course, but with the equivalent surge of emotion:

"You can never again in life afford to depend on the love of somebody, you must always be prepared henceforth to be disappointed, and then if you are disappointed you will be able to bear it because you knew that it might happen."

When I reached my bedroom I opened the window and flung that golden ten-shilling piece out into the deep April dusk. My old nurse came in at that moment with my money box.

"Put it in, put it in," she sniffed fussily.

When I told her I had thrown the half-sovereign away she said it was meant as much for Frank and Viola as for me, and that it wasn't mine to do what I liked with. I was not impressed and told her I hoped some poor person would find it. The money had been given to *me* by Mr Coward. He had not given it to Frank and Viola. The only faint consolation I had was the knowledge that Nanny was annoyed and that I had successfully baffled that annoyance.

The theorists about childhood will find in this incident confirmation of their Oedipus-complex. I can assert with a completely clear knowledge of my reaction and an equally clear memory of it that jealousy of my father did not enter into it. I was never jealous of my father. I had no possessive love for my mother. She was for me somebody who understood my motives and who always presumed my reasonableness. Many years later she related an incident that happened some time early in my third year. She had told me to hand her something or pick up something at a moment when I was much pre-occupied with my alphabet blocks. 'Monty cannot be told,' I had replied. Instead of snapping a sharp order, she had sensibly added 'to help mother', whereupon I had immediately hurried to do what she wanted. I do not remember that particular incident, but I do remember my early dislike of obedience merely for the sake of obedience without the reason for such obedience being made clear to me, and I remember the feeling of a physical *contra naturam* which made me say 'cannot be told' instead of 'will not be told'.

Yet I was entirely without any desire to have my own way for the sake of having my own way. If it was made clear to me that something I wanted to do could not be done because it interfered with the convenience of other people I was always ready to give in by ceasing to want whatever it was. I have fortunately always been able to control my desires. If I have wanted to acquire something and found it impossible to acquire I have ceased to want it. I know that many people when frustrated allow the frustration to cuddle itself within themselves for some psycho-analyst to wheedle it out of them, thus giving him the satisfaction of supposing he has released them from an inhibition. I have not yet been lucky enough to obtain direct evidence from the patient himself of any such achievement by psycho-analysis. I am not presumptuous enough to deny the possibility of a cure by psycho-analysis, but the experience of my own introspection, when I do very rarely indulge in it, has convinced me that my own memory of my thoughts and behaviour when young are much more reliable than any theories I have read. When psycho-analysis became the fashion in the early 'twenties I read everything Freud and Jung and Adler and others of them had written. When I

N

moved my library from the Channel Islands to the Outer Hebrides I left behind on the island of Jethou about two dozen volumes on psycho-analysis; they had ceased to provide me with any food for thought.

So I am not prepared to be told by some devotee of psycho-analysis that the Oedipus-complex entered into the failure of my mother to resist my father's wish for her to do what somebody presumably of importance to his career wanted him to do. What I learnt that evening was something completely objective about human behaviour, which was of great benefit to my happiness in the future, however painful the lesson was at the time.

I have used this incident in *Sinister Street* but much changed in background and detail to suit a piece of fiction. As I have told it now it is autobiography; as I told it in *Sinister Street* it was a personal experience transformed to fit a created character who was as real to me as myself but whose thoughts and behaviour in a novel were not hampered by being myself.

It was about this time that Mrs Frith came to us as Cook. I called her Mrs Frith in *Sinister Street* because I could not find a name that did not somehow detract from the invaluable service she performed for me by letting fresh air into that house and lightening the oppression of my old nurse's rule. Ellen had gone by now, and the housemaid whose name I have forgotten was colourless and subservient to Nanny. I remember that Mrs Frith on one occasion alluded to her as no better than a guttered candle. I thought at the time she said 'gutter candle' and asked for elucidation, which was immediately given. That was one of Mrs Frith's virtues. She always gave me an intelligible reply. She never left the third person of the verb 'to be' in the air when asked to answer why. With Nanny, 'because it is' was the equivalent of Amen.

Scherazade did not prolong her Arabian Nights to a more entranced listener than Mrs Frith enchanted for me the hour before it was time for bed. It happened that when Mrs Frith came to us I had recently unearthed *Roderick Randam* from my father's library, and for me Mrs Frith was a figure in what was my first encounter with a writer like Smollett who called a spade a spade. Mrs Frith was an antidote to my old nurse's retention of that prurient early Victorian prudery which called trousers 'unmentionables' or the legs of a piano 'limbs'.

That exaggerated niceness went with her as far as to call dripping 'honey', it may be remembered. I was too young to rebel openly against Nanny's euphemisms, and indeed if it had not been for Mrs Frith I might have been lost in a forest of inhibitions from which I should have had to wait for Freud to show me the way out.

Not that Mrs Frith ever attempted to enlighten me about what today is called 'sex'. What she did was to disembarrass my mind of the notion that the bodily functions were something of which one should be ashamed. I regarded her as old, but children regard anybody over twenty as old, and anybody over fifty as very very old. Looking back now, I doubt if she was much more than in her mid-thirties, but she was large and plump with a ringing laugh and reminded me of the women drawn by Doré in the courtyards of inns through which Don Quixote passed.

I told one of her stories in *Sinister Street*, but even in 1912, although Queen Victoria had long left us, it had to be bowdlerised. Here is the story as she told it to me as one of her great adventures when she was fourteen or fifteen years old.

"When these new open drawers came in there was nothing I wanted so much as a pair for myself because I was quite a big girl by now and I kept on at my Ma to let me have a pair until she said 'If you don't keep quiet, Mabel, I'll give you more open drawers than you want over my knee.' Well, there was a Sunday School Treat where we used to live and we were all going down to Margate. 'Well,' I said to myself, 'I'm going to wear a pair of open drawers for the Treat, and if my Ma won't buy me a pair I'll get hold of a pair of hers.' And that's just what I did. So when she was out I went to her room and I got hold of a pair of hers and hid them under the mattress of my bed until the morning came for the Treat, a lovely fine morning it was too. I'd worried a bit in case my Ma noticed one of her pairs was missing, but she didn't, and I put 'em on and I wasn't half proud of myself when I started off for the Treat. Well, when we got to Margate we went on the pier and we paddled and then we had a whopping good feed and afterwards some of us girls went behind one of these breakwaters as they call them to break water ourselves. (A Gargantuan laugh as she said this.) Well, I thought to myself I'll make the other

girls jealous and while they was unbuttoning themselves I
upped with my frock and petticoats and of course I didn't
have to unbutton nothing. And it didn't half make them
jealous. But you'll hear how they paid me out. Well, I have to
laugh now, but I didn't laugh at the time, I tell you.

"Well, the next item for the Treat was a donkey-ride, and
what did those girls do but tell the donkey-boy to see if he
would make me fall off of my donkey and he'd see what he
would see. Well, I got up side-saddle on my donkey and off
we went. I hung on to these things that stick up in front of the
saddle, and then, whoops! suddenly my donkey kicked up his
legs and off I came head over heels with my clothes over my
head and my B.T.M. in the air. That donkey-boy had stuck
a pin into the donkey's behind to make him kick up his legs
and throw me off. Well, it was a minute or two before I could
disentangle myself and everybody was laughing and the boys
was all jeering and my young brother Charlie was scowling
because the other boys was all jeering at him because his
sister had made such a poppy-show of herself.

"Well, when we got home that evening what did Charlie do
but tell our Ma what had happened, and meantime she'd
found out a pair of her own drawers was missing. 'All right,
Mabel,' she says to me. 'All right, my girl, it'll save me the
trouble of taking them down,' and with that she put me on
the kitchen-table and gave me such a belting as I've never
forgotten to this day. And Charlie looking on and enjoying
it.

"And that wasn't the worst of it. I used to hide behind a
pillar-box or anywhere I could when I was going to Sunday
School because the boys used to holler after me 'There goes
the girl who showed her bottom at the Sunday School Treat!'"

To my sorrow Nanny managed after about a year's warfare
with Mrs Frith to get her sent away for drinking, but I must
add that the scene in *Sinister Street* in which her final departure
is described is fiction, not fact. Nevertheless, I have no doubt
that the reason why my old nurse managed to eliminate Mrs
Frith was her knowledge of Nanny's own devotion to gin.

I cannot recall where my father and mother spent their
summer holiday. Possibly they stayed with John Bolton in
Scarborough while Nanny, Frank, Viola and myself were in

rooms. We stayed with a Mr and Mrs Denton, who had a
stationer's shop below. We stayed there twice again in the
'nineties and as they both have vivid memories I shall keep
Scarborough for my second octave.

During August we were on tour, and I have a sharp recollection of A. E. W. Mason, who had joined my father's Company
in the previous year and by now had been promoted to 'second
walking gentleman'. In other words, he was playing Careless
in *The School for Scandal* and Fag in *The Rivals*, or it may be
that he was by now 'first walking gentleman', in which case he
would have been playing Sir Benjamin Backbite, Falkland,
and Hastings in *She Stoops to Conquer*. I remember that in
Hastings (the town) he shared rooms with Sydney Paxton, a
grandson of the Crystal Palace architect, who played Crabtree
and the rest of the so-called 'heavy utility' parts. Mason was
very good-looking, not long down from Trinity College,
Oxford, and always immensely kind to myself. Later he joined
the Company my father had formed for my Aunt Isabel and
was her leading man.

The son of the house where Mason and Paxton were lodging
was the leader of a band of brigands whose territory was an
undulating stretch of wasteground opposite, and to my tremendous satisfaction I was allowed to accompany the brigands on
their expeditions as a kind of camp follower. "You kid ain't a
brigand yourself, mind," I was warned by the leader who,
I suppose, was about twelve. "You can't be a proper brigand
till you've taken the oath." I begged to be allowed to take
the oath but I was told that I wouldn't have enough blood
at my age with which to sign my name. This was a disappointment, but I recognised the awe-inspiring priority conferred
by age and was only too happy to be accepted as a camp
follower.

Another place we went to that August was Great Yarmouth,
which is distinguished in my memory from all other seaside
places by the number and variety of its goat-carriages that
in those days were the delight of children as yet too small to
ride on donkeys. They were to the donkey what the camel at
the Zoo was to the elephant. The average goat-carriage of a
seaside place was a kind of miniature dogcart; but at Yarmouth
there were miniature coaches drawn by four goats, landaus,

victorias, wagonettes, hansom-cabs, and I do not know how many types of vehicles besides. To be sure, the proprietor held on to one of the leaders and the four goats harnessed to the coach never moved at a faster pace than a slow walk; yet the thrill of driving that four-in-hand has lasted for more than seventy years.

The next distinction of Yarmouth was the number and variety of the penny-in-the-slot machines outside the doors of the Aquarium, which, as I remember it, was a combination of theatre, concert hall and side-shows, with two or three tanks of weary-looking fish to justify its name. Those penny-in-the-slot machines may have provided the first impulse I ever had to make enough money to be independent. It used to seem to me that life could offer nothing fairer than enough money to spend the whole of one's leisure in putting pennies in slots, for with my rare pennies I was always perplexed which set of performing puppets I should conjure into motion. My favourite was one which showed the last moments of a condemned murderer. When the penny was dropped in the slot and a handle had been turned, the figure of the murderer, who was leaning over a table sunk in his own gloomy thoughts, jerked slowly and painfully upwards to perceive the door of the condemned cell open and the hangman advancing slowly and jerkily to seize him for the fatal rope, which could be seen through the open door. Alas, the skill of the designer had not been capable of reconstructing the whole macabre scene, for no sooner had the hangman reached his victim than he shot back again through the doors, which closed behind him and left the condemned man bending once more over his table, reprieved until the next penny stirred him into apprehensive life again.

An absurd adventure happened to me at Yarmouth that summer when I was taken on the switchback by my old nurse, for when we had hurtled up and down to the far end Nanny absolutely refused to make the return journey. There was for me an embarrassing argument between her and the conductor, and at last when he told her firmly that there was no possible way of getting back to the ground except by making the return trip in the car she declared she would walk back, and walk back she insisted on our doing. She grasped me firmly by the hand, and we slithered and slid down the artificial undulations in what for me was a nightmare of anxiety. I can still hear the shouts of the indignant attendants urging us to hurry, because we were holding up the next trip.

"Well, what a shocking waste of sixpence," Nanny sniffed when we emerged from the switchback.

I need hardly add that when we got back to the lodgings she claimed that she had had a terrible experience walking along the switchback because *I* had been frightened to make the journey again in a car.

We must have gone back to London with Nanny at the very beginning of September 1889, for among the very few letters left undestroyed by my mother I find one from W. G. Wills addressed to her at the Aquarium Theatre, Great Yarmouth:

> 6 *Penywern Rd*
> *Earls Ct Rd*
> *S. Kenton*
>
> *Aug.* 30. 89

My dear Mrs Compton,

I shall have the greatest pleasure in doing the portrait—let the nurse come on Tuesday next and I shall take a first sitting—I am going for a week to Paris but will complete picture when I come back—I shall want about three sittings.

I sent the missing pages (1st Act) of 'Clarissa' to your sister yesterday.

> *Kind regards to Mr Compton*
> *Yours cordially*
>
> *W. G. W.*

William Gorman Wills had been engaged by my grand-father at an annual salary as dramatist to the Lyceum Theatre, and wrote for him *Medea in Corinth*, *Charles I* and *Eugene Aram*. Later for Irving he wrote *Faust* and was the author of *Olivia*, in which Ellen Terry made a success before she joined Irving. This was a dramatisation of *The Vicar of Wakefield*, and as good a dramatic version of a novel as I know. His brother, the Reverend Freeman Wills, wrote *The Only Way* for Martin Harvey.

Wills was the complete Bohemian and never did justice to

his great talents, which included a gift for making delightful pastel portraits of children. He made one of my cousin Sidney Crowe sitting among dandelion blow-balls which had great charm. He was a good balladist too. 'I'll sing thee songs of Araby' was the most popular. It was typical of Wills that when Queen Victoria commanded his attendance to make portraits of the royal children he pleaded a prior engagement.

Wills was extremely absent-minded; he may have inherited that from his father who was a Church of Ireland parson and distinguished philosopher. It is related of James Wills in the *Dictionary of National Biography* that once he boiled his own watch instead of the egg he was meaning to boil.

It was typical of W. G. Wills that some of the pages should have been missing from the first act of the dramatisation of *Clarissa Harlowe* he was making for my Aunt Isabel, in which A. E. W. Mason would play Lovelace.

Wills was one of the only two painters who had the courage to go into the witness-box and testify for Whistler in the action he brought against Ruskin for libel, for which a clod-plated jury awarded him one farthing damages.

How well I remember that September morning when, after taking the chocolate-and-blue omnibus from the Cedars Hotel, West Kensington, to the top of Earl's Court Road, we walked along to Penywern Road. The door was opened by a charwoman who showed us up to a room at the back on the first floor which was completely empty of furniture, carpet or curtains. In fact, the only thing in the room was a Spanish onion on the chimney-piece into which was stuck a penknife. Presently a worried-looking man with a frowzy grey beard shuffled into the room in a dressing-gown and dilapidated carpet slippers to say that the sitting would have to be postponed because the bailiffs had just taken away all the contents of his house. I can see now the indignant twitching of my old nurse's snub nose as she flounced out of the room with me, muttering to herself over the disgraceful business which she seemed to suppose somehow reflected on her management. I remember turning in the door and looking back at the grey marble mantelshelf on which reposed that Spanish onion spitted by the penknife and envying the discomfited painter his freedom, my own being at the mercy of my sniffing nurse with her eternal tut-tuts.

One day not so far hence I would be reading Murger's *Vie de Bohême* and George du Maurier's *Trilby* and as I read them I would be remembering that Spanish onion as a symbol of Bohemia.

Alas, I never was painted by W. G. Wills, and two years after that visit to 6 Penywern Road he died.

It was in that August of 1889 that Mrs Maybrick was tried for the alleged poisoning of her husband with arsenic, and probably because my old nurse was so fervidly in favour of hanging her I was a champion of Mrs Maybrick's innocence. I hesitate to claim for myself at the age of six a clearer head than that possessed by Mr Justice Stephen or the Home Secretary, but what I believed at the time I still believe today.

The only plays I remember going to see during that autumn were *Doris*, which had succeeded *Dorothy* at the Lyric, and *Our Flat*, a farce at the Strand Theatre. I recall nothing of the former except that we sat in a box on the prompt side. *Our Flat* was in my juvenile opinion the funniest play I had ever seen. I laughed so much that Nanny threatened me with being taken home if I did not make less noise; we were sitting in the stalls. The story of *Our Flat* was the effort of a newly married pair to entertain a rich relative from whom they had expectations. As with W. G. Wills either the bailiffs had removed their furniture or for some reason they had to improvise furniture. I recall an armchair made by covering a hip-bath with a rug into which the rich relative when he sat down collapsed with his legs in the air. This seemed to me a veritable Everest of lofty humour; I did not suppose I should ever witness anything funnier.

I note in the Chronicle of the *Annual Register* for 1889 that on November 21st the students of Glasgow University made a strong demonstration against the Senate for attempting to carry out the graduation ceremony in a small building— Randolph Hall—instead of Bute Hall. Principal Caird and other professors were mobbed and narrowly escaped being severely handled. Some of those students may still have been about when I became Rector of Glasgow University forty-two years later, and I regret I never had an eye-witness' account of what must have been a stirring scene.

Just below this entry on the following day is a note that the trial began in Hungary of 57 women charged with poisoning their husbands and other relatives. There were originally 80 implicated, but of these 23 had either fled or died before proceedings were started. The poisons were obtained from two professional fortune tellers, who were arrested in 1882, and who died in prison during the seven years spent in collecting evidence. I have never read any account of this trial and commend it to the attention of the publishers and authors who serve up so regularly mixed grills of murders with which we are already familiar.

I think it was in this autumn that Lady Emily Cherry first began to ask me to tea. She had known my mother when she was Lady Emily Leslie and she had recently come to live in Fairholme Road, West Kensington. Her son Charles Cherry had just gone on the stage, where later in America he was very successful. Her younger daughter Gladys was about eighteen months older than myself and would become a dear and mischievous girl friend for the next five or six years. One day she would be a survivor from the *Titanic*.

Lady Emily's drawing-room was for me a wonderful escape from Nanny. At this date it was fashionable to decorate the curtains with odd insects in wool and I greatly admired a large spider which was supposed to be crawling up one of Lady Emily's curtains. To my delight one afternoon when Nanny came to call for me Lady Emily presented me with this spider.

"No, no, he asked for it. Mustn't ask. Mustn't ask," Nanny sniffed.

"But he did not ask for it, Nurse," Lady Emily insisted.

"Yes, yes, my lady, I know the way he asks for things. Tut-tut-tut."

"No, Nurse, he did not even hint at asking for it. I wish him to have it."

So I was able to carry that precious spider back to Avonmore Road, only to have it taken from me the moment the area door was closed behind us. It was then that I missed Mrs Frith most acutely, for she, I knew, would have put up a fight for me to keep that spider. As it was the spider vanished into some unreachable drawer at the top of the tallboy in my mother's room.

My old nurse's capacity for thwarting my desires was endless. On my last birthday I had been given a clockwork mackerel which when wound up swam with a stolid click to one end of the bath, when on being turned round it swam back to the other end before its mechanism ran down. Of course Nanny had to keep the key which wound up the mackerel and only allow it to perform as a 'treat'. I should have been justified in hating my old nurse, but I did not hate her. I merely regarded her as a necessary blot on life like a November fog or a rainy day in summer, for which there was no remedy except growing older. And that would take a despairingly long time.

That Christmas we were again at Southport. The old comedies to be revived that year were *The Love Chase* by Sheridan Knowles and *The Wonder* or *A Woman Keeps a Secret* by Mrs Centlivre. In both seventeenth-century costumes were worn.

In November 1889 the *Annual Register* records:

"An epidemic of influenza prevailed to an extraordinary extent in a large number of cities of Russia and Siberia. At St Petersburg it was especially severe, more than 50 per cent of the population from the Imperial family and Ambassador downwards being attacked. It was ascribed to the long delayed frost, which had not set in at the usual period."

This was the Russian influenza which would reach Great Britain very soon after this and remain the most virulent and lethal influenza epidemic until the Spanish influenza of 1918. One of its first victims was my father, who never fully recovered from it for the rest of his life. Like all actors, at any rate in those days, the idea of not appearing and so disappointing an audience was abhorrent. Moreover, with two plays to revive he felt he was inflicting too much on his Company to ask them to undertake understudies. Therefore he started to act again far too soon, and when the C.C.C. went on to the next town he must have been off again, because in a life of A. E. W. Mason by R. L. Green I read that Alfred Mason played Alfred Evelyn in Lytton's *Money* at twenty-four hours' notice.

I only vaguely recall my father's illness in Southport, but I have a vividly disagreeable memory of my own. This was on the Sunday morning, when on going into the sitting-room of the lodgings I saw that a newspaper which my old nurse had put in front of the fire to make it burn up had caught alight. I rushed across the room to batter it down before the pelmet by which so many chimneypieces were adorned in those days began to burn. Unfortunately for me I seized hold of the poker that was propping up the newspaper by the hot end and my left hand was badly burnt.

The maddening thing was that Nanny insisted the accident had occurred because I was playing with the fire. This lie she told to protect herself against any suggestion that it was her fault for leaving the newspaper in front of the fire when she went out of the room. My mother certainly did not believe her and it has always been a puzzle to me why she was ready to leave her three children in the charge of a woman over sixty who could tell such a lie. I suppose the reason was that Nanny was a competent and economical housekeeper and that her devotion to gin was at this date unsuspected.

I remember my father's taking me to a chemist to have the burns dressed and waiting for some time in acute pain before he opened the shop-door on that Sunday morning.

I do not remember positively what town we went to from Southport, but I am almost sure that it was to Huddersfield, and that we stayed there with the Mallinsons, Alec Mallinson being my father's most intimate friend. Later we were three nights in Stratford and three nights in Leamington. Frank and I had the *Measure for Measure* room in the Shakespeare Hotel (today *Measure for Measure* is the name of the bar) and I remember wishing it was *A Midsummer Night's Dream*, even although it was the middle of January. I also remember the landlord of the White Lion (or was it Red?) whom we went to call on telling my father that next time it was his turn to stay at the Lion instead of at the Shakespeare.

In Leamington I had my seventh birthday on the Friday of that week, and chose for my birthday present a box of Richter's stone-bricks, the price of which was 7s. 6d. Those bricks were a pleasure to me for a long time and one day I would buy an enormous box of Richter's stone-bricks, the price of which was £20. Martin Secker and I used to play with them when I lived in Herm.

The other thing I remember from those three nights in Leamington is a Chatto and Windus yellowback about mysterious events in Peru. There was a picture of a cloaked assassin on the cover and to this day I regret I did not have time to finish the story, though I have forgotten the name of the book and its author. Now I shall never know whether that cloaked assassin lurking in the shadows of a street was successful in eliminating the hero. However, the yellowbacks of Chatto and Windus did not go in for unsatisfactory endings and I feel sure that virtue triumphed.

Nanny with Frank, Viola and myself were to go back to London after Leamington and we all went to the railway station to see the Company off on the Sunday morning. And then another catastrophe happened to me. The train started unexpectedly before I had kissed my mother good-bye. I called after the cruel train, "I haven't kissed you good-bye," and this shook Nanny's sense of decorum.

"Don't be such a mollycoddle," she snapped angrily with a crackle of tut-tuts. "And on a Sunday morning too!"

W E probably went to the Drury Lane pantomime about a week after we got back to London. It must have been thought of as a way of mitigating the sadness of parting from my mother. We sat in the stage-box on the prompt side. The stage-box in those days looked directly on the stage from behind the footlights and the orchestra. Is there a stage-box left in the two or three eighteenth-century theatres still in existence?

By this date the Harlequinade had shrunk to a couple of scenes; the time had long gone by when the Clown went right through the pantomime as in the days of Grimaldi, and as he still did in the pantomimes preserved from the past in the books of words for toy theatres. At the end of what was called the Transformation Scene, which consisted of raising one by one a series of gauzes to reveal fairies reclining in enormous roses and water-lilies, came a procession of all nations or whatever subject had been chosen for the procession that year. Then the Clown, Pantaloon, Columbine and Harlequin appeared, the Clown opening with the time-honoured greeting of 'Here we are again' and proceeding to throw crackers to the children in the audience, often able to reach as far as the dress circle, which was a pretty good throw from the stage at Drury Lane. This was followed by a front-cloth street-scene in which the Clown always burnt everybody with a red-hot poker and always stole a string of sausages from a butcher's shop. Columbine was continually pirouetting backwards and forwards along the street and Harlequin was playing all sorts of tricks on shop-fronts with his wand. Pantaloon and a gawky Policeman were always the butts of every joke and they were always being burnt more than anybody else by the Clown's red-hot poker. The street-scene gave way to an interior which ended in a riotous trap-act with Harlequin whizzing up into the air through a star-trap and diving head foremost through a wall just as the Clown was going to catch him. That second scene vanished early in the 'nineties, and by the beginning of this century nothing was left of the Harlequinade except a brief street-scene. In a few years or so even that vanished, and today the Harlequinade is extinct.

This year Harry Paine, the last of the great clowns, came into our box, all dressed to go on and cry 'Here we are again' when his cue came. This was as big a thrill for us once upon a time as it would be today for a small boy if the latest pop-singer emerged from a radiogram.

The Drury Lane pantomime that year was *Jack and the Beanstalk*. I remember all sorts of people climbing up the bean-stalk, including Dan Leno as Jack's mother, and an exciting scene in the giant's abode at the top when Dan Leno was throwing pots and pans at him. However, it is Jack who stands out in my memory. Jack was played by Harriet Vernon, a very handsome woman not far from six feet tall with a rich bust above perfect legs, and I fell madly in love with her. I had been in love with Minnie Terry when I was five and she was about seven, but this was a grand passion, and I made up my mind that when I grew up I would marry Harriet Vernon.

I said nothing about this in the train on the way back from the matinée, but when the area door was closed behind us in Avonmore Road I confided in my brother Frank, who was four months away from his fifth birthday, that I intended to marry Harriet Vernon one day.

"You won't," he declared. "I'm going to marry Harriet Vernon."

I was staggered for a moment by this confident prediction.

"You won't. You're too small," I protested.

"So are you too small," he said defiantly.

There is only one way to settle a *tu quoque* when one is young. It must be fought for. In a trice we were locked in a furious duel, rolling over and over one another on the area doormat and on the linoleum beyond like a couple of cavemen.

I am under the impression that with the advantage of age and weight I compelled my young brother to renounce his claim to Harriet Vernon's hand, but it may have been that, when after a day or two the shape of Harriet Vernon's volup-tuous figure began to fade, we both of us forgot about our ambition to marry her.

Whether an account of that visit to the pantomime of *Jack*

and the Beanstalk was incorporated in the first Sunday letter I wrote to my father and mother I do not know. What remains with me to this day of that first Sunday letter is writing the date 1890 instead of 1888 and 1889. The emotion of entering upon some tremendous new era with that 90 I can still re-conjure. Children who had been born in 1893 and wrote 1900 for the first time may have had a richer thrill. I have asked several people what they felt when they wrote 1900 for the first time, but none of them has been able to recall doing so. What I envy is the child who will be born in 1993 and at the age of seven after writing 1999 the previous year writes 2000 for the first time. And what I should like to know and never shall know is whether when 2000 comes it will be called two thousand or twenty hundred.

Yet somebody of eighty setting out to write his autobiography in 2000 will probably have to chronicle a childhood in the 1920s seemingly much less farther away from his present than I in trying to recall that childhood of the 1880s and the awe with which that child wrote the date on his first Sunday letter of 1890.

Although the monotony of existence in London was intense I can remember how agreeably that monotony was broken up by the variety of itinerant vendors and craftsmen that brought colour even to Avonmore Road.

I was no longer afraid of being stolen by gypsies; it was now a pleasure to see a caravan coming round the corner and to hear presently some sharp-featured gypsy man beside it call 'Chairs to mend? Any chairs to mend?' It was interesting to stand and watch fine flaunting gypsy women with plumed hats and richly coloured shawls sitting on the front-door steps of one of the houses while they deftly plaited the cane seats of broken chairs.

It was not less interesting to see the knife-grinder wheeling before him his barrow with treadle and grindstone and hear him cry hoarsely 'Any knives or scissors to grind?' And it was fascinating to watch him grinding them.

Then there would be grubby old men with bulging dis-reputable sacks, wheezing out 'Any rags, bottles, or bones?' and equally grubby men not so old shouting, 'Old iron! Old iron! Any old iron?'

The tinker's arrival was quite an event. His children, an eager tousle-headed swarm, would go dashing along the street, seeking custom all the way while the tinker himself stood in the middle of the road and shouted 'Any pots, pans, or kettles to mend?' And the tinker's wife wheeled along the barrow with the furnace and the swinging tools.

The catsmeat man crying 'Meat! Meat! Catsmeat!' And the man selling fly-papers who always wore a battered old top-hat round which was a fly-paper spotted with trapped flies, calling 'Catch 'em alive-oh.' And the milkman yodelling 'Milk-ho' as he passed along, his barrow clanking with cans. And the sweep with his brushes over his shoulder and his face as black as the inside of a chimney whooping 'Sweep! Sweep!' And best loved of all, the muffin man. I hear now his clear bell ringing in the November dusk and see him pause for a moment before he disappears round the corner and turn his head, on which is balanced his load wrapped in green baize, to see if some hesitant purchasers do, after all, want muffins or crumpets for tea that afternoon.

What child today after coming down in a lift from some flat high up could walk out into the street and meet a girl carrying two big baskets on a yoke, her apron stained with the juice of fruit, and hear her cry, 'Fine strawberries!' or 'Cherry Ripe!'? Perhaps the lavender-girls still go crying their bunches along a Kensington street, crying them with that old tune as fragrant as lavender itself; even if they do, the tune will be drowned by the noise of passing cars.

The mention of a tune reminds me of the German band. German bands were a feature of the London streets right up to the outbreak of the First World War. A German band consisted of four or five middle-aged men with peaked caps blowing brass instruments. The German band visited Avonmore Road once a week regularly at the same time on the same day and played for about a quarter of an hour while one of them took round the hat.

Then there was the gentleman in a top-hat with bells round it who played simultaneously a drum, a pair of cymbals, a penny whistle, a concertina, and a triangle. I seem to remember that his equipment was called a panharmonica. The drum was on his back and he beat it by working the drum-stick with one

o

of his feet, and above the drum were the cymbals, worked in the same way.

People nowadays talk about barrel-organs when they are thinking of piano-organs. The barrel-organ which made a noise like a harmonium was nearly obsolete by 1890; the much gayer piano-organ, which had an individual sound of its own like no other instrument, had displaced it. The Italian with his hurdy-gurdy on one leg strapped from his shoulder with a monkey sitting on top of it was seldom seen by now; the Italians all had piano-organs. The dancing bear was already a rarity, but one still appeared occasionally.

One more of these figures from the past I must mention and that is the crossing-sweeper. Our particular crossing-sweeper swept a double crossing at the end of the first part of Avonmore Road where it forked to the left to continue as Avonmore Road and to the right where it turned into Lisgar Terrace. This was a strategic position because he could hope for pennies from people crossing from Lisgar Terrace who wanted to catch an eastward omnibus or from people bound for Hammersmith Broadway. Our crossing-sweeper wore a greenish frock-coat that was much too big for him and a bowler hat.

Lisgar Terrace was a line of grey brick houses facing a high blank wall with a slit at one end of it through which the big Burne-Jones pictures were taken out to be placed in a vehicle waiting to carry them off to some exhibition. The Grange was a red-brick Queen Anne house in which Burne-Jones lived and painted and in which once upon a time Samuel Richardson lived and wrote. The lovely garden today is covered with ugly blocks of flats and the Grange itself is to be pulled down. The members of the Fulham Borough Council were too frightened of not being returned at the next election to resist a piece of vandalism. Beyond the garden of the Grange was the garden of Otto House, a large grey stucco private asylum. One of my dreads at night was that one of the lunatics would escape and hide under my bed.

Opposite the Grange was a row of cottages with little front-gardens and one or two tiny shops among them, one of which sold penny packets of flower seeds. When I expressed a desire for a window-box in which I might sow two or three packets of these seeds, for once in a way my old nurse offered no opposition and she herself bought a pot of musk which still had its exquisite scent. The sudden fading of the scent from musk everywhere is a botanical mystery nobody has been able to explain. Beyond the cottages on the left-hand side of North End Road going toward the Hammersmith Road were three or four large houses set back from the road in spacious tree-shadowed gardens. Today grim blocks of flats have taken their place.

At the corner North End Road made a narrow and insignificant entrance into Hammersmith Road, and at this corner was the shop of Williams, our ironmonger. I am sure if I smelt that smell of metal today I should suppose myself back again watching Mr Williams himself, a thin man with mutton-chop whiskers, serving Nanny with tacks or nails or whatever she was asking for.

Most of our shops, however, were in that terrace of shops opposite West Kensington District Railway Station. At the corner of this and Gwendwr Road was Schneberger, the confectioner in whose window there was always a wedding cake, and from the door of which as one entered came a delicious perfume of warm bread and chocolate. As for the young women who served the customers, with their complexions like pink fondant, their elaborately built up coiffures resilient and blonde as the finest sponge cake, and their fingers like sugar icing, they seemed animated confectionery themselves. Nanny of course disapproved of them and always embarrassed me, who greatly admired them, by being at her sniffiest when she was ordering a Madeira cake, the only cake considered digestible by children.

Beyond Schneberger's was Pearson's dairy. Mr Pearson himself was as pale as the milk from one of his cans, and Mrs Pearson was just as pallid. When she sat in her little glass sentry-box of an office, adding up her accounts, she used to look as unreal as a wax figure from which the pigment had faded. Did Mr and Mrs Pearson grow to look milky because they sold milk or had he and she felt irresistibly drawn towards selling milk by a natural affinity with the commodity itself?

Beyond Pearson's was a stationery shop kept by an elderly maiden lady. In the shop parlour at the back was a circulating library where for 2d one could borrow one volume of a three-volume novel for three days. I never did borrow one of those volumes, most of which looked old and tattered and very dull. I used to wonder why grown-up people read these stupid books called novels when they might read a story like *Roderick Random* or *Oliver Twist*. Miss Dash was never to be seen without a red woollen shawl round her shoulders and she used always to be knitting when a customer entered. I used to think she was like the Sheep in *Alice Through the Looking Glass* and she had the same stupid and rather large face.

The other two shops I recall from that West Kensington of long ago are the barber's, of which the proprietor had the absurdly appropriate name of Cutbush, and the chemist whose name I have forgotten; the great attraction of his shop was a big jar of leeches. There was another chemist in Hammersmith Road with the splendidly appropriate name of Feltwell, and he, or rather I suppose his grandson, is still there. Feltwell the chemist's shop in Hammersmith Road opposite the turning down Blythe Road is the only shop left of all those shops I should soon have to pass four times a day for eight and a quarter years of school.[1]

On the morning of May 5th, 1890, my father told me to bring my Tennyson birthday book with me because I was going to see a famous novelist who would put his name in it. We took the red omnibus from the corner of Avonmore Road to where Church Street (now called Kensington Church Street) joins High Street and walked along to the Round Pond because we were too early for my father's appointment with Mr Henry James in De Vere Gardens. My father was always glad of an excuse to visit the Round Pond. Perhaps it held memories of skating there long ago with that athletic father of his, not one of whose sons, let it be added, followed his example in later life. My father used to ride, but he was not in the least interested in games of any kind, outdoors or indoors. He was persuaded to take up golf when he was over fifty, but did not have much aptitude for it, and for him as for the jockey there was just enough sport about it to spoil a good walk and in my father's case a good talk as well.

As we were going down the Broad Walk my father said:

"When I was a year or two older than you are now your

---

[1] To my distress when I drove round West Kensington in the spring of 1962 I found that Feltwell had recently vanished.

Uncle Henry and I were walking with your grandfather in Kensington Gardens when we met a friend of his, a very tall gentleman with white hair. After your grandfather and he had talked for a while this tall gentleman with white hair asked us boys about ourselves and we told him we were going back to school next day. 'Ah, that calls for a little contribution,' he said. 'Let me see if I have the needful.' With that he felt in his pocket and took out a red purse and divided the money in it between us two boys. There was over ten shillings, which was the biggest tip either of us had ever had. That was Mr Thackeray, and he was a very great novelist."

This must have been in September 1862 soon after Thackeray went to live in the house he had built for himself at 2 Palace Green. He died there in the following year when he was only fifty-two.

This tale of a great novelist made me think it was worth while to have been given the responsibility of bringing my birthday book. Great novelists were evidently grown-ups with a grasp of what life meant to the heavily handicapped young.

We passed the woman who sold balloons by the gate of the Broad Walk. Normally I should have hinted to my father that a penny invested in a balloon would have shown a good return in the pleasure it would give me, but with the prospect opened up by a great novelist's bounty I did not hang back for a moment to contemplate that great polychromatic bunch of balloons before we crossed the road to turn down De Vere Gardens. Henry James lived at Number 34, a house about half way along on the right-hand side. In May 1890 he had a fairly full dark-brown beard and I recall a slight restless anxiety in his manner. He may have been embarrassed by the presence of a small boy. The purpose of my fathers' visit was to discuss a dramatisation James was making of his own book, *The American*.

While my seniors were gravely talking I looked around the room, much interested by the variety of the great novelist's accommodation for his work. On the right of the window was a desk at which he could write, standing; along the wall on the left there was a day bed with a swivel-desk attached on which he could write, lying; in front of the window was a large knee-hole desk at which he could write, sitting. Observing my eyes wandering round these engines of his craft, Henry James explained to me with elaborate courtesy their purposes.

Then I brought out my birthday book. I was an old hand at this business of asking people to write their names on the date they were born. After the first entry made by Judge Hughes I had Sarasate and Sir Charles Hallé and several other distinguished names. To his name, in the space for his birthday on April 15th, James added the date on which he wrote it— May 5th, 1890. Tom Hughes had protested against the Tennyson quotation from *The Princess* by his name; Henry James might well have protested against the quotation from *Maud* opposite his name—'A stony British stare.'

Alas for my hopes, no red purse was taken out of the great novelist's pocket and emptied into my hand. I decided that great novelists were unreliable folk. Indeed, I never again asked anybody of note to sign my birthday book and the small volume disappeared for over fifty years. Then one day it turned up from a hamper that was being unpacked in my Barra house. Bob Boothby[1] was staying with us at the time, and I asked him to restart the signatures. That was in the middle of the Second World War and since then I have well over two thousand five hundred names in it. I regret that I let the birthday-book blush unseen for so many years. I might have had a fine crop of signatures.

In a letter to his brother William, written a week before that meeting with my father, Henry James confided in him as something 'extremely secret, silent and mysterious' that 'the enterprise conceived by me with a religious and deliberate view of gain over a greater scale than the Book (my Books at least) can ever bring in to me' was on 'a good and promising footing'. In the same letter he says that *The Tragic Muse* which he had just sent his brother was to be his last long novel.

Henry James gave my father this novel, and I tackled the three dark-blue volumes, only to decide that they were unreadable, and I must confess that although they have now been on my own shelves these forty years I have continued to find them unreadable.

To his sister James wrote from Venice on June 6th to tell

[1] Lord Boothby.

her that the business arrangements had been concluded and
to say he had been ravished by her letter after reading the
play. It made him feel as if there had been a triumphant
première and that he had only to count his gold. That autumn
Henry James went up to Sheffield, where my father was playing
at the Theatre Royal, in order to read his play to the Company.
James sat on the stage with his back to the empty auditorium
and by the illumination of the two gas-jets of what used to be
called a T-light, he read *The American* to the Company sitting
round in a semi-circle. The reading began at eleven and
continued till nearly three. When it was over my father called
on the author to take a quick walk before they went back to
dinner at half-past three.

"Well?" James asked anxiously, as they walked along the
London Road, "What . . . er . . . what is your . . . er . . . first
immediate impression, my dear Compton?"

"The play is too long," said my father.

"Too long?" the playwright gasped. Then he stopped to
hold my father's arm in an almost agonised appeal. "Too
long?" he repeated in bewilderment. "But did you not tell me
yourself, Compton, that the performance must occupy two and
three-quarters hours including the entr'actes? And now do I
understand you to say that it is too long?"

"Yes, it is much too long," he was told. "It took you nearly
four hours to read it to the Company. Add the intervals to
that, and if the curtain went up at half-past seven it would
be midnight before it came down on the last act."

"But what . . . what shall we, as they say, do about it?" the
playwright asked, dazed by so unexpected a criticism.

"We must cut it," my father said.

Henry James pressed a hand to his heart. "Cut it?" he
quavered. "Did I . . . did you, my dear Compton, say 'cut it'?"

"By an hour," my father replied firmly.

"But who will perform . . . this . . . this monstrous piece of
surgery?" James asked.

"My wife is good at cutting," he was assured.

So for the next two months a long correspondence went on
between my mother and Henry James, much of it in the shape
of very long and very elaborately phrased telegrams from the
playwright in which he would surrender two or three words

at a time. It is much to be regretted that my mother did not preserve this correspondence.

We shall meet Henry James again in January 1891 when he came up to Southport for the first performance of *The American*. To return to Sheffield for a moment. After dinner my father asked James if he would care to see *The School for Scandal*, which was being performed that night. So James went and at the end of the performance came round to my father's dressing-room. For some time he talked about anything except the performance while my father was taking off his make-up with the bear's grease he always used. At last, like every other actor-manager that ever was, he had to ask what his guest thought of the play.

"How did you enjoy *The School for Scandal*?"

Henry James shook his head in retrospective perplexity.

"A curious old play," he commented at last, half to himself. "A very curious old play."

Henry James had something approaching horror of the eighteenth century. Many years later, when my mother begged his good offices to draw William Heinemann's attention to my first novel *The Passionate Elopement*, which had just been sub-mitted for his approval, he kindly wrote to Heinemann but expressed his concern at my wasting any of what he called my 'latent energy' on that 'monstrous century'.

This year my father and mother had spent Holy Week at Killarney, after which the C.C.C. would have played in Dublin, Belfast, Cork and Limerick, arriving in London late on May 4th. That was my brother Frank's fifth birthday. May 5th fell on Monday that year and I think the Company must have been playing that week at the Camberwell Theatre. All the other suburban theatres then in existence were almost exclusively melodrama houses.

It must have been in this week that my mother announced that we children had to give up calling her 'Mumma' and my father 'Pappa'. In future we were to call them 'father' and 'mother'. This was very difficult at the time and caused my brother and myself many gulpings before we could address either of them naturally in so formal a way. On the other hand my sister Viola, who was now three and a half, took the new style of address with an aplomb which my brother and I considered showing off. What we called Viola's affectation was beginning to be a matter of genuine concern to us. She had a habit of chewing her food with what seemed to us intolerable deliberation. My father had told us that Mr Gladstone ascribed his good health to masticating every mouthful thirty times before he swallowed. It failed to impress us, and we supposed that my sister's slow mastication was inspired by a wish to show off in front of father. In fact it was due to adenoids which were removed some months later. When we urged her not to think that she was Mr Gladstone she used to raise her hand with a menacing gesture and continue to chew with exasperating placidity. She had another habit of suddenly coming out with a long word upon which she had been ruminating as she chewed. I remember one moment in particular when after chewing with relentless deliberation and silence all through dinner she suddenly ejaculated 'hippopotamus'. It was idle for us to challenge her to define 'hippopotamus'. She merely raised a hand to shake at us and then relapsed into silence and mastication.

Even in the holidays my father was loth to give up the hour of three for dining, but exceptions were occasionally made for family dinners which were held at seven o'clock. That June, when he and my mother came back from tour, there was a family dinner party for which my cousin Sidney Crowe, who was now in her Aunt Isabel's Company and was to join my father for his next tour, was anxious to display her skill in making a lemon sponge. This lemon sponge, in two shapes each holding I suppose about a quart, was put to set out on the sill outside the kitchen window. There my brother discovered the delectable liquid and at intervals during the afternoon he visited those shapes until he had drunk every drop of at least half a gallon of liquid lemon sponge; it may have been more.

At these family dinners it was the custom to let my brother and myself come down into the dining-room for dessert in spite of a fusillade of tut-tuts from Nanny at the lateness of eight o'clock as an hour to be eating fruit. As a punishment for scoffing those quarts of unset lemon sponge Frank was not allowed to come down to dessert that evening, and from seventy-two years ago I hear the echo of his yells as he was led away from the promised land. Even Nanny, who could usually find an excuse for him, could find no excuse for his raid on that lemon sponge.

And as I write these words I hear news of that cousin of mine who has just had her ninety-first birthday. She is in a nursing home after a stroke and is living in the past when she and I were in Malvern together, talking of me as if I were still two years old.[1]

That summer we went to Folkestone, where the Compton Comedy Company would open their autumn tour at the Pleasure Gardens Theatre on August bank holiday. My father was not well; about a week after we arrived toward the end of June he developed a bad carbuncle with other complications. Before that I recall walking with him on the Leas and his meeting a friend who had been at Kensington Grammar School with him over twenty years before. When they went their ways my father asked me if I knew who that was.

"That was Mr Condy. You've heard of Condy's fluid?"

Heard of it? It was one of Nanny's favourite forms of medical torture. To gargle with that horribly positive taste of nothing needed all the honey and borax we could get out of a teaspoon to counteract the taste of Condy's Fluid. To meet Mr Condy himself was as impressive an experience as it would have been to meet Dr Gregory of the powder.

The next incident I recall is of Major-General A. L. Playfair's visiting my father in our rooms in a narrow street just off the front. One could see the English Channel gleaming beyond the end of it. With the General was his son Arthur, who was then about twenty. Arthur was already on the stage and wanted to join the Compton Comedy Company, but there was not a vacancy. I can see Arthur Playfair looking rather embarrassed and wearing an unusually high choker collar. Later he was a very successful actor and was a loss to the London stage when he died in 1918.

For some reason the General took a fancy to me and I was invited to call on him next day where he was staying in rooms on the Leas. The hour named was ten o'clock and I was congratulated by the General when I arrived on the very stroke of the appointed hour. He and I then took a walk together three or four times a week. He was a tall, thin, extremely

[1] She has since died.

distinguished figure with a grey moustache and an ebony cane. He had served through the Indian Mutiny, had been at the siege of Lucknow and had recently retired from the Bengal Staff Corps. By him I was fired with an ambition to enter the Indian Army, the particular regiment I aimed for being the 1st Bengal Lancers, Skinner's Horse.

"Capital choice. Capital choice," said the General. "You couldn't pick anything better than the yellow boys, the old canary birds as we used to call them."

I was fascinated by that yellow uniform which I had seen in a coloured plate of the Indian cavalry regiments published by the *Boys' Own Paper*.

I recall from one of those walks we took together the General's indignation because Lord Salisbury had given Heligoland to the Germans in exchange for some disputed territory in East Africa.

"We'll pay for that one day," he growled, thumping his ebony cane on the ground. I seem to remember also the General's approval of an order to muzzle all dogs.

One day the General asked me if I would like a box of soldiers, and together we visited a toyshop. After a great deal of hesitation between various boxes, during which instead of getting impatient the General encouraged me to consider well my choice, I finally decided on a box of Highlanders charging at the double with fixed bayonets and a Highland band playing, each instrumentalist except the pipers with a music-stand. Then after deciding on these two boxes, which cost 3s. 6d. each, I was for a moment tempted by the penny boxes of about ten minute soldiers. For seven shillings I could have an enormous army. Then I rejected the penny boxes.

"Quite right. Quality before quantity, sir. I'm glad you have so much common sense."

I used that companionship with Major-General Playfair in *Sinister Street*, but dated it two years later because I did not think it would sound a plausible experience for a child of seven.

I was never to enter the Indian Army, but fifty-six years after those absorbing walks with him along the Folkestone Leas I would follow the steps of the Indian Army all over the East and I wish the General could have been still alive to hear my tale;

I owed that gallant figure so many hours of magic long ago.

When my father fell ill and was unable to take myself and my brother for walks my mother found a charming and youthful French governess at a girls' school who taught there only in the mornings and was free to look after us in the afternoons. We always called her Mademoiselle, and I cannot recall her name. In the mornings Frank and myself often had to go for walks with Nanny, Viola being now wheeled in what was called a mailcart. One day I was suddenly filled with a new menace to existence. Would people be supposing that Nanny was our mother? Even Frank, who was not at odds with her like myself, was filled with consternation at the idea of such a mistake being made, and we both of us used to let Nanny with our sister in her mail-cart get as far ahead as possible so that people might suppose the pair of us were not attached to her. And when she would turn round and call 'Come along, you two boys, don't dawdle' we used to scowl and hope that such scowls would make it evident to passers-by that Nanny was not our mother. We were deeply distressed by the notion that anybody so old and so ugly could be mistaken for our mother; social prestige did not enter into it. The anxiety was purely aesthetic.

I peer back into the past of that Folkestone summer and see the purple clematis on almost every other house, and the tamarisks of the lower Sandgate road, and the white tents of Shorncliff camp with the scarlet figures moving about among them like toy soldiers, and a polo game the niceties of which were explained to me by General Playfair.

I think it must have been in this summer that the Duke of Edinburgh opened some addition to Radnor Park. Somehow I managed with other small boys to get in front of the respectful crowd awaiting the Duke's arrival in a carriage and pair. He was in an Admiral's uniform and as I reconjure that portly bearded figure stepping down out of the carriage his uniform glows with a blue nearer to ultramarine than the navy blue to which it turns when one is older.

One afternoon Mademoiselle took me to tea at the school where she taught; Nanny did all she could to prevent my brother Frank's sharing in these walks, for she was extremely jealous of Mademoiselle.

I imagine that the half-dozen or so schoolgirls with whom we had tea were boarders, and after tea we went up to the recreation room where there was a swing. The petticoats of one of the smaller girls taking her turn on the swing shot up and revealed a tear in her white drawers. I was much embarrassed by this and quickly turned my head away to seem preoccupied by the view of the houses opposite. Then suddenly came a chorus of shocked 'oo's' from the other girls and the little girl who had offended their modesty was hustled out of the room in disgrace. After this the other girls started a discussion about the shameful business. I remember one in particular who must have been nearly fourteen being particularly eloquent about it all. She had a long sharp nose and a pale face and she seemed to feel it was necessary for me to be made to realise that for a girl to behave as Dorothy (or whatever her name was) had behaved had upset the rest of her companions. I can hear that horrible girl explaining to me that letting a boy see what he had seen of Dorothy was something beyond the bounds of decent behaviour. And I can see her (she was wearing a light blue sailor's top) pointing to the placket of her own navy blue skirt and saying that of course she realised one could sometimes see a glimpse of a small bit of her petticoat through it. Of course, she would not show even a tiny bit of her petticoat on purpose, but if it showed for a moment by accident she did not feel that it was anything to feel ashamed about. But what Dorothy had done! To swing high like that when she must have known there was a tear in her—well, where there was a tear.

With a memory of Mrs Frith's downright language I said, "But she didn't know there was a tear in her drawers."

"Oh, *you* don't mind what you say, do you? Well, fancy letting a boy see what you said even if they weren't torn by swinging high like that!"

At this point Mademoiselle came back, and the girl with the pale face and the long sharp nose tried to involve her in the prurient discussion. Mademoiselle, however, merely shrugged her shoulders, and said it was time for me to be going home. On our way out we passed a small room at the end of the passage and there sitting with tear-stained face was poor Dorothy all alone.

This incident, so trivial, made a deep impression upon me. It was the first opportunity I had been given to appreciate how much pleasure people could derive from the misfortunes of others. I was distressed by the realisation of this and I felt very sorry for the poor little girl. Yet, at the same time, even as early as this I was critical of my own reactions because I realised that even while I was disliking the attitude of those chattering girls I had, unwillingly perhaps, enjoyed that prurient discussion.

It might be going too far to claim that I made a resolve never to deceive myself about my own self if I possibly could, but I do know that round about this time I began to be critical of other people's motives and to justify such criticism by my ability to criticise my own motives and behaviour. Thus expressed in the language of maturity these emotions of a seven year-old boy may sound unreal because of course at this date they were merely unformulated emotions. Nevertheless, I know that as early as this I was capable of self-criticism.

It must have been some days after the tea-party at the girl's school that while I was walking round the pond in Radnor Park I fell into a day dream and walked into it. I can see now the lump of grey clay on the heel of my boot as I pulled myself out again, soaked up to the shoulders.

My brother Frank let out a roar and as we walked back to our lodgings he bellowed all the way "my brother is drowned". It was idle for Mademoiselle to say "Veux-tu te taire, mon petit. Monty is not drowned. He is walking home with us. Ton frère n'est pas noyé. Monty is not drowned. He is walking home with us at this moment." Frank continued to roar that his brother was drowned; Mademoiselle could not quieten his yells.

Back in the rooms my father, laid up with a carbuncle, heard the noise along the narrow street and limping to the window in his dressing-gown heard with alarm the bellowing of Frank about his drowned brother; it was a relief to see me walking along in my wet clothes with Mademoiselle holding Frank's hand and a tail of curious small boys following behind.

Nanny, of course, was extremely scornful of my Johnny-Head-in-Air behaviour. She was always a believer in the moral benefit of *Struwwelpeter*. Although I had long ceased to suck my thumb I did bite my nails, and she was insistent on the likelihood of the Long-Legged Scissor Man's arriving to cut off my thumbs in the way he cut off Conrad's thumbs for sucking them.

"Biting your nail's just as bad," she would mutter, and proceed to smear the tips of my fingers with bitter aloes, which as far as I was concerned was a worthless deterrent because I did not very much dislike the taste of bitter aloes.

Frank and I suffered a good deal from what we considered Viola's self-righteous showing off by reciting at the least excuse the preliminary verse of that old German book:

> When the children have been good,
> That is be it understood,
> Good at meal times, good at play,
> Good all night and good all day,
> They shall have the pretty things
> Merry Christmas always brings.

We were particularly offended by our small sister's declaiming in the last line 'What Merry Christmas always brings' and refusing to listen to our protests against putting in a 'what' that did not exist on the printed page.

Viola had heard at a matinée of *The School for Scandal* Lady Sneerwell's exit line 'The torments of shame and vexation[1] on you all.' Suddenly when Frank and I were teasing her she rounded on us, being then not quite four, by saying with dramatic intensity: "The torments of shame and vaccination on you all!" Nor was she in the least impressed when we taunted her as another Mrs Malaprop.

"I'm *not* Mrs Malaprop!"

"Yes, you are. You said 'vaccination' when you ought to say 'vexation'."

"I'm *not* Mrs Malaprop. I'm Julia Melville," she would declare.

We gave it up.

It was when my father was laid up with the carbuncle that one day he tossed across the table to me a volume with the label of a Folkestone circulating library on it.

[1] In the old prompt books 'vexation' was substituted for 'disappointment' which appears in the printed text.

"Here, *you'd* better read this book. It will interest you more than me," he said.

That volume must have been a first edition of *Treasure Island* and when I read it I entered a new world of enchantment cast by the magic of words. The thrill of Squire Trelawney's reply when asked by Dr Livesey if he had ever heard of Captain Flint is with me now:

"Heard of him! Heard of him, you say! He was the blood-thirstiest buccaneer that sailed. I've seen his topsails with these eyes off Trinidad, and the cowardly son of a rum-puncheon that I sailed with put back—put back, sir, into Port of Spain."

What an awe-inspiring thought it would have been if I had known that just after Henry James had received my father and me on that May morning of this very year the famous novelist would be writing a long letter to the author of those words that breathed life to the small boy who read them a couple of months later.

I do not remember where we went after the C.C.C. had played the opening week of their autumn tour at Folkestone, but it would have been to other towns on the south coast. At any rate, they played in Portsmouth some time in the middle of September. I was with them; Nanny had gone back to Avonmore Road with Frank and Viola.

I went to a matinée but forget which play it was. What I do remember are the pillars of the old Portsmouth theatre not much thicker than masts and my saying that I had found it difficult to see because one of those pillars was in the way. Thereupon my father told a story about when he was a very young actor and was playing the hero in some melodrama in this old Portsmouth theatre. Ada Blanche (I am almost sure) was the name of the actress playing the heroine; she caused a bit of a sensation many years later by joining the Salvation Army. The heroine was in the villain's toils and the hero was waiting in the wings to rush on in answer to her agonised cry for help and save her. But when the heroine had demanded of Heaven in a scream of despair who would save her, just as the hero entered from the prompt side a bluejacket entered from the O.P. side, shouting 'I will, you bastard,' and immediately knocked the villain as flat as we can see one knocked out today in a television Western. The bluejacket had been sitting in the gallery and had become so much agitated by the heroine's plight that he had descended by one of the pillars into the pit, as he would have descended a mast, and had made his way through the pass door on to the stage. I remember thinking my father had made a mistake in saying 'bastard' instead of 'bustard', and at the same time wondering why somebody should call somebody else a bustard.

When the C.C.C. moved on I was left to stay for a while with my aunt Kate Crowe. George Crowe, my godfather, was in a nursing home with some incurable complaint, from which he would die early in the following year and my aunt was living in Southsea with Josephine Dolling, whose brother Robert had been priest in charge of the Winchester College Mission in Landport for five years. Five years had still to run before Dr Randall Davidson, the new Bishop of Winchester, would destroy the work of ten years for the sake of a third altar in St Agatha's, the church he had raised the money to build by his eloquence in the pulpit and the beauty of his life and example. I have always felt that Dr Davidson's humility and charity when he became Archbishop of Canterbury were inspired by remorse for the great wrong he had done when he destroyed the ten years' work of a priest in his diocese to gratify what he considered expedient authority. He was a very different man as Archbishop of Canterbury from what he had been when he was Queen Victoria's favourite clergyman, known in disrespectful Anglo-Catholic circles as 'God's butler'.

In 1890 St Agatha's was still a temporary church with a corrugated iron roof and packed so full at evening service with sailors, soldiers and the poor of Landport that a ceremonial procession could hardly make its way round it. I was allowed to think that by wearing a surplice and singing in the choir I really was a chorister.

My cousin Sidney Crowe had joined my father's Company at the same time as George Harrison Hunter, the son of an Edinburgh doctor, had joined it. Sidney would marry George Hunter a year or two later, disastrously for herself, for he was a liar and a braggart. If ever I write a book called *Great Liars I have Known*, George Harrison Hunter will earn a chapter in it.

Dolling kept open house at St Agatha's and there were usually two or three Winchester men staying there. I recall

P

from this autumn of 1890 hearing Hunter holding forth to them about the wonders of his own school, which had been Fettes. I can see now the expression on the faces of two of these Winchester men while they summoned all the manners that had gone to the making of them with which to listen politely while George Hunter bragged on and on about the perfection of Fettes; I can hear now one Wykehamist turn to another after Hunter had left the room and say. "This man seems to think a lot of this place called Fettes. Have you ever heard of it?" The other shook his head.

"Nor have I," said the first Wykehamist.

Then they both shook their heads, puzzled presumably by the ability of somebody to suppose Winchester men could be impressed by the imaginary merits of any other school. Eton was recognized. Harrovians could be alluded to with a compassionate smile at their lack of manners. Were there any other schools? Oh yes, there was a place called Rugby.

When I was back in London a young and handsome governess used to come every day to give me lessons. At last I had somebody who was able to stand up to the unreasonableness of my old nurse. Lilian Champion was the daughter of a retired Colonel of the Indian Army who I imagine had recently died. Her childhood had been spent near Falmouth and her description of the Cornish sands implanted in my mind a determination to live in Cornwall one day, an ambition I should not achieve until the autumn of 1907. As I look back at my life I realise with gratitude that I have been able to carry out all the resolves I made at different times during my youth. One of the first was that as soon as I was independent I would never allow myself to be tied to London.

Miss Champion married an officer of the Dorset Regiment who was killed in South Africa. Later she took up professional typewriting and it was to her that I sent the manuscript of my first novel *The Passionate Elopement*. I owed much to Miss Champion, who was my governess until I went to St Paul's Preparatory School a year after she came to us. She was living with her mother and therefore she was only able to come five days in the week to give me lessons. So my old nurse still had plenty of opportunity to be unreasonable.

I remember going to two plays in London during that autumn

of 1890. The first was *A Pair of Spectacles*, which had been adapted by Sidney Grundy from a French comedy. John Hare played the lead, but I remember more vividly Charles Groves as Uncle Gregory from Yorkshire and the exact tone of his voice as he kept saying grimly 'I know that man. He comes from Sheffield.' I was interested to see Charles Dodsworth again. He had been at the Strand with the Compton Comedy Company in 1886 and he had given my father an ivory paper-knife cut from an elephant's tusk with the foot of the tusk for a handle. I loved this paper-knife dearly. I did not want to cut a book with it; I merely wanted to stroke it. So of course Nanny had to lock it up. I have very few relics of my father's past possessions, but that paper-knife is on the table beside me as I write about it.

My father's elder brother Charles was John Hare's business manager at the Garrick. He wrote two or three novels. I tried when young to read one of them called *Scot Free* but found it, as indeed I found all novels at that age, very dull. I still did not regard the works of Dickens or Smollett as novels.

Poor Charles Compton was the typical unsuccessful literary man (literary gent, as R. L. S. would have called him) of the period. He did a certain amount of reviewing and had occasional articles in the *Fortnightly Review*. He had married a barmaid, a most delightful woman. Aunt Lizzie was a great favourite with us as children, and I realise now how much she must have wanted children of her own. Charles Compton, like too many relations on my father's side, had a passion for instructiveness. I have always fancied it was a Symonds inheritance. This instructiveness was a trial to my mother, and thank heaven neither my brother nor myself ever suffered from it. Charles Compton's literary hero was George Meredith, and I am sure that today he would have been a devoted admirer of Dr Leavis, and the school of Cambridge criticism.

The other play I went to that autumn was *Antony and Cleopatra* at the Princess's Theatre in Oxford Street. We sat in a box on the prompt side nearest the stage, and I can see Mrs Langtry with the asp as if it were but yesterday instead of over seventy years ago. Charles (?) Coghlan was the Antony; he was pulled up into a tower to die. The play opened with

the scene between the triumvirs at the end of *Julius Caesar*.
I was much impressed by hearing Lepidus say 'Prick him down,
Antony.'

I also remember from that autumn seeing thousands of the
Salvation Army arriving at Olympia, of all places, to attend
the funeral of Mrs Booth, the General's wife. Another memory
of that autumn is reading about the mutilated body of Mrs
Hogg being found on a rubbish heap in Kentish Town and of
her baby being found dead on another rubbish heap. Why that
murder committed by Mrs Pearcey should have made such
an impression on me I do not know; perhaps it was that my
old nurse always called her Mrs Peacey and I got her mixed
up in my mind with the redoubtable Charles Peace who was
her star criminal. And I dare say the picture of Mrs Pearcey
cutting Mrs Hogg up in her kitchen and wheeling away her
mangled body with the baby on top of it in Mrs Hogg's own
perambulator was impressive. With a touch of macabre humour
she called herself Mrs Wheeler as an alias. Mrs Pearcey was
hanged at Newgate for her crime before the year was out.
That I remember because Newgate had made an impression
when we passed it once or twice on the way to Liverpool Street
station. There was a kind of playground beside it in which the
Bluecoat boys could be seen playing football. That December
when Mrs Pearcey was hanged was terribly cold, and when
we went up to Southport just before Christmas I fancy it was
snowing.

Henry James's play *The American* was produced on January
3rd, but I was not taken to the first night, and so I did not have
an opportunity of seeing how the author bore what in a letter
to Edmund Gosse he called 'the vulgar ordeal'. Five days later
he was writing to Mrs Hugh Bell from De Vere Gardens:

"I flung myself upon Compton after the 1st act: 'In heaven's
name, is it going?' 'Going?—Rather! You could hear a pin
drop!' Then . . . the applausive house emitted agreeable sounds
from a kind of gas-flaring indistinguishable dimness and the
gratified Compton publicly pressed one's hand and one felt
that really as far as Southport could testify to the circumstances,
the stake was won. . . . The great feature of the evening was
the way Compton 'came out' beyond what he had done or
promised at rehearsal, and acted really most interestingly and

admirably—if not a 'revelation' at any rate a very jolly surprise."

Henry James came back to rejoin the Company at Huddersfield, where I was to celebrate my eighth birthday before going down to London. To Robert Louis Stevenson he wrote on January 19th:

I have "been out of town for several days on a base theatrical errand—to see my tribute to the vulgarest of the muses a little farther on its way over the provincial circuit and re-hearse two or three portions of it that want more effective playing. Thank heaven I shall now have no more direct contact with it till it is produced in London next October."

Five years later Melpomene and Thalia would invite Nemesis to punish Henry James for calling them the vulgarest of the muses. The attitude of Henry James towards the theatre reflected the New Englander in him. He was continually excusing himself for stooping so low, and the explanation he offered was that he needed the money the theatre might give him. In fact, although his novels did not bring him much money, he had enough private means to live confortably, and there was really no excuse for talking as if he were a respectable young woman whom poverty had turned into a prostitute. He always felt impelled to stress his awareness of having allowed himself to come into contact with an inferior social world and to apologise for doing so as he might have apologised for being intimate with a tradesman. The puritanism of New England, which through the years had developed into the exclusiveness of Eastern American 'society', was able to accept as the most intelligible excuse for 'vulgarity' the prospect of financial gain.

Nearly twenty-five years after that week in Huddersfield he would be writing to me from Carlyle Mansions, Cheyne Walk:

My dear 'Monty Compton!'

For that was, I think, as I first heard you named—by a worthy old actress of your father's Company who, when we were rehearsing 'The American' in some touring town to which I had gone for the purpose, showed me with touching elation a storybook she had provided for you on the occasion of your birthday. That story-book weighted with my blessing on it, evidently sealed your vocation—for the sharpness of my sense that you are really a prey to the vocation was what, after reading you, I was moved to emphasise . . . you are so rare a case of the kind of reaction from the theatre—and from so much theatre—and the reaction in itself so rare—as seldom taking place; and when it does it is mostly, I think, away from the arts altogether—it is violent and utter. But your pushing straight through the door into literature and then closing it so tight behind you and putting the key in your pocket, as it were—that strikes me as unusual and brilliant!

I remember well that book. It was one of the five-shilling volumes of G. A. Henty. Blackie used to publish these volumes every year—two at six shillings and one at five shillings. All were in 'cloth elegant', but only the six-shilling volumes were allowed olivine edges, which was a sort of greenish gilt. The six-shilling volumes had twelve full-page illustrations, the five-shilling volumes only eight. In these days a six-shilling book was sold over the counter for 4s. 6d. and a five-shilling book for 3s. 10d.

My present that Christmas was given me by Miss Elenor Aickin, whom I have already mentioned. It was called *For Name and Fame or Through Afghan Passes*, and was a story of the 9th Foot or Norfolk Regiment. It has not been on my shelves these sixty years and more, and as it does not figure in the catalogue of my library I made in 1899 I fancy I must have given it away when I suddenly grew tired of Henty in the summer of 1897.

There is still, however, on my shelves a copy of Scott's *Tales of a Grandfather*. It is inscribed:

Dear Monty from Little Auntie,
Xmas. 1890

Of the 1192 pages few are not begrimed with the finger marks of youth, and to have reached such a state of degraded filth this volume must have been continuously read over a period of years. The grimiest page of all is that which sums up the effect of the Battle of Bannockburn:

"The English, after this great defeat, were no longer in a condition to support their pretentions to be masters of Scotland, or to continue, as they had done for nearly twenty years, to send armies into that country to overcome it. On the contrary, they became for a time scarce able to defend their own frontiers against King Robert and his soldiers."

It is significant that, while the account of the '45 is heavily thumb-marked as far as the Battle of Falkirk, the pages which tell of the Battle of Culloden are almost the cleanest in the book, showing that I seldom brought myself to the pitch of being able to bear the reading of it. In memory the capture of Edinburgh Castle by Sir Thomas Randolph seems to last for pages of excitement, and I can hardly believe that the whole desperate enterprise was carried through in a page and a half as by referring to that old copy of *Tales of a Grandfather* I find it was.

That book, given to me by my Aunt Isabel, was to have an even profounder influence upon the future course of my life than *The Heroes* of Charles Kingsley given to me by that god-mother of mine two years previously.

After my first reading of *Tales of a Grandfather* I kept pressing my father to know why he did not call himself Mackenzie. I had been perfectly clear about what my real name was since I was two years old, and it may be remembered that when I walked into the police station near St Mary Abbot's Church I told them the four names which will be found in my baptismal register.

However, when I went to Colet Court I was entered as 'Compton' and it was not until I went to St Paul's in May 1894 that I was 'Mackenzie'.

EIGHT YEARS OLD 1891

I HAD written an account of the Drury Lane Pantomime in that January of 1891 under the impression that it was *The Yellow Dwarf*, when I was taken round to Marie Lloyd's dressing-room by Harry Paine the great clown. Then on checking my reference I found that the Drury Lane pantomime of 1891 was *Beauty and the Beast*. *The Yellow Dwarf* was the following year. I have no recollection whatever of *Beauty and the Beast* and I think we must have stayed on with my parents on tour and that for some reason we did not go to the Drury Lane pantomime this year.

It must have been in that spring of 1891 that our house in West Kensington was entirely redecorated. At the same time some furniture which had been lent to my parents by Kate and George Crowe when they first acquired 54 Avonmore Road was needed by my aunt for a house she had taken with Josephine Dolling in Edith Road. It was just as well, because during those years in the 'eighties pieces of furniture bought by my father at second-hand shops all over Great Britain and Ireland used to arrive at intervals until it became a puzzle where any more were to go.

My mother did not go back on tour after Holy Week, which was very early that year. My cousin Sidney took her place as my father's leading lady for the rest of the tour. Those were the days when Maples was in its prime and my mother must have greatly enjoyed herself, for she loved spending money as much as I have always liked spending it. I should surmise that my father named a certain sum as the amount to be spent on redecoration, but that she began to draw upon her marriage settlement when she exceeded his permitted amount. My father was extremely careful with his money, although when he did buy anything he always bought the best to be got. I did not inherit from him much financial prudence, but I did share his taste for the best that could be got.

Lincrusta was the latest craze for wall-paper, and the walls of the drawing-room were covered with a wiggle-waggle of flesh-coloured lincrusta moulding which appeared rich and beautiful to us. In the angle of the walls on the left of the fire-place was what Maples called a Cosy Corner, in which four people could sit in comfort on well-sprung settees, the backs of which were padded and finished off by shelves for china. There were french-windows opening on a balcony from which steps led down into the tiny garden. One of our regrets in childhood was that the gardens grew longer and longer until Avonmore Road reached the seventies, beginning with Number 56, next door, from which the Robins family had departed by now.

The chairs were Louis Quinze, and there was a yellow satinwood Mezzler piano which I always found heavy going when I had to perform one of my pieces practised on the Brinsmead with pleated crimson front in the morning-room.

The dining-room was distempered in a light *café au lait* which set off admirably the two marquetry corner cupboards and the Sheraton sideboard, and also the George Morland coloured prints. The front-hall was distempered in ivory. On the walls were two long prints of Maclise's pictures of Nelson's death and the meeting of Wellington and Blücher at Waterloo. There was also a large full-length portrait of Adelaide Neilson, and over the hat-rack there was a mezzotint inscribed *Not Worth Powder and Shot* in which a highwayman was pulling up his horse behind a ragged old man with a fiddle tramping across a desolate dusky moorland. This used to worry my logic. Why should a highwayman suppose that anybody worth robbing would be tramping along like that by himself at dusk? The only other picture I remember was a print of a Scottish painter's evocation of the scene when Walter Scott as a youth had a word of thanks from Robert Burns for being the only person present who knew the name of the author of some poem.

On the first floor at the back was my father's library. This was now distempered in a Wedgwood blue above a lincrusta dado that tried to simulate panelling. In the hearth on either side of the asbestos gas-fire were tiles representing scenes from the *Idylls of the King*—Geraint and Enid, Lancelot and Guini-vere, Elaine the lily maid of Astolat, Gareth and Lynette, and of course Arthur with Excalibur and the lake beside the sea. Against the wall opposite the fireplace was a mahogany chest of three large drawers, the top one of which pulled out and became a writing-desk. Above the drawers was a bookcase which held among other books the works of Byron in several volumes, among which I would soon discover for myself the fascination of *Don Juan*, and read it over and over again. There were also two volumes of *Bentley's Miscellany* in which were Harrison Ainsworth serials—*The Tower of London* and *Jack Shepherd*.

This piece of furniture had once upon a time belonged to Lord Nelson and behind every handle of the drawers was a brass tablet stamped with his crest.

There was also a Chippendale bookcase which contained the numerous volumes of Oxberry's Drama, every play in which I read at least twice, my favourite of all about this time being *Una or One O'clock* by 'Monk' Lewis. This was a Gothic melodrama in which a four-post bed sank down with its terrified occupant to a haunted cellar. I have not read *Una* for nearly seventy years, and I am a little vague about the plot.

Two other books which had been birthday presents that year had a great influence over my dreams of the future. One was *The Swiss Family Robinson*, which filled my fancy with the delight of living on a desert island, and reinforced the effect of an abbreviated *Robinson Crusoe* with coloured plates which I had been given the year before. The other book was a Blackie publication in 'cloth elegant' called *Historic Boys* by E. S. Brooks. He must have been an American writer because the stories originally appeared in the *St Nicholas* magazine. Marcus Aurelius the Boy Magistrate, Baldwin of Jerusalem the Boy Crusader, Frederick of Hohenstauffen the Boy Emperor, Giovanni de' Medici the Boy Cardinal (afterwards Pope Leo X) Louis XIV the Boy King and Charles XII of Sweden the Boy Conqueror made the greatest impact on my imagination— most of all Frederick Stupor Mundi and Marcus Aurelius. The book is still on my shelves and looking through it I found myself lost again in these twelve tales. *Historic Boys* should be reprinted for children of today; it is an admirable stimulus to history.

To return to my father's library. There were two corner-cupboards, one of Dutch marquetry and the other of English marquetry. In one of these my father kept his cigars, of which more presently. In this room was one of my mother's wicker rocking-chairs, the other was in her bedroom. They had been sent over to her from America and had been her own mother's once upon a time.

Next door to the library was my parents' bedroom and my father's dressing-room. My mother must have had a wonderful time showing Maples how to fit out a wardrobe and a quantity of drawers going right up to the ceiling.

Upstairs again was the night-nursery at the back, and in front the room in which I had been sleeping for the last three years. The bathroom was also on this floor. It was now decided that my brother and I should sleep in what had been the day-nursery and was in future to be the 'boys' room'. The morning-room in the basement was to become the school-room though it remained the dining-room for Frank, Viola and myself.

Next to the 'boys' room' was the 'servants' bedroom' where the cook and the house-parlour-maid slept.

I think it was now that the Whistle was installed. On every floor there was a pipe at the top of which was a mouthpiece with a plug in it. My brother and I considered it an exquisitely enjoyable piece of humour, only very occasionally to be indulged in, to whistle down to the kitchen and when it was answered to blow down it instead of speaking. I wonder if anywhere in London today a whistle still exists. I cannot recall hearing any small boy or girl being told to whistle down and ask Cook to do this or that. It had at least the advantage of sparing the legs of a maid who would otherwise have had to climb perhaps three flights of stairs to find out what was wanted.

A great event of 1891 was going to see the Oxford and Cambridge boat race from Hammersmith Bridge. The two boats passed under the bridge absolutely level, and at the finish there was barely half a length between them. This Oxford victory was the first of a sequence of nine that would last throughout my schooldays and prevent my ever suffering the mortification of a Light Blue triumph. I do not know why I was 'Oxford'. Perhaps Oxford's loyalty during the Great Rebellion made me suspect Cambridge as a nest of Round-heads; or perhaps it was temperamental instinct. It may be that like Gilbert's little Liberals and Conservatives one is born a natural Oxonian or a natural Cantab. There must have been a strong prejudice in favour of Oxford because my old nurse was 'Oxford' and that would ordinarily have been enough to make me 'Cambridge'.

For some reason or other, I remember that a horse called *Common* won the Derby. This was at the end of May, just after I had the accident to my hand about to be related, and perhaps being confined to a sofa I read the *Daily Graphic* more thoroughly than usual. About the same time I read with great interest about an attack on the Orient express by brigands somewhere in Turkey, when after looting the train they carried off some German passengers and held them to ransom. It seemed a pity that exciting things like that did not happen on our railways at home. In my early boyhood I was always regretting that stage-coaches had passed away. If we only had brigands they could compete with the highwaymen of once upon a time.

On a sunny afternoon in that May of 1891 I was walking along Avonmore Road and saw a seedy-looking fellow with a barrow of flowers leave his barrow and go down the area-steps of one of the houses and as I passed the area I saw that he was picking the tulips from a window-box. So I went up the front steps, pressed the bell, and informed the maid who opened the door that somebody was picking the flowers in the area. She looked down over the parapet and asked the flower-thief what he was doing. He dropped the tulips in his hand, ran up the area-steps and wheeled away his barrow at a run. The maid congratulated me on my observation and said I must come in and be thanked by Mrs X—, I do not remember her name.

Mrs X was extremely pleasant and said she should like to reward me for my courage. I did not think I had done anything particularly brave in ringing her front-door bell, but little boys do not find it easy to make nothing of their behaviour with grown-up slickness and so I suppose I just stood there looking embarrassed. I think, or at any rate I hope, I should have refused a monetary reward, but when she offered me a round board with hooks and a set of rings for what was called on the outside of the box 'Quoits At Home' I accepted the present gratefully. For some time I had been thinking how nice it would be to have a quoit-board and indeed had marked down a quoit-board as a reward for not biting my nails for a month. Now I could go on biting my nails and yet become the owner of a quoit-board. I thanked Mrs X, no doubt as clumsily as children in those days used to thank the donor of a present or the hostess of a party, and went home with my treasure.

I decided that the place to hang the quoit-board was high up beside the bay-window in the morning-room, for which purpose I climbed up on a table. When I had hammered in a nail and hung up the quoit-board I stepped back to admire the effect and stepping back too far felt myself falling. In an effort to avoid this I grabbed one of the hooks of the quoit-board and when I hit the back of my head on the floor I saw that my right hand was gashed from just above the wrist to a third of the way up the middle finger. And as I held up my hand I cried, "I can see the light through it. I can see the light through it."

Hearing my cries, Cook and Hetty the maid came running from the kitchen. One of them fetched a bowl of water, but the gash was hardly bleeding at all; just an occasional thin trickle of blood made its way up through the water. On either side of the deep gash, which had in fact almost torn my hand in half, the skin was curled in a white fringe.

It was decided that I must be taken at once to Dr Collison-Morley. Miss Champion had already gone home, my mother was out. The last person I wanted to go with was my old nurse.

"You take me, Hetty," I begged. "And don't tell Nanny what's happened."

I felt I could not stand the sniffing and tutting of Nanny over what she would imply was a deliberate plot by me to take up her time when she was so busy. I was given the co-operation that throughout my youth I was always given so generously by cooks, housemaids and parlour-maids, a co-operation that was to last all my life between myself and those in my service.

"I'll catch it from HER," said Hetty. "But never mind, the sooner Dr Morley sees that hand of yours the better."

So away went Hetty and I down Matheson Road, across

North End Road, and past the Cedars Hotel to Edith Road
at the corner of which lived Dr Collison-Morley.

Dr Morley was the family doctor of half West Kensington
in those days. The only other doctor I remember was Dr Birch
at the corner of Gunterstone Road. Dr Morley was an outstanding figure. He looked so tall and spare in his short frock-
coat, or rather riding-coat, for I believe that would have been
a more accurate name for it, when he used to go round with
springy steps upon his daily visits to his patients.

In all the years we lived in Avonmore Road, that is from
1886 to 1901, I never saw Dr Morley in any other garb but
that black riding-coat, which by constant exposure to the
weather had taken on the greenish hue that the finer cloth of
once upon a time used to acquire without the cloth's wearing
out. It might snow or blow. It might pour with rain. It might
freeze. The only concession Dr Morley ever made to the
weather was to carry an umbrella. If he possessed a greatcoat
he was never seen in one, and I believe he carried an umbrella
to protect his silk hat more than himself. Perpetual exercise
had kept his figure as trim as an athletic young subaltern's.
Long service in India had turned his complexion to parchment,
and like parchment his skin was stretched tight across his high
cheekbones. He had a nose like the Duke of Wellington's, and
indeed in many respects he bore a resemblance to the Iron
Duke. He was a widower, with two sons and an elder daughter
who kept house for him. His two sons were still both at St
Paul's when I went there in 1894. Lacy the elder was an
albino and a fine classical scholar; he was a scholar of St
John's College, Oxford. The younger, Harold, was a brilliant
artist who was killed at Loos in the First World War.

The surgery in Edith Road was a tiny room, but it was so
full of objects of interest that one never noticed time pass when
one was waiting for the doctor to come in. There were yellowing
photographs of regimental groups and Indian scenes, curious
weapons and jars and a framed coloured print of two officers
of the 78th Foot, which became the Second Battalion of The
Seaforth Highlanders. Neither officer was in the kilt; both
were wearing trews with the Mackenzie tartan. Since reading
Tales of a Grandfather, and deciding that Mackenzie was a more
important part of my name than Compton, this print absorbed

my attention when I had to go and see Dr Morley for a tonic to be prescribed or for my eczema to be looked at. How vividly I remember the way in which he used to come bustling in from the dispensary, nearly always drying his hands on a small towel. He had beautiful slim hands, the colour of old ivory and the lightness of his touch as he felt the side of one's neck to detect the presence of swollen glands was immensely reassuring.

It needed all Dr Morley's gentleness, when my hand was unwrapped on that afternoon in May seventy years ago, to hold out my hand for him to look at the gash.

"This will take a bit of stitching," he murmured to himself.

By now I was crying again.

"Now hold out your hand, and *don't* move it," he said as he threaded the needle.

Before he could put in a stitch he had to smooth as well as he could the corrugated white skin on either side of the gash, and I continued to cry. However, I managed to hold out my hand for the six stitches it required. Then a sling was made and Hetty was told that I was to be kept lying down when I got home.

A sofa was brought into the newly distempered dining-room for me. Probably the library and my mother's room were still in the hands of the workmen. So she slept in the room I had had and I slept in the dressing-room off it.

The next day when Dr Morley came to look at my hand he said to my mother,

"He was wonderfully brave when I was stitching him up."

This was too much altogether for my reverence for the truth.

"I wasn't," I protested. "I cried all the time."

"Ah, but you held out your hand and didn't move it when I was stitching you up."

I was puzzled. For me tears were the stigma of cowardice, and I still could not understand being called brave when I had wept so copiously. It was a long time before I had had enough experience of life at school to grasp what Dr Morley had meant by saying I had been brave about those stitches.

I recall lying on that sofa in the dining-room and reading the *Boys' Own Paper* in which *The Cockhouse of Follsgarth* by Talbot Baines Reed was running as a serial at this date. I have never understood why *The Fifth Form at St Dominic's* has always been considered Talbot Baines Reed's best school story. For me *The Cockhouse* every time, and indeed next to it I used to enjoy *The Master of the Shell*. *The Cockhouse at Follsgarth* tells the story of the feud between the Classical side and the Modern side at a public school, and significantly the chaps in the Classical side were all decent chaps and the chaps in the Modern side were a pretty caddish lot. What a much better showing Yorke, the Captain of the Classical Fifteen, made compared with Clapperton, the Modern Vice-Captain!

Wally Wheatfield, D'Arcy, Ashby and Fisher II were the spirited Classical juniors. Percy Wheatfield (Wally's twin brother), Cash, Cottle, Lickford and one whose name I have forgotten (I have not read the book for nearly forty years), were the equally spirited Modern juniors.

The only criticism I had to make of *The Cockhouse* was that instead of the 'right-o' of my time (the O.K. of today) the chaps said 'all serene'. I could not understand how the author of such a jolly good story could suppose that boys ever said 'all serene'. Schoolboy slang, indeed all slang, is a dangerous toy for authors because nothing dates a book so fatally as the use of outdated slang. In the United States the dating is even more swift in coming, though English slang is becoming more ephemeral all the time.

My earlier youth was lucky in coinciding with the palmy days of the *Boys' Own Paper*, the first rival of which was *Chums*, that too in its early days a good boy's paper. So I escaped wretched papers like the *Magnet* in the same way as I escaped *Peter Pan*. The fact that Billy Bunter is from time to time presented on television shows that his author was closer in touch with today than the really *good* writers of school stories in the nineteenth century.

The other consolation for my damaged hand was the *Strand Magazine*, with the first adventures of Sherlock Holmes, and I think about now the weekly serialisation of *The Sign of Four* in *Tit Bits*.

My mother ran a magazine club in the C.C.C. She and my father were responsible for *Temple Bar* and the *Cornhill*; other members, the juniors sharing a magazine between them, took in the rest of the magazines. These circulated during the current month, at the end of which they went back to their subscribers. The *Strand Magazine* was a novelty and I begged that it might be taken in by us as well as *Temple Bar* and the *Cornhill*, which I found heavy reading. This request was granted. The *Strand* was read in its turn on tour, but we had our own copy in Avonmore Road and it was one of the great pleasures of my youth.

When the end of the tour came toward the end of June we went to Cromer. I think, but I cannot be quite sure, that we were again in Prospect Villa. My father had acquired a bicycle with those cushion tyres that would so soon be displaced by pneumatic tyres. The cushion tyres were an improvement on the solid tyres of the boneshaker safety bicycle, but they were not enough of an improvement to make bicycling a luxurious form of exercise. My father got rid of his cushion-tyred bicycle about a month later and never mounted a bicycle again in his life. He used to come back from solitary rides and try to pretend that he had enjoyed them by telling us stories of what he had seen and encountered in the course of his morning's exercise, but he always ended up by saying he could not understand how people could argue that bicycling was a good substitute for riding a horse.

I had a bad time of it during that July. Dr Fenner, a good-looking youngish medical man to whom I had been taken to show my gash, declared that it would leave a bad scar to judge by the way it was healing and he wanted to open it again. When, owing to my dread of such an operation, this idea was abandoned, Dr Fenner insisted that there was a danger of my right hand's becoming useless for ever and that it was vital for the fingers to be pulled back four times a day, a duty which was laid upon my father to carry out; as the pain for me was agonising it was not a pleasant duty. However, it was carried out, and I owe to Dr Fenner the restoration of as much mobility to the fingers of my right hand as the uninjured ones of my left hand have. Luckily for me I was naturally left-handed and therefore the temporary uselessness of my right hand was less of an inconvenience than it might have been. Nevertheless, it remains to this day a most formidable scar.

One of the things that made Cromer dear to us as children was that it had no pier, but only a wooden jetty. One had to pay twopence to go on a pier, and two pennies were not

Q

so easily come by; a jetty was free. Moreover, it was easier to fall into the sea off the end of a jetty than off the end of a pier. Not that we wanted to fall into the sea, but we respected the sensation of feeling that one so easily might.

Another great advantage of Cromer was that the sands were not at the mercy of the tide. In all the South Coast watering places shingle was the enemy. How poignantly sad it was when the tide refused to be really low until the moment when it was time to go home for dinner. That sitting down to a long meal of roast meat and beastly cabbage and boiled potatoes with the thought that half a mile away there was a glorious expanse of sand, marvellously empty at that hour, was an intolerable weight upon one's spirits. We had probably spent the morning huddled on a narrow strip of hot shingle with nothing to do except listen to nigger minstrels.

Cromer must have been one of the first seaside places in England that made golf an outstanding attraction. In those days all golfers used to wear red coats on the same principle as red flags were carried in front of steam-rollers, and in my mind's eye I see the green shapes of the East Cliff dotted with scarlet figures like Shorncliff Camp. I suppose there were niggers and pierrots and camera obscuras and all the other joys of the beach, not excluding the gentleman who for a penny allowed you to look through a microscope at eels in vinegar or mites in cheese, but they are not associated in my memory with Cromer. I recall walking up the slopes of the East Cliff among the dangerous balls of the golfers to have tea at the lighthouse, and I recall walking along the West Cliff where the cockchafers seemed more dangerous than the balls of the golfers. I remember one of my American cousins alluding to them as maybugs. I also seem to recall a signpost just before one took the path along the West Cliff which said 'To Gunton, Runton and Trunch'. If I have the names wrong, I must be forgiven by the patriots of Cromer.

I recall, too, the way the country always seemed to be over-flowing from behind into the little seaside town. I can see now the fields of poppies and ox-eyed daisies on the way to the railway-station, which was quite a long way off. I can smell now the honeysuckle in the July dusk mingling its sweetness with the salty air.

And there is another scent I recall from those far off days—the scent of the small pink convolvulus, which would in time become the pestilent bindweed of my gardening days and lose its delicate perfume. Oh yes, and the scent of lady's bedstraw which only a year after this would always be associated with the blessed relief of the summer holidays at July's end.

I have not revisited Cromer since 1895 and I suppose that today it is a much larger place than it was then, but I have made it a rule not to revisit the glimpses of the moon if I can help it, because the place as it is gets confused with the place as it was, and one's memory of what was is disturbed.

One more memory of Cromer in 1891, and that is of going for a walk with my father and meeting by a stile Beerbohm Tree, Viola Tree and a red setter dog. While the two actor-managers talked Viola, whose hair was as red as the dog's, eyed me suspiciously while I looked at her, wondering if every girl called Viola had to have red hair. The Viola of my sister was pronounced Veeola. Dear Viola Tree, she is one of those I miss most from this world, though many years would go by after I saw that little girl with red hair standing by a stile before she became a close friend.

From Cromer we went to the Isle of Man, where the Compton Comedy Company would rehearse for a week and then play at the Grand Theatre, Douglas, during the first week of August. I suppose they must have played elsewhere through August; but then the tour would have stopped because my father had taken a lease of the Opera Comique for the London production of *The American* at the end of September, in which the leading members of the Company would be acting. We crossed to Douglas from Fleetwood. I was sea-sick and there was a thick mist so that we were a long time before we made the harbour. I see myself looking at the paddle of the steamer and wishing it would start churning up the water again so that we could go ashore instead of rolling about like this in the fog.

We stayed at the Castle Mona Hotel, a large grey Gothic building at the far end of the bay. Lodgings were impossible to secure in this favourite resort of Lancashire, which at this date surpassed any other seaside resort, even Blackpool, in the variety of its diversions; and Lancashire could fairly consider that it knew more about amusement and amusing itself than any other county in England except Yorkshire. There was something exotic about Douglas to my youthful imagination, and those dance halls and music halls nestling in the fuchsias and rich foliage of that bay seemed like visions from the Arabian Nights when they were lit up by jewelled fairy lamps. I shall always regret that I was born much too late to see candles in the footlights of a theatre; but I am glad that I was born early enough to have seen flickering fairy lamps and gas footlights.

In 1891 there was plenty of dancing in Douglas, and some of those places of amusement along the front had splendid ballrooms. I can recall the name of only one of them, the Derby Castle, where there was a good variety programme every evening.

Somehow or other I attracted the attention of a young lady who was singing at the Derby Castle, and somehow or other, though I confess I do not know how, I managed to be allowed to accompany Miss Mabel Allen every evening, wait in her dressing-room while she did her turn, and afterwards escort her home along the front. She must have been staying in the same hotel as we were, but I am puzzled to know how I continued to be allowed out till about nine o'clock. Later Miss Allen married Mr Alfred (?) Hemming, the manager of the Grand Theatre and a great friend of my father's.

On the Sunday my parents went to lunch with the Governor and my mother was wearing a black lace hat with a red rose in it. I looked at her and said,

"You are pretty with that red rose."

She blushed with pleasure, and I can hear my father saying,

"You are more pleased with that little compliment than you've ever been."

And I remember wondering why a simple statement of fact should be considered a compliment.

In the Castle Mona Hotel the head waiter was the greatest artist at folding table-napkins I have known, so much the greatest that I have forgotten any others. He could build up the most marvellously complicated shapes with about half a dozen napkins, the size of wedding-cakes. I can still see his little room and the table covered with green baize and the window

looking out on the blue water of the bay, and his deft fingers
turning this napkin into a boat, that napkin into a water-lily,
with less effort than most people would have taken to roll a
cigarette.

Some twenty-five years ago I mentioned the Castle Mona
Hotel in a broadcast talk, and here is an extract from a letter
I received:

*"At the time to which you were referring I happened to be (out in
the big world for the first time) at the Castle Mona Hotel, and remember you so very well as a very, very sweetly inquisitive little boy (about
seven years old?) brimful of questions. I wonder if you remember such
a very trifling incident as speaking to a young lady in the office, enquir-
ing her name, and when being told it was Salisbury adding: 'Does
the Salisbury Hotel, London, belong to you?'"*

It is as well that one who indulges in reminiscences of other
people should occasionally be presented with somebody
else's memory of himself. I shudder to think of the questions I
must have asked Miss Mabel Allen at the Derby Castle, and
marvel at her infinite tolerance; and how mortified I should
have been if I in the glory of eight had heard that Miss Salisbury
thought I was only seven!

My hand must have been better by the end of that fortnight
in Douglas because, although my arm was still in a sling, I
remember kissing a round-faced girl of about my own age in
the excavation made for a sand-castle. This girl belonged to
Belfast, but, perhaps tactfully, her name has deserted my
memory. I remember her protesting but I cannot believe that
her resistance was genuine because obviously if she had really
minded being kissed she could easily have pushed off a boy
with his arm in a sling.

I fancy we went to one or two resorts on the South Coast
after leaving Douglas, but which they were I do not remember.
Anyway, we were back by the beginning of September when
my father was busy rehearsing *The American* for its production
at the Opera Comique at the end of the month.

My mother, who was expecting a baby at the end of
November, was not acting; with her I went to be interviewed
by Mr James Bewsher, the headmaster of Colet Court, which
had been started as a preparatory school for St Paul's soon

after St Paul's moved in the middle of the 'eighties from the city to its present position. The boys of Bewsher's, as Colet Court was then always called except by the masters, were originally accommodated in a large red house still to be seen at the corner of Talgarth Road and Gliddon Road, close to the Baron's Court Station which did not exist in those days.[1]

James Bewsher was a younger brother of Samuel Bewsher, the Bursar of St Paul's, to whose enterprise Colet Court owed its existence. He was a very kindly man with a slight Lancashire accent. I suppose the Bewsher brothers came to London when the great Frederick Walker ceased to rule Manchester Grammar School and became High Master of St Paul's.

I can hear now Mr James Bewsher asking my mother if I could read, and I can see now the amazed expression on her face as she told him that I had been reading since before I was two. No doubt he looked politely incredulous, but at any rate I was to be accepted as a pupil at Colet Court when the Michaelmas term began on Tuesday, September 15th.

Some time before school started my father took my brother Frank and myself to a rehearsal at the Opera Comique. The theatre was almost completely underground and situated where the clearance was made of so much of a piece of old London for the new Kingsway thoroughfare. As I remember we walked up from the Temple station along Holywell Street to reach the theatre, but my topographical memory for this part of London has been blurred by so many years of familiarity with the Aldwych of today that I cannot be completely sure. I remember the narrow Holywell Street with its furtive book-shops where Victorian pruriency was given an added itch and rubber goods were slipped quickly across the counter. After the rehearsal, which was a short one, we walked with my father along the Strand to Coventry Street.

On the way we managed to get him into the Lowther Arcade, which was opposite Charing Cross Station and had several toyshops for children. Here I persuaded him to buy for me a horseguard on sentry duty in Whitehall. The guardsman could be lifted from his black horse, the saddle having a hole into which a spike between the guardsman's legs fitted.

[1] It is no longer to be seen. It was demolished to make way for the stream of traffic along Talgarth Road today.

He cost one shilling, which seemed a tremendous price for a single toy soldier. However, in spite of being a motionless sentry he was a splendid addition to my toy army because he was very difficult to knock down with a marble and was therefore the undefeated hero of many battles.

Before we turned into the Lowther Arcade my father had been telling us about the house at 16 Charing Cross where he had been born and with my heart set on bringing something out with me from the Lowther Arcade I had listened with as rapt an expression of attention as I could muster, though every time I had ever passed Charing Cross beside my father on the top of an omnibus he had always told me about that house where he was born. And my tact was rewarded.

From Charing Cross we walked along past Morley's Hotel and the National Gallery to reach Coventry Street by way of Leicester Square. Here we were taken into Scott's, where our parent ordered for himself a dozen osyters. In those days a dozen Whitstable natives at Scott's cost 3s. 6d., and that was considered a very high price to pay for a dozen oysters. After we had sat watching my father eat his oysters we told him that we wanted to know what an oyster tasted like.

"No, no," he said. "You boys wouldn't care for them at all."

"But you don't know," we protested. "We haven't tasted them."

"I think they ought to be allowed a taste, Mr Compton," suggested the head waiter who had overheard our request.

"Oh, very well," said our parent. "Give them one each."

We tasted our first oysters.

"But they're frightfully nice," I declared.

"I like them frightfully too," Frank agreed warmly.

"I think they deserve another couple each, Mr Compton," the head waiter again suggested.

"Oh, very well," our parent said. "And you'd better bring me another half-dozen."

We hastily swallowed our couples before my father had had time to squeeze the slice of lemon on his, and asked if we couldn't have six more like him.

The head waiter hurried off and presently came back with nine for each of us.

"For goodness' sake!" our parent protested.

"Six of them are on the house, Mr Compton," said the head waiter with a benevolent smile.

My father shook his head, but in fact he was proud of our accomplishment. Some days later we accompanied him to the City, where he was closeted awhile with the manager of the Union Bank. No doubt he was making arrangements for an overdraft, if necessary, should business at the Opera Comique prove less lucrative than he hoped. Then we went on to visit an old friend of my father's who had a wholesale wool store. Here, while he and Mr Pratt were in colloquy together in Mr Pratt's office, we enjoyed ourselves by pushing over bales of wool at one another until Mr Pratt and my father emerged.

"I hear you boys like oysters," said Mr Pratt.

Obviously our parent had not been able to resist bragging about our recent performance in Scott's to his old friend, who owned an oyster-bed at Whitstable.

"Rather!" we agreed warmly.

Next Christmas and for several more Christmases my brother and I would receive a barrel of fifty Whitstable natives from Mr Pratt.

Although it will be going a month or two beyond the point where this first octave of my life will stop this is an appropriate moment to relate the story of our first cigars.

One morning I received the exciting news that I was to go to the play that evening because the Prince of Wales was to be there. I sat in a box on the O.P. side Naturally, at school next day I spoke of my experience. One small boy, unwilling to allow me as much glory as I thought I deserved, asked if I knew that the Prince of Wales paid half a crown for every cigar he smoked. I expressed disbelief, but his statement was supported by others, and I was left under the impression that, in spite of my having sat in a box opposite another box in which the Prince of Wales was sitting, I was nevertheless fundamentally ignorant of royal behaviour. I asked my father how much he paid for his cigars.

"It depends on the cigar. I have some good cigars for which I paid fourpence; I have some cigars for which I have paid as much as a shilling. But I haven't many of those," he added hastily, for extravagance was to him one of the deadly sins,

and he was obviously afraid that such an admission might set a
bad example to his eldest son.

"The Prince of Wales pays half a crown for his cigars," I
announced.

"Yes, well, but the Prince of Wales is the Prince of Wales."

The retort was a feeble enough truism, but I was not surprised by it, I had realised for a long time that grown-ups
when cornered took refuge in truisms, however feeble, in
order to block further exploration or inquisition by the young.

While *The American* was running, my father continued to
dine at, for him, the sacred hour of three o'clock in the afternoon, except of course on matinée days when he used to eat
at Gow's or Simpson's in the Strand between the performances.
After his dinner at home he always smoked one cigar, and it
was my brother Frank's duty to collect the stub of this cigar
when his father had left the house for the theatre. Then when
an opportunity occurred Frank and I would smoke that stub
in one of our father's Petersen pipes, a habit which somehow
or other he discovered.

"And so you boys enjoy smoking?" he enquired.

We probably told him we thought it was 'ripping' or
'spiffing'.

"Well, since you both enjoy smoking so much I will give
you two of my cigars to smoke."

With this he went to that corner cupboard of Dutch marquetry in which he kept his cigars, and extracted two of the
largest he had. They must have been two of those shilling ones
of his, and it must have cost him a pang to administer the
lesson he believed he was about to administer.

"Light them properly," he commanded.

He passed us a big Bryant and May's box of safety matches,
one of which would light a cigar properly, whereas it takes
three of the matches in the shrunken boxes of today to light
a cigar as it should be lit before it is put between the lips.
When he saw that we were puffing away, my father lit a cigar
for himself from the same box. I wish I could remember what
the brand was, but I know it took a full hour to smoke that
cigar.

Soon I noticed a questioning look in the paternal eye, and
this in turn was gradually succeeded by a puzzled and finally

by a baffled expression. At this date my father was on the
edge of thirty-eight, and I was conscious of the emotion of
triumphing over his venerable age. I realised that he was
searching our complexions for that greenish pallor which in
the *Boys' Own Paper* always appeared on the cheeks of young
readers who defied the threat of early blindness and stunted
growth; this the Editor continually insisted was the inevitable
result of smoking in early youth. Alas, for our poor father's
self-abnegation in parting with two of his best and biggest
cigars for a lesson to his offspring. Our cheeks remained rosy,
our foreheads dry.

"Are you feeling all right?" he asked when the cigars had
been smoked. We beamed at him gratefully: filial good manners
forbade us to crow over a parent whose morale was for the
moment a wreck.

After my father went out on tour again we discovered a key
that could unlock the marquetry cupboard, and from time to
time at rare intervals we helped ourselves to cigars. On his
return home he evidently suspected that somebody (and he
may reasonably have concluded that it was one or other of
his sons) had been helping himself to his cigars, for when we
next opened the cupboard we found written on the flap of
every box the number of cigars he had left in it. We recognised
those figures as the writing on the wall, and after that we
regretfully left his cigars alone.

I reflect with a touch of complacency that two of the great
pleasures of my life which are still enjoyed as much as ever
were first appreciated seventy years ago. I hope that some of
the devoted addicts to non-smoking will be warned by this
cautionary tale. The smoking of the pipe of peace was not an
empty name for an empty gesture. If the fanatics of nicotine
prohibition succeed in their campaign they will make the
world safe for madness and for war.

Miss Champion was still with us that autumn, giving lessons
to my brother Frank and sister Viola, but she was to leave us
at the end of the year because her invalid mother needed her.
When that first September morning of school arrived she
asked me if I would like her to accompany me. There was
nothing I should have liked better, but some instinct warned
me that I should be wise to reach school without a feminine

escort. I declined her offer and set out alone on the first of what before I had finished with them would be 7500 of such walks between Avonmore Road and first Colet Court and then St Paul's, backwards and forwards twenty times every week of twenty-five terms until the end of my second octave; since when I have never once walked it again, though I have passed along it occasionally in an omnibus or taxi.

And as the ginger-headed foxy-faced porter of Colet Court in his green uniform asks 'New boy?' and I murmur 'Yes' I bring my first octave to an end.

POSTSCRIPT

IT was a temptation to continue this first octave to the end of my ninth year, but on consideration I decided that it would be easier for readers to have my schooldays contained in a single volume.

Apart from an odd letter, and two or three tattered programmes which escaped my mother's periodic fits of destructiveness, I have had nothing with which to check my dates. My mother destroyed a number of letters she had from Whistler, all of them illustrated by drawings in the margin, and when my Bateman grandmother died my mother and her sister Isabel destroyed the whole of the correspondence that would have been an invaluable help in telling the story of the years at the Lyceum. When she was eighty-five she wrote a very brief account of those years which I shall print in my second octave at the appropriate moment.

The present fashion in autobiography strongly favours poverty as a prelude to success, and I feel I should apologise for having, as it will seem to many, been born with a silver spoon in my mouth. In fact, there was often much unhappiness in my childhood, but I am temperamentally incapable of dwelling upon unhappiness; I sympathise with the sundial's preference for sunny hours. A leading critic once told me that I would never reach the top as a novelist because I had never known deep mental suffering. That may be true. At the same time, some temperaments enjoy mental suffering as much as some people enjoy being ill.

I remember the poet Walter Turner saying to me on one occasion:

"You always feel well, don't you?"

I reminded him that from time to time I did suffer extreme physical pain.

"Yes, I know, but when you're not in pain, you feel well," he insisted.

I agreed that this was true.

"I never feel well," he said.

And a few months later he died.

This was the first time I had ever heard Turner allude to his ill health, and his courage made a deep impression on me.

I have known, like most of us, many other people who have obviously derived a gratifying sense of importance from being able to enlarge on their physical discomforts.

I should agree with that critic I mentioned about the advantage to a creative writer of an unhappy childhood, and I believe that the contemporary passion for turning childhood into an Eden before the Fall will have an adverse effect on the creative literature of the future, however advantageous it may be to technological achievement. I am not afraid to prophesy the inevitable victory of science over art and the humanities in the course of the years to come. I cannot imagine that the creative urge of young people in that future will be satisfied by writing novels or even poetry when some great secret of the universe may be unlocked by them. Yet the victory of science over the arts and the humanities may send mankind along an evolutionary path that far hence will leave it much in the position achieved by bees and ants and termites long since.

If I subtract the eighty years I hope to have lived when this first octave is published from the year of my birth I shall be back in 1803. Superficially it seems a much longer stretch of time from 1803 to 1883 than from 1883 to 1963. Yet if one considers the scientific advance achieved within those two stretches of time the latter period, the years of my own life, is twenty times as long.

Every age is an age of transition, said Goethe. That may be true, but he was thinking of transition in terms of contemporary locomotion. Transition is hardly the word for the rate at which we are now moving. The circumstances of the present are all in favour of out-growing and outliving everything more rapidly than ever before in the history of mankind. And the disconcerting part about this outgrowing and outliving is that there is no perceptible development of the inward man that is pretending to keep pace with the development of the outward man. We are like children who have too many toys, and we outgrow our old toys not because the imagination has exhausted itself in playing with them, but because we are continually being presented with new toys.

I ask myself in the mood of pessimism which, with me, usually succeeds the completion of a mental task, whether in this case that strain upon the memory has been justified, whether indeed it may not have mustered an assemblage of trivialities that were not worth assembling. A few octogenarians may enjoy comparing my experience of a time they knew with their own experience of it, but will it have the slightest interest, let alone importance, for those even twenty years junior to myself? I re-read the opening apology and prologue and am inclined to delete it as the expression of a too facile optimism. However, let it stand. Optimism returns with the prospect of beginning my second octave. I will face the fact that autobiography is a form of self-indulgence and claim that after over fifty years of trying to entertain the public I am entitled to entertain myself by revisiting the glimpses of the moon on paper. Yet even as I make that claim I am sharply aware that, however much I may be writing to indulge myself, I shall be disappointed if the result is tedious for the reader.

I have never had the slightest desire to go on the stage. Indeed, from the age of two I have been strongly prejudiced against the stage as a profession for myself. Nevertheless, in such an inheritance as mine there must be an irresistible desire to entertain and a constant dread of failing to hold the attention of the audience one is seeking to entertain, be they readers or listeners. It may be this characteristic which has led various critics to suggest that I have never grown up. Certainly I have to admit that many prejudices conceived in childhood have survived through my life. I can echo the words of Seneca: *Tenacissimi sumus eorum quae pueri percipimus*: 'we cling most closely to what we observed in boyhood', and I believe with my Pauline predecessor, John Milton, that the child will show the man.

During the first vital eight years of their lives most men are entirely educated by women. Mother, nurse and governess, or if the nurse and governess be omitted, his mother and in so many cases school-teacher have built the foundation on which the average man stands to survey the world; and what a fortunate thing that is for the human race, since there is little doubt that if the earliest years of a man had always been handed over to the education of his fellow-men, humanity might not yet have emerged from the neolithic age. Woman is the mainstay of civilised human progress, and her profoundest instincts are always on the side of sane evolution. If the present trend towards the insect state be halted it will be through the conservative instinct of woman. But let us remind ourselves that whether humanity follows the path of the bees and ants or of the spiders and earwigs, woman will still be ultimately in control. Looking back on my life I perceive that I have learnt everything I know about the realities of existence from women, and if I wanted a proof of this it would lie in the fact that I have never yet succeeded in shocking a woman, though often enough I have often been able to rub the tender bloom from the romance or sentiment of the male. Men distrust a cynic because they think he is deliberately choosing a base motive to exploit their actions. Women distrust a cynic for the same reason that they distrust one another.

During my second octave, throughout all of which I was being almost entirely educated by men, I was without realising it continuously at war with the male's surrender to the herd. I say without realising it because, apart from a very few exceptions, I got on well both with my schoolmasters and schoolmates. I did not have to endure again anything like the difficulty of what life had been with my old nurse. Indeed, that experience remains for me unique. I have already explained why I did not make more of it in this first octave.